An A–Z of Community Care Law

of related interest

Community Care Practice and the Law
Michael Mandelstam with Belinda Schwehr
ISBN 1 85302 273 X

Equipment for Older or Disabled People and the Law
Michael Mandelstam
ISBN 1 85302 352 3

An A–Z of Community Care Law

Michael Mandelstam

Jessica Kingsley Publishers
London and Philadelphia

First published in 1998 by
Jessica Kingsley Publishers Ltd,
116 Pentonville Road,
London N1 9JB, England
and
325 Chestnut Street,
Philadelphia, PA 19106, USA.

www.jkp.com

Second impression 1998
Third impression 2000

Library of Congress Cataloging in Publication Data
A CIP catalog record for this book is available from the Library of Congress

British Library Cataloguing in Publication Data
Mandelstam, Michael, 1956–
An A–Z of community care law
1. Community health services – Law and legislation – England
2. Community health services – Law and legislation – Wales
I. Title
344.4'2'03212

ISBN 1 85302 560 7

Printed and Bound in Great Britain by
Athenaeum Press, Gateshead, Tyne and Wear

CONTENTS

Acknowledgements

This book has been made possible by the conversations I have had in the course of my work with many local authority staff, voluntary organisations and solicitors. In particular, it has benefited from the proofreading and comments of my father. None of the views expressed represent those of any employer or contractor, past or present, for whom I have worked – and all errors are mine.

Disclaimer

Every effort has been made to ensure that the information contained in this book is correct, or at least represents a reasonable interpretation. However, not only is a book of this nature likely to contain errors, but the law is continually changing and is also – as the book reiterates many times – characterised by various uncertainties. Furthermore, particular situations and disputes possess their own unique set of circumstances, and the reader should seek professional advice when attempting to solve particular problems, formulate legally sound policies, challenge decisions etc.

INTRODUCTION

This book is intended to be a concise and practical guide to the complex field of community care law.

STRUCTURE OF THE BOOK

The book consists of one main A–Z section (preceded by three 'at-a-glance' lists of entries: general terms, Acts of Parliament, and cases). At the back of the book is a list of other items of legislation and guidance, which do not have their own entries. The A–Z list contains entries dealing with the following:

1. Specific services referred to in legislation (e.g. **home adaptations, home help, NHS continuing care, residential accommodation**);
2. Provision of those services (e.g. **duty, necessary, needs, power**);
3. Judicial review: concepts used by the law courts when they decide whether authorities have behaved lawfully (e.g. **illegality, unfairness, unreasonableness**);
4. Key aspects of community care, not necessarily referred to by legislation, but governing the delivery of community care in practice (e.g. **criteria of eligibility, delay (waiting times), priorities, resources**);
5. General considerations (e.g. **central government, knowledge of law, right answers**);
6. Legislation (e.g. *NHS and Community Care Act 1990*);
7. Case summaries (e.g. *Gloucestershire, Sefton*).

The text within each entry attempts not only to give a legal explanation, but also to indicate the consequences in everyday practice. Summaries of legal cases have been included to give the reader a feel for the issues coming before the courts and how they are dealt with. For reasons of space, it has not been possible to list every last service that might be provided under legislation; instead, for the most part, only those terms actually appearing in legislation have been included. For example, 'recreation' is listed because the term appears in the legislation, but all the possible recreation activities which exist (from bingo to swimming) are not. Arguably, the duties and powers in community care legislation are so wide that local authorities have very extensive powers indeed to provide all manner of service.

HOW TO USE THE BOOK

The book is designed to work on a number of levels to suit differing readers' needs.

It will be particularly useful for the busy practitioner, who does not have the time to read through a book on the subject. For example, a community care manager in social services might have to ask the following sorts of question: 'How long is it **reasonable** to **delay** in providing a service?'. 'Is it **illegal** to **withdraw** services such as **home help** because we have fewer financial **resources** than anticipated?'. 'Can we make a **rigid policy** never to provide **equipment** costing under £20?'. The emboldened terms in these questions could be looked up quickly.

Similarly, a community **physiotherapist** working in the NHS, having denied further treatment to a patient on the grounds that it will not be productive, might suddenly be threatened with **judicial review** (which she knows nothing about) and worry about whether her **record-keeping** will reflect an integrity of **clinical judgement**. A manager of **community health services** might face the same threat when she is forced to **ration** the provision of **incontinence** pads to patients in the community.

The book functions as a reference facility, designed to provide 'a five-minute guide' to any particular issue. From one perspective this reflects the approach to law and legislation often forced upon practitioners: namely, highly pressurised and fragmented. However, there is also extensive cross-referencing between entries in the A–Z list, allowing the reader – from either necessity or interest – to build up a more coherent picture of the community care legal framework. It should be emphasised that there are not necessarily 'right answers' to all the questions people ask about community care; indeed, it is the very legal uncertainty which lies behind the procession of community care cases through the law courts. However, even where absolutely certain answers are not available, it at least helps if the people who are making decisions, or those who are challenging them, know the type of questions to ask when attempting to assess just how sound a decision really is.

CROSS-REFERENCING

Within the main A–Z section cross-referencing is indicated by **emboldening**, except in the case of legislation and court cases when *italics* are used. Cross-referencing is made not only to the exact same word, but also to a common root: for example, the word 'assessed' might be linked to the entry word: **Assessment**. Generally speaking, words are emboldened only once within each entry. Emboldening has been added to quotations from legislation but not from law reports. Cross-referencing is generally contextual rather than literal: for instance, in the phrase 'authorities need to be cautious', the word 'need' (i.e. in the sense of 'should') would not be cross-referenced to the entry word **Need** which is about what people require.

ABBREVIATIONS AND USAGE OF PARTICULAR TERMS

For the most part, abbreviations have been avoided. One notable exception is that the term *CSDPA 1970* has been used instead of the *Chronically Sick and Disabled Persons Act 1970* (except in the case of its own entry). Another is *HASSASSA 1983*, which is the shortened form of *Health and Social Services and Social Security Act 1983*.

The term 'local authority' is used mainly to refer to local authorities (i.e. local councils) in respect of their social services functions only. It will be clear from the context where the term is used to refer to local councils as a whole. The terms 'housing authority' and 'education authority' refer to a local authority exercising either its housing or education functions. Sometimes one and the same authority is a housing, education and social services authority – i.e. unitary and metropolitan councils exercise all these different functions under various legislation.

SCOPE OF THE BOOK: COMMUNITY CARE IN A BROAD SENSE

The preferred aim of community care policy is, in principle at least, to enable people to remain in their own homes. Therefore, although community care embraces, legally, only services for adults provided by social services departments, the book also considers community care in a wider sense, by covering to some extent the provision of welfare services for disabled children and other children in need, provision of home adaptations by housing authorities, and provision by the NHS. Regrettably, for reasons of space and ease of use, the book applies specifically to England and Wales (though references to Welsh guidance are omitted), and only at a general level to Scotland and Northern Ireland.

WHOM IS THE BOOK FOR?

The book is aimed at a wide range of interested parties involved in the social care, health care and housing fields – including managers and practitioners, voluntary organisations and advice agencies, lawyers, service users, private sector providers, lecturers and students.

Examples of professionals within local authorities and the NHS, for whom the book will be relevant, include chiropodists, commissioning officers, care managers, district nurses, environmental health officers, general practitioners, home care managers, housing grants officers, NHS consultants in elderly care and rehabilitation, occupational therapists, physiotherapists, policy-makers, practice nurses, social workers, speech and language therapists, technical officers, and so on.

REASON FOR WRITING THE BOOK

The approach of the book reflects the fact that community care is increasingly being placed under the microscope by local authorities, the law courts, voluntary organisations and lawyers, in their attempt to ascertain rights and obligations – as resources diminish, disputes escalate and local authorities struggle to keep their practices and procedures on a sound legal footing.

By pointing out what is lawful and unlawful, the book is relevant to 'both sides' – i.e. those making decisions and those challenging them. In principle at least, this could contribute to a better quality of decision-making which, though inviting fewer challenges, would be of benefit to service users as a whole. As to wider issues affecting community care, such as the lack of resources, they lie ultimately in the political rather than the judicial domain.

AT-A-GLANCE

LIST OF TERMS IN A–Z LIST

Migration of services
Minor works assistance
Mixed economy of care
Mobile homes
Mobility
Monitoring officers
Museum attendants
Necessary
Needs
Needs-led assessment
Negligence
NHS services for residents of homes
Night-sitter services
Nursing attention
Nursing care
Nursing equipment
Nursing homes
Nursing services
Nursing treatment
Occupational activities
Occupational therapists
Old people
Ombudsman
Ordinarily resident
Ordinary needs
Other circumstances
Otherwise available
Outings: disabled people
Owner/tenant certificate
Palliative health care
Parliament
Participation of service users
Partnership
Passing the buck
Personal care
Personal information
Physical health
Physiotherapy
Policies
Policy guidance
Politics
Power (energy)
Power (legal)
Practical assistance
Practice guidance
Precedents
Predictability of law
Preferences
Preparation and cooking of food
Prevention of illness
Primary health care
Principal family room
Priorities
Private law
Procedures
Professional judgement
Psychological need
Public housing allocation
Public law
Publicity
Qualified duty
Radio
Rate-capping
Rationing
Reasonable
Reasons
Reassessment
Record-keeping
Recovery
Recreation
Referral
Registered social landlords
Registers of disabled people
Regulations
Rehabilitation
Relevant factors
Relief of poverty
Removing people
Remuneration
Renovation grants
Repair of a dwelling
Requirements (NHS)
Requisites
Residential accommodation
Residential homes
Resources
Respite care
Review of needs and services
Right answers
Rigid policies
Safety
Safety, comfort or convenience
Safety net
Satisfied
School-leavers: disabled
Screening
Semantic distinctions
Sensory impairment
Service provision
Settled residence
Shall
Shams
Shopping
Shouting loudest
Shower
Sight impairment
Social activities
Social care
Social Fund
Social rehabilitation
Social services committees
Social services directors
Social services functions
Social treatment of disorder
Social work services
Social workers
Sleeping room
Specific duty
Speech and language therapy
Speech impairment
Standards
Standing
Statutory duty: breach of
Statutory guidance
Statutory instruments
Stoma care
Strip wash
Subjective
Substantially and permanently handicapped
Supervision orders
Support
Target duty

AT-A-GLANCE

CASES IN A-Z LIST

Aldabbagh: *R v London Borough of Islington, ex parte Aldabbagh* (1994) 27 Housing Law Reports 271 (High Court).

Ali: *R v Inner London Education Authority, ex parte Ali* [1990] 2 Administrative Law Reports 822 (High Court).

Avon: *R v Avon County Council, ex parte M* [1994] 2 Family Court Reporter 259 (High Court).

Beckwith: *R v Wandsworth London Borough Council, ex parte Beckwith* [1996] 1 Family Court Reporter 504 (House of Lords).

Beckwith (no.2): *R v Wandsworth London Borough Council, ex parte Beckwith* (1995) 159 Local Government Review Reports 929. (High Court).

Bedfordshire: *X and others (minors v Bedfordshire County Council, M (a minor) and another v Newham London Borough Council and others, E (a minor) v Dorset County Council, and other appeals* [1995] 3 All England Law Reports 353 (House of Lords)

Berkshire: *R v Berkshire County Council, ex parte P* [1997] Crown Office Digest 64 (transcript, CO/526/96) (High Court).

Bexley: *R v London Borough of Bexley, ex parte B* [1995] 1 Current Law Year Book 3225 (transcript, 31 July 1995).

Birmingham: *R v Birmingham City Council, ex parte A (Minor)* [1997] 2 Family Court Reporter 357 (High Court, Family Division).

Bradford: *R v Bradford Metropolitan Borough Council, ex parte Sikander Ali* [1994] Education Law Reports 299 (High Court).

Bristol: *R v Bristol City Council, ex parte Bailey and Bailey* [1995] 27 Housing Law Reports 301 (High Court).

British Oxygen: *British Oxygen Co Ltd v Board of Trade* [1971] Appeal Cases 610 (House of Lords).

Bruce: *R v Department of Health and Social Security, ex parte Bruce* (1986), The Times, 8 February 1986 (and transcript, CO/123/86) (High Court).

Bucke: *R v Essex County Council, ex parte Bucke* [1997] Crown Office Digest 66 (transcript, CO/526/96) (High Court).

C: *R v Secretary of State for Education, ex parte C* [1996] 1 Education Law Reports 93 (High Court).

Caddell: *R v Lambeth London Borough Council, ex parte Caddell, The Times, 30 June 1997 (High Court).*

Cambridge (High Court): *R v Cambridge Health Authority, ex parte B (A Minor)* [1995] 1 Family Law Reports 1055

Cambridge (Court of Appeal): *R v Cambridge Health Authority, ex parte B (A Minor)* [1995] 6 Medical Law Reports 250 (Court of Appeal).

Carroll: *R v London Borough of Lambeth, ex parte Carroll* (1987) 20 Housing Law Reports 142 (High Court).

CCSU: *Council of Civil Service Unions v Minister for the Civil Service* [1985] Appeal Cases 374 (House of Lords)

Cleveland: *R v Cleveland County Council, ex parte Cleveland Care Homes Association and Others* (1993) 158 Local Government Review Reports 641 (High Court).

Cocks: *Cocks v Thanet District Council* [1983] 2 Appeal Cases 286 (House of Lords).

Collymore: *R v Warwickshire County Council, ex parte Collymore* [1995] Education Law Reports 217 (High Court).

Cumbria (High Court): *Cumbria Professional Care Limited v Cumbria County Council* [1996] 12 Current Law 505 (transcript, 30 September 1996, CO/3677/95).

Cumbria (Court of Appeal): *Cumbria Professional Care Limited v Cumbria County Council* (1996) (transcript, 18 April 1997 1996, LTA 96/7317/D).

Daykin: *R v Kirklees Metropolitan Borough Council, ex parte Daykin* [1996] 3 Current Law 565 (transcript, CO/2944/95) (High Court).

Devon: *R v Devon County Council, ex parte Baker and Johns; R v Durham County Council, ex parte Curtis and Broxson* (1992) 158 Local Government Review Reports 241 (Court of Appeal).

Durham: see Devon

East Sussex (High Court): *R v East Sussex County Council, ex parte T* (1997) The Times, 29 April 1997

East Sussex (Court of Appeal): *R v East Sussex County Council, ex parte T* (1997), *The Times*, 2 October 1997 (transcript, 31 July 1997, QBCOF/97/0714/D)

Enfield: *Barrett v Enfield London Borough Council* [1997] 3 Weekly Law Reports 628 (Court of Appeal)

Essex: *W and others v Essex County Council and Golden* (1997), *The Times*, 16 July 1997 (High Court).

Farley: *R v Staffordshire County Council, ex parte Farley* [1997] 7 Current Law 572 (transcript, 8 April 1997, CO/4413/96)

Fox: *R v Ealing District Health Authority, ex parte Fox* [1993] 1 Weekly Law Reports 373 (High Court).

GLC: *Bromley London Borough Council v Greater London Council* [1983] Appeal Cases 768 (House of Lords).

Gloucestershire (High Court): *R v Gloucestershire County Council, ex parte Mahfood and Others* (1995) 160 Local Government Review Reports 321

Gloucestershire (High Court no 2): *R v Gloucestershire County Council, ex parte Royal Association for Disability and Rehabilitation* (1995) (transcript, CO/2764/95)

Gloucestershire (Court of Appeal): *R v Gloucestershire County Council, ex parte Barry* [1996] 4 All England Law Reports 422.

Gloucestershire (House of Lords): *R v Gloucestershire County Council, ex parte Barry* [1997] 2 All England Law Reports 1.

Goldsack: *R v Cornwall County Council, ex parte Goldsack* (1996) (transcript, 28 June 1996) (High Court).

Good: *R v Kirklees Metropolitan Borough Council, ex parte Good* [1996] 11 Current Law 288 (transcript, CO/436/96) (High Court).

Gorenkin: *R v Newham London Borough Council, ex parte Gorenkin* (1997), The Times, 9 and 13 (note of clarification) June 1997 (transcript, CO/1564/97) (High Court).

Hammersmith and Fulham: *R v Hammersmith and Fulham London Borough Council, ex parte M (and other cases)* (1997), The Times, 19 February 1997 (Court of Appeal).

Hammersmith and Fulham (no 2): *R v Secretary of State for Health, ex parte London Borough of Hammersmith and Fulham (and others)* (1997), The Independent, 15 July 1997 (High Court)

Harcombe: *R v Somerset County Council, ex parte Harcombe* (1997), The Times, 7 May 1997 (transcript, CO 4005/95) (High Court). (And see article in: The Times, 29 April 1997).

Hargreaves: *R v North Yorkshire County Council, ex parte Hargreaves* (1994) 26 Butterworths Medical Law Reports 121 (High Court).

Hargreaves (no 2): *R v North Yorkshire County Council, ex parte Hargreaves* (1997), The Times, 12 June 1997; The Independent, 20 May 1997 (transcript, CO/181/95) (High Court).

Haringey: *R v Haringey Council, ex parte Norton* (1997) (transcript, 15 July 1997, CO/555/97) (High Court)

Harow (two linked cases):

R v Brent and Harrow Health Authority, ex parte Harrow London Borough Council (1996), The Times, 15 October 1996 (High Court).

R v Harrow London Borough Council, ex parte M [1997] 1 Education Law Reports 62 (High Court).

Hendry: *R v Leeds City Council, ex parte Hendry* (1993) 158 Local Government Review Reports 621 (High Court).

Hendy: *R v Bristol Corporation, ex parte Hendy* [1974] 1 Weekly Law Reports 498 (Court of Appeal).

Hillingdon: *R v Hillingdon London Borough Council, ex parte Governing Body of Queensmead School* (1997) The Times, 9 January 1997 (High Court).

Hincks: *R v Secretary of State for Social Services and Others, ex parte Hincks and Others* (1980) 1 Butterworths Medico-Legal Reports 93 (Court of Appeal).

Hooper: *Avon County Council v Hooper and Another* [1997] 1 All England Law Reports 532 (Court of Appeal)

IRC: *R v Inland Revenue Commissioners, ex parte National Federation of Self-Employed and Small Businesses Ltd* [1982] Appeal Cases 617 (House of Lords).

Khan: *R v Secretary of State for the Home Department, ex parte Khan* [1984] 1 Weekly Law Reports 1337 (Court of Appeal).

Kingston upon Hull: *R v Secretary of State for the Environment, ex parte Kingston upon Hull City Council* [1996] Crown Office Digest 289 (High Court).

Jennifer Lewis: *R v London Borough of Ealing, ex parte Jennifer Lewis (1992) 24 Housing Law Reports 484* (Court of Appeal.

Lancashire: *R v Lancashire County Council, ex parte Royal Association for Disability and Rehabilitation and another* [1996] 4 All England Law Reports 422 (Court of Appeal). Heard with the Gloucestershire case.

Leaman: *R v London Borough of Ealing, ex parte Leaman* (1984), The Times, 10 February 1984 (and transcript, CO/562/83) (High Court).

M: *R v Lancashire County Council, ex parte M* [1989] 2 Family Law Reports 279 (Court of Appeal).

Macwan: *R v Brent London Borough Council, ex parte Macwan* [1994] 2 Family Court Reporter 604 (Court of Appeal).

Manchester: *R v Secretary of State for Health, ex parte Manchester Local Medical Committee and Others* [1995] 2 Current Law Year Book 3621 (transcript, CO/189/94) (High Court).

McMillan: *R v London Borough of Islington, ex parte McMillan* (1995) 160 Local Government Review Reports 321 (High Court). Heard in the High Court with the Gloucestershire case.

Newcastle: *R v Newcastle-upon-Tyne City Council, ex parte Dixon* (1993) 158 Local Government Review Reports 441 (High Court).

Northavon: *R v Northavon District Council, ex parte Smith* [1994] 2 Family Court Reporter 859 (House of Lords).

O'Rourke: *O'Rourke v London Borough of Camden* (1997), The Independent, 17 June 1997 (House of Lords).

Oxfordshire: *R v Oxfordshire County Council, ex parte W* [1987] 2 Family Law Reports 193 (High Court).

Patchett: *Patchett v Leathem* (1948), The Times Law Reports, 4 February 1949 (High Court)

Powys: *R v Powys County Council, ex parte Hambridge* (1997) (CO/280/97: judgment expected October 1997).

Quinn: *Chief Adjudication Officer and Another v Quinn* [1996] 1 Weekly Law Reports 1184 (House of Lords).

Re J: *Re J (a minor) (wardship: medical treatment)* [1992] 4 All England Law Reports 614 (Court of Appeal).

Redbridge: *R v London Borough of Redbridge, ex parte East Sussex County Council* [1993] Crown Office Digest 256 (High Court).

Redezeus: *R v Sunderland City Council, ex parte Redezeus* (1994), 27 Housing Law Reports 477 (High Court).

Richmond: *R v Richmond upon Thames London Borough Council, ex parte McCarthy and Stone* [1991] 4 All ER 897 (House of Lords).

Rixon: *R v London Borough of Islington, ex parte Rixon* [1997] 1 Education Law Reports (High Court).

Sefton (High Court): *R v Sefton Metropolitan Borough Council, ex parte Help the Aged and Others* (1997) The Times, 27 March 1997; The Independent, 18 April 1997 (transcript, CO/3036/96)

Sefton (Court of Appeal): *R v Sefton Metropolitan Borough Council, ex parte Help the Aged and Others* (1997) (transcript, 31 July 1997, QBCOF 97/0819/D)

Shah: *R v Barnet London Borough Council, ex parte Shah* [1983] 2 Appeal Cases 309 (House of Lords).

Southwark: *Southwark London Borough Council v Williams* [1971] 1 Chancery 734 (Court of Appeal).

Staffordshire: *Staffordshire County Council v J and J* [1996] 4 Education Law Reports 418 (High Court).

Steane: *Steane v Chief Adjudication Officer* [1996] 1 Weekly Law Reports 1195 (House of Lords).

Tameside: *Secretary of State for Education and Science v Tameside Metropolitan Borough Council* [1977] Appeal Cases 1014 (House of Lords).

Tilley: *Attorney General ex rel Tilley v London Borough of Wandsworth* [1981] 1 All England Law Reports 1162 (Court of Appeal).

Tower Hamlets: *R v The Mayor and Burgesses of the London Borough of Tower Hamlets, ex parte Bradford* [1997] Crown Office Digest 282 (High Court).

Tucker: *R v London Borough of Sutton, ex parte Tucker* [1997] Crown Office Digest 144 (transcript, CO/1075/96) (High Court).

Vicar of Writtle: *The Vicar of Writtle and Others v Essex County Council* (1979) 77 Local Government Reports 656 (High Court).

Woolgar: *R v Hertsmere Borough Council, ex parte Pettina Woolgar* (1995) 160 Local Government Review Reports 260 (High Court).

Wyatt: *Wyatt v Hillingdon Borough Council* (1978) 76 Local Government Reports 727 (Court of Appeal).

Zakrocki: *R Secretary of State for the Home Office, ex parte Zackrocki* [1996] Crown Office Digest 304 (High Court).

AT-A-GLANCE

ACTS OF PARLIAMENT IN A–Z LIST

Access to Personal Files Act 1987

Carers (Recognition and Services) Act 1995

Children Act 1989

Chronically Sick and Disabled Persons Act 1970

Community Care (Direct Payments) Act 1996

Data Protection Act 1984

Disabled Persons (Services, Consultation and Representation) Act 1986

Disability Discrimination Act 1995

Health Services and Public Health Act 1968

Health and Social Services and Social Security Adjudications Act 1983

Housing Act 1985

Housing Act 1996

Housing Grants, Construction and Regeneration Act 1986

Local Authorities Goods and Services Act 1970

Local Authority Social Services Act 1970

Local Government Act 1972

Local Government and Housing Act 1989

Mental Health Act 1983, s.117

National Assistance Act 1948

NHS Act 1977

NHS and Community Care Act 1990

Registered Homes Act 1984

A–Z LIST

- **ABSOLUTE DUTY:** see **Duty: absolute**

ACCESS

Access (physical). Access by a **disabled occupant** to and from a dwelling, and to different parts of it, underlies the list of statutory purposes for which a housing authority has a duty to approve an application for a **disabled facilities grant** – if various other conditions are also met (*Housing Grants, Construction and Regeneration Act 1996*, s.23).

Access to Personal Files Act 1987. This Act governs access to personal information generally. Specifically, access to social services information is covered by the *Access to Personal Files (Social Services) Regulations 1989* (SI 1989/206). See: **Information: personal**

ACCOMMODATION

Accommodation: boarding for old people. In order to meet the needs of **elderly people**, local authorities have the **power** to **make arrangements** to provide assistance in finding suitable households for boarding (Approval under *Health Services and Public Health Act 1968*, s.45).

Accommodation: children. A local authority has a **duty** toward 'any child' in need in its area to provide accommodation in certain circumstances (e.g. where there is nobody with parental responsibility) (*Children Act 1989*, ss.20,22). In addition, the courts (*Tower Hamlets* case) have ruled that accommodation could in certain circumstances also be provided for a child and his or her **family** under the **general duty** – to safeguard and promote the welfare of **children in need** (which **may** include provision for the whole family) – contained in s.17 of the *Children Act 1989.*

Accommodation: disabled facilities grants. Making a dwelling or building suitable for the accommodation of the *disabled occupant* is one of the statutory purposes for which a housing authority **may** approve an application for a **disabled facilities grant** – i.e. a **discretionary**, rather than a **mandatory**, grant (*Housing Grants, Construction and Regeneration Act 1996*, s.23).

Accommodation: NHS provision. The Secretary of State has a **duty** – exercised by health authorities – to provide hospital or other accommodation 'to such extent as he **considers necessary** to meet all **reasonable requirements**'

(*NHS Act 1977*, s.3). This is a vague duty, difficult to enforce in the law courts because of the wide **discretion** it confers. This difficulty has been confirmed in cases such as *Cambridge and Hincks* – although the health service ombudsman attempted to give the duty some substance in his **Leeds investigation**.

Accommodation: nursing home: see **Nursing homes**

Accommodation: public housing: see **Housing allocation; Housing Act 1985; CSDPA 1970**

Accommodation: residential: see **Residential accommodation**

■ ACT UNDER

Local authorities have a **duty** to 'act under' the general **guidance** of the Secretary of State under the *Local Authority Social Services Act 1970*, s.7(1). Guidance – such as community care policy guidance – issued under this **legislation** is sometimes referred to as statutory guidance, and regarded by the law courts as imposing stronger obligations than guidance which is not issued under the 1970 Act.

The term 'act under' suggests something short of 'follow to the letter'. Nevertheless, in practice, the law courts have found that failure to follow guidance can in some circumstances amount to **unlawfulness** (e.g. the *Hargreaves*, *Rixon* and *Fisher* cases).

■ **ADAPTATIONS:** see **Home adaptations**

■ ADDITIONAL FACILITIES

This term refers to **equipment** provided for **disabled people** under s.2 of the *CSDPA 1970*, and for **elderly** people under the *Health Services and Public Health Act 1968*. In both Acts the additional facilities are for people's 'greater **safety, comfort or convenience**'. Under the 1970 Act, the authority has to be **satisfied** that it is **necessary** for it to meet the person's **needs**.

Meaning of 'additional'. The word 'additional' has not been examined by the courts in this context, but might be interpreted by local authorities in two different ways: *first*, as an extra item needed (and therefore an extra cost) on account of the person's **disability**; or *second*, as an item which is a specialist (i.e. rather than an **ordinary**) item, and likewise needed because of the person's disability. (A similar, though not identical, dichotomy of interpretation arose in the *Hargreaves (no.2)* case, about **holidays** under s.2 of the CSDPA 1970 – although in the case of holidays the word 'additional' does not appear in the legislation).

The practical consequences of the two different interpretations are as follows. Under the *first*, authorities could provide both ordinary equipment (not designed specially for disability or frailty) such as electric tin-openers, footstools, jar-openers, non-slip bath mats and portable heaters – as well as specially designed equipment such as hoists or kettle-tippers. Under the *second*, authorities could only provide the latter, specialist type of equipment.

Although, as already mentioned, the meaning of the term 'additional' has not been clarified by the courts, it is possible that the second interpretation might be deemed too restrictive. In addition, there might be practical problems with it, because it depends on distinguishing specialist, disability equipment from ordinary equipment. Yet disputes in the field of VAT have shown that this distinction can be difficult to make, in those circumstances when zero-rating depends on equipment having been designed solely for disabled people. For instance, in one case involving overbed tables, a VAT tribunal decided that though of particular value to disabled people, they were also useful to all sorts of other hospital patients as well; therefore zero-rating could not apply.

On the other hand, the first interpretation might make local authorities anxious about opening the **floodgates**, being asked to furnish disabled people's homes from 'top to bottom', and having to **relieve poverty** by meeting the costs of everyday items. Nevertheless, such a fear is almost certainly ill-founded, since, under the *CSDPA 1970*, the need for the item still must stem from the person's disability – and, in any case, the authority still has first to decide according to its **criteria of eligibility:** (a) whether there is a need for the item at all, and (b) whether it is necessary for it to make arrangements to meet the need.

ADEQUATE

An imprecise term occurring in legislation.

Adequate: home help. Local authorities have a **duty** to provide home help for households on a scale 'adequate' for the area (*NHS Act 1977*, schedule 8). This appears to be a **general** or **target duty** towards the local population, which might be more difficult to enforce than a **specific duty** towards individuals. It resembles the duty of authorities to ensure that sufficient schools are available for the area – which the court in the *Ali* case characterised as a target duty only.

Adequate: staff. Local authorities are under a **duty** to secure the provision of adequate staff to assist the **director of social services** in his or her functions (*Local Authority Social Services Act 1970*, s.6).

In general this is a duty enforced with difficulty against authorities. However, in some limited circumstances, this section of the 1970 Act might be capable of being used in both **judicial review** and investigations of the **local ombudsman** as evidence of failings. For example, records of **social services committee** meetings might show (a) an awareness of long-standing staffing problems resulting in poor services, and (b) inaction on the part of the committee, over a substantial period of time, in attempting to remedy the situation.

ADJUSTMENT TO DISABILITY

Local authorities have a **duty** to **make arrangements** to provide facilities (whether at centres or elsewhere) for **social rehabilitation** and adjustment to **disability** – including assistance in overcoming **communication** and **mobility** limitations – for disabled people who are **ordinarily resident** in the area. In respect of those not ordinarily resident, there is a **power** only (Direction and Approval under *National Assistance Act 1948*, s.29).

This broad duty empowers local authorities to provide a wide range of services – including, for instance, daily assistance with walking (as in the *Goldsack* case), or even **communication aids** or **speech and language therapy** (e.g. if these were not forthcoming under other **legislation**).

ADVICE

When authorities seek to make best use of **resources** and yet still assist people as far as possible, advice about different ways of dealing with problems and difficulties is crucial. At least part of good advice-giving relies on staff having access to, and disseminating, good quality **information**.

Advice: children. In respect of **children in need** who are living with their **families** in the area, local authorities have a **duty** to make 'such provision as they consider **appropriate**' for various services including advice (*Children Act 1989*, schedule 2).

Advice: disabled people. Local authorities have a **duty** towards **disabled people** who are **ordinarily resident** in the area – but only a **power** towards those not ordinarily resident – to **make arrangements** to provide advice (Direction and Approval under *National Assistance Act 1948*, s.29).

Advice: elderly people. In order to meet the **needs** of **elderly people**, local authorities have the **power** to **make arrangements** to provide advisory services (Approval under *Health Services and Public Health Act 1968*, s.45).

Advice: illness. For the prevention of **illness**, the care of people who are ill, and the **after-care** of people who have been ill, local authorities have the **power** to **make arrangements** to provide advice to prevent the **impairment** of physical or mental **health** of adults in **families** where such impairment is likely, or to prevent the break-up of such families, or for assisting in their **rehabilitation** (Approval under *NHS Act 1977*, schedule 8).

AFTER-CARE

A term occurring both in community care (social services) and **NHS legislation**.

After-care: illness (NHS). To 'such extent as he **considers necessary** to meet all **reasonable requirements**', the Secretary of State has a **duty** – **delegated** to health authorities – to provide such facilities for the after-care of people who have suffered from **illness** 'as he **considers** are **appropriate** as part of the health service' (*NHS Act 1977*, s.3). This is a vague duty, difficult to enforce in the law courts because of the wide **discretion** it confers on authorities, as illustrated in the *Cambridge* and *Hincks* cases. Nevertheless, the **health service ombudsman's Leeds investigation**, which attempted to put some substance into the duty, referred specifically to the failure to provide after-care.

After-care might cover services (in or out of hospital) such as **continuing care, rehabilitation, respite care,** and so on.

After-care: mental disorder: see **Mental disorder**

After-care: non-residential services. Local authorities have a **power** to **make arrangements** for the provision of non-residential after-care services for people who have been suffering from **illness** (Approval and Direction under *NHS Act 1977*, schedule 8).

After-care: residential accommodation. Local authorities have the **power** to **make arrangements** to provide **residential accommodation** for the after-care of people suffering from **illness** (Approval under *National Assistance Act 1948*, s.21).

AGE

The terms 'age' or 'aged' occur at various points in the **legislation** but are not defined in terms of years. See also: **Elderly people**

Age: home help. Local authorities have a **duty** to provide, or **arrange** for the provision of, **home help** for households 'on such a scale as is **adequate** for the **needs** of their area' – which is **required** because of the presence of a person who is 'aged' (*NHS Act 1977*, schedule 8).

Age: laundry facilities. Local authorities have the **power** to provide, or **arrange** for the provision of, **laundry facilities** for households for which **home help** is being, or could be, provided for a person who is 'aged' (*NHS Act 1977*, schedule 8).

Age: residential accommodation. Local authorities have a **duty** to **make arrangements** to provide **residential accommodation** for people who, because of age, are in **need** of **care and attention** not **otherwise available** to them (Direction under *National Assistance Act 1948*, s.21).

ALCOHOL AND DRUGS

Department of Health **guidance** issued in 1993 attaches a high **priority** to tackling the misuse of alcohol and drugs – and states that the **criteria of eligibility** of local authorities should be 'sensitive to the circumstances of alcohol and drug misusers' (LAC(93)2).

Later guidance on the purchasing of treatment for drug misusers urges that both health authorities and social services departments 'should identify gaps in their current service provision and ensure that **appropriate**, effective and accessible services are developed'. This should include, for example, practical **co-operation**, long-term **partnership** (where possible), and a user-centred approach (see LAC(97)9 and accompanying guidance book).

Alcohol and drugs: illness (non-residential services). For the prevention of **illness**, the care of people who are ill, and the **after-care** of people who have been ill, local authorities have the **power** to **make arrangements** for the provision of 'services specifically for persons who are alcoholic or drug-dependent' (Approval under *NHS Act 1977*, schedule 8).

Alcohol and drugs: illness (residential care). For the prevention of **illness**, the care of people who are ill, and the **after-care** of people who have been ill, local authorities have the **power** to **make arrangements** for the provision of **residential accommodation** 'specifically for persons who are alcoholic or drug-dependent' (Approval under *National Assistance Act 1948*, s.21).

Alcohol and drugs: payments to voluntary organisations. The Secretary of State has the **power** to make a specific grant to local authorities, to enable them to make payments to voluntary organisations which provide care and services for people who are, have been, or are likely to become, dependent on alcohol or drugs (*Local Authority Social Services Act 1970*, s.7E).

■ ALDABBAGH CASE

A housing case illustrating **unlawful delegation** of decision-making.

One aspect of the case focused on the housing authority's **policy** which stated that decisions in relation to rent arrears of over £50 should be delegated to, and be decided by, a neighbourhood manager. In fact, the arrears were above £250 but the decision was taken by an officer at a lower level. This meant that the decision had been taken 'without authority' and so was unlawful; especially since the decision might have been different if the manager had taken it.

■ ALI CASE

This education case explored the notion of **target duties**, referring to them as less than **absolute**, couched in 'broad and general terms', and possessing a 'degree of elasticity'. It referred to these duties as being a 'common feature of legislation which is designed to benefit the community', such as s.1 of the *NHS Act 1977*.

■ **ALLOCATION OF PUBLIC HOUSING:** see **Housing allocation**

■ ALTERNATIVE REMEDIES

Authorities sometimes attempt to deflect **judicial review** challenges by claiming that they should be resolved via an alternative channel such as **complaints** procedures or the Secretary of State's **default powers**. The courts state sometimes (e.g. *Birmingham, Good* cases) that such other channels should be used or at least exhausted first, but at other times (e.g. *Devon* case) that certain types of dispute (e.g. involving points of law) are more appropriately dealt with via judicial review.

■ **AMENITIES (IN RESIDENTIAL CARE):** see **Residential accommodation**

■ ANY PERSON

The term 'any person' in **legislation**, in combination with the word **'shall'**, might indicate the existence of a strong, **specific duty** towards individual people – rather than a **general duty**, more difficult to enforce, towards the local population or other group of people as a whole.

For example, the **duty** to carry out a community care **assessment** is owed to any person who **appears** to be in need of **community care services** (*NHS and Community Care Act 1990*, s.47). Whereas the duty of a health authority to provide services under the *NHS Act 1977* is towards the local population as a whole.

■ APPEARANCE OF NEED

It is appearance of **need** which triggers the **duty** to carry out a community care **assessment**: 'where it appears to a local authority that **any person** for whom they may provide or arrange for the provision of **community care services** may be in need of any such services' (*NHS and Community Care Act 1990*, s.47(1)).

Therefore, no request is required, nor strictly speaking is the person's consent to the assessment (though an authority might not get very far without such consent or co-operation). The duty is not tantamount to **assessment on request**. Nevertheless, the duty would appear to be extensive, since it arises on an appearance of possible need, rather than actual need. The following should be borne in mind both by authorities when formulating, and by users of services when challenging, **policies** on assessment:

(1) **Appearance of need: broad or narrow approach?** On the one hand the term 'appears' is **subjective**, in that the appearance is in the eye of the authority, not that of the person in need or an independent onlooker. On the other hand, the very breadth of the term can make it difficult for local authorities to restrict its application. Thus, when the NHS and Community Care Bill was passing through **Parliament**, the government made it quite clear that although the duty did not amount to assessment on request, it came near, since it was intended to be wide-ranging and not to be interpreted narrowly so as to deny people assessments.

(2) **Restrictive approaches in practice.** Even so, some authorities seem precisely to be attempting a restrictive approach when reworking policies in the light of reduced **resources** in order to deny assessment to certain groups of people. It seems that some authorities reduce **waiting lists** – on which people have waited for months or years – not by finally assessing people, but by re-categorising what is meant by 'need' and 'appearance of need' in the light of revised policies and **criteria of eligibility**. In this way, a number of those waiting are simply removed from the list.

(But if, for example, the long **delay** is due to **maladministration**, and if a complainant would have been eligible under the old policy, then the **local ombudsman** might recommend that the local authority pay compensation – since the maladministration would have deprived the complainant of a service.)

(3) **Simple assessment or pre-assessment screening?** In practice, on the basis of a quick telephone conversation involving questions such as 'can you make a cup of tea unaided?', an authority might decide that a person does not appear to be in need of services, and thus is not entitled to even an assessment. Alternatively, recognising the extensive nature of a term such as 'appears' and the legal difficulty in denying people assessments, another authority might claim that the very same telephone conversation actually constitutes an assessment, albeit a simple one.

Both practices might be adopted by authorities so that they can manage large numbers of enquiries and applications within limited resources. Both also illustrate the thin line between assessment and **screening**. One danger that local authorities run by adopting either practice has been exposed by the local ombudsman on occasion: namely that their initial information-gathering is insufficiently thorough to justify decisions about people's (potential) needs.

(4) **Appearance of need: looking away.** If an authority wilfully 'looks away' or 'sticks its head in the sand' so as to claim that particular people do not appear to be in need, then it might be subject to adverse findings by the local ombudsman or even **judicial review** by the law courts. For instance, in order to clear a long, 'low priority' **waiting list**, an **occupational therapist** might be carrying out simple assessments for people's **bathing** needs, under strict instructions to 'ignore' any other needs for **community care services** which she comes across during assessment. Arguably, such a policy might be of dubious legality.

Indeed, the *Gloucestershire (no.2)* case emphasised the strength of the duty to assess people in apparent need. The judge ruled that the duty to assess (or reassess) a person who appears to be in need could not be discharged by simply sending a letter offering **reassessment**, and stating that unless a reply was received, **home help** services would remain **withdrawn** or reduced. This was because once the appearance of need had been established – which it clearly had because these people had already been receiving services – the duty to assess could not be discharged simply on the grounds that people did not respond to a letter.

■ APPROPRIATE

The vague term 'appropriate' is used sometimes in **legislation** to qualify a **duty**.

For example, to 'such extent as he **considers necessary** to meet all **reasonable requirements**', the Secretary of State has a **duty** – exercised by **health authorities – to provide such facilities for the prevention of illness**, the care of those who are ill, and the **after-care** of those who have been ill 'as he **considers** are appropriate as part of the health service' (*NHS Act 1977*, s.3). Similarly, housing authorities must be **satisfied** as to whether proposed **home adaptations** are **'necessary and appropriate'** to meet the needs of a **disabled occupant**, before approving applications for **disabled facilities grants** (*Housing Grants, Construction and Regeneration Act 1996*, s.24).

Nevertheless, although the term 'appropriate' is vague, its very vagueness might mean that authorities cannot dismiss its effect, in relation to a duty, with impunity. For instance, the *Tower Hamlets* case involved s.17 of the *Children Act 1989*, which states (amongst other things) that local authorities have a **general duty** to promote and safeguard the welfare of **children in need** by providing a 'range and level of services appropriate to those children's needs'. The judge found that in failing even to consider whether to provide **accommodation** for the child and his parents, the authority had interpreted the scope of s.17 too narrowly.

■ **APPROVALS:** see **Directions**

■ **APPROVED SOCIAL WORKERS:** see **Social workers**

■ **ARRANGE:** see **Make arrangements**

■ ASSESSMENT

Assessment is crucial to community care. Despite the fanfare of publicity about the implementation of mainstream community care, the *NHS and Community Care Act 1990* did not, in the main, introduce any new services. Instead, it put in place a gateway of assessment, through which people must pass if they are to gain access to **community care services** provided under other, previously existing, **legislation**. The entries immediately below outline the legal foundation for this gateway and also some of the practical implications.

Assessment: appearance of need: see **Appearance of need**

Assessment: care management framework: see **Care management**

Assessment: carers: see **Carers**

Assessment: existence of duty. Assessment is a duty towards individual people imposed on local authorities. Where:

> 'it **appears** to a local authority that **any person** for whom they **may** provide or **arrange** for the provision of **community care services** may be in **need** of any such services, the authority (a) shall carry out an assessment of his **needs**

for those services; and (b) **having regard** to the results of that assessment, shall then decide whether his needs **call for** the provision by them of any such services (*NHS and Community Care Act 1990*, s.47(1)).'

This two-part duty seems straightforward, but authorities sometimes fail to perform it. For instance, in the *Daykin* case the recommendation of a local authority's advocacy officer was ruled not to be an assessment, because, under the council's **policy** of **delegation**, it was not her responsibility: she had no authority. This meant that no assessment and decision about services had in fact been made. In the *Berkshire* case, it was alleged that the assessment did not take account of needs but merely listed services already being provided. And, in the *Tucker* case, the second part of the duty – the decision about what services are called for – had still not been performed two years after the first part (the assessment of need) had been completed.

In addition, assessment involves the following:

(1) **Assessment of disabled people.** If 'at any time during the assessment', it appears to an authority that the person being assessed is **disabled**, then the authority has a duty to decide what services the person **requires** under s.4 of the *Disabled Persons (Services, Consultation and Representation) Act 1986*, and to inform the person of what is happening and what his or her rights are under the 1986 Act. The services referred to by s.4 of 1986 Act are those provided under s.2 of the *CSDPA 1970*.

It would appear that many local authorities **breach** their **statutory duty** in this respect, and fail to tell disabled people what is going on. It seems that occasionally local authorities even receive legal advice neither to tell people, nor to record, that an assessment involves the 1970 Act, because decisions are more easily challenged if that Act is involved. However, any such advice is an encouragement to breach the law. It might also lead an authority into further trouble, since the **local ombudsmen** and the courts are not impressed by vague, inadequate **record-keeping**.

(2) **Assessment on request of disabled people under the 1986 Act.** Perhaps confusingly, authorities remain anyway under a free-standing duty to assess **disabled people** under s.4 of the 1986 Act, if they are requested either by a disabled person or by a **carer** providing substantial care on a regular basis. Thus, the effect of the 1990 Act is to make this request unnecessary (for adults) – but only assuming a community care assessment is under way. However, should a community care assessment not be forthcoming for some reason, then this duty to assess on request might still be of use to disabled people. For instance, it seems that in practice some authorities bypass the 1990 Act altogether, and continue to regard assessment under the 1986 Act and *CSDPA 1970* as a separate procedure, legally and administratively.

The duty under the 1986 Act remains more relevant to children, since the *Children Act 1989* does not contain the same provision for 'automatic' assessment for *CSDPA* services, which the 1990 Act contains (see e.g. *Bexley* case).

(3) **Assessment under the CSDPA 1970.** Even under s.2 of the *CSDPA 1970* itself – without reference to the 1990 and 1986 Acts – an authority has a duty to assess, even though the term 'assessment' is not mentioned. This is because the authority has to be **satisfied** about whether it is **necessary** to **make arrangements** to provide for a person's needs; yet it could scarcely satisfy itself without carrying out some form of assessment. Thus, a refusal to assess and to provide under the Act might be regarded by the courts as avoidance of the duty placed on authorities and even as **unreasonable**, as illustrated by the judge's comments in the *Bexley* case. The local authority had claimed that it was making provision under the **general duty** imposed by s.17 of the *Children Act 1989*, but not under the

specific duty of the 1970 Act – even though the **practical assistance in the home** at issue fell plainly within the ambit of the 1970 Act.

(4) **Invitation to the health authority and housing authority.** If during the assessment it appears to a local authority that the person might need services from the health authority or housing authority, then it has a duty to notify and invite either of these 'to assist, to such extent as is reasonable in the circumstances, in the making of the assessment'. When deciding about the provision of services, the local authority must then 'take into account' what services are 'likely to be made available' by the health authority or housing authority' (*NHS and Community Care Act 1990*, s.47(3)).

It should be noted that (a) there is no explicit duty placed on the health authority or housing authority to respond to the invitation, let alone provide services; and (b) the courts are wary of enforcing **co-operation** between authorities (e.g. *Northavon* case).

Assessment: level. Community care **guidance** envisages different assessment levels, from the quick and simple at one extreme, to the comprehensive and multi-disciplinary at the other (SSI/SWSG 1991a). In practice, local authorities attempt to steer a middle course between assessing people too superficially and failing to identify **needs**, and assessing them in excessive depth, intrusively and time-consumingly.

Assessment: mental disorder. Local authorities have a **duty** to **make arrangements** for the provision of **social work** and related services to help in the assessment of **mental disorder** (Direction under *NHS Act 1977*, schedule 8).

Assessment: nature of duty. The **legislation** does not specify what assessments should consist of, although the Secretary of State has the **power** to issue **Directions** about how they should be carried out or the form they should take. No Directions have been issued. In their absence, authorities are under a **duty** to carry out assessments in the form and manner that they **consider appropriate** (*NHS and Community Care 1990*, s.47).

Instead, **guidance** must be looked to in order to understand the Department of Health's intentions. This might seem odd; however, during the passing of the 1990 Act through **Parliament**, the government explained that rather than place local authorities in a legal and bureaucratic straitjacket, it wished to give them flexibility to innovate and develop best practice. Thus, it is guidance rather than legislation which introduces and explains terms such as **needs-led assessment, screening, priorities,** levels of assessment (see above), **criteria of eligibility** etc. Furthermore, guidance emphasises the importance of the **participation** of service users in assessments, the seeking-out of their **preferences** by authorities, and a broad view of **need** (e.g. DH 1990, SSI/SWSG 1991a). Such considerations appear to preclude cavalier and superficial approaches to assessment.

Assessment: needs-led: see **Needs-led assessment**

Assessment: on request: see **Assessment: existence of duty**

Assessment: resources. At the heart of the *Gloucestershire* case was the question of the extent to which local authorities can take account of **resources** when assessing **need** and when deciding whether or how to meet it. See: **Resources**.

ASYLUM-SEEKERS

Several cases have been heard about the provision of **residential accommodation** for asylum-seekers under s.21 of the *National Assistance Act 1948*: see *Hammersmith and Fulham, Hammersmith and Fulham (no.2)* and *Gorenkin* cases.

AVON CASE

This case shows (a) how fine the line is – in some circumstances – between a person's **preferences** and **psychological needs**; and (b) that local authorities might need to have good **reasons** for not following the recommendations of a **complaints** review panel.

(1) Preference for residential home. The case involved a 22-year-old man with Down's Syndrome, for whom the local authority was under a duty to **make arrangements** for **residential accommodation** under s.21 of the *National Assistance Act 1948*. The man had an 'entrenched' **wish** to go to a particular home, but the council had decided to place him in a cheaper one which would still, it claimed, meet his **needs**.

The dispute went to the **complaints** procedure review panel – which recommended that the council make arrangements for provision at the man's **choice** of home. The panel found, having consulted expert opinion, that the **assessment** should be based on current need, including psychological, educational, social and medical needs, and that the entrenched position of the man formed part of his psychological need. The **social services committee** of the council, worried about setting costly **precedents**, rejected the panel's findings.

(2) Psychological need. The judge stated that needs 'may properly include psychological needs', and that the authority was not therefore being forced to pay more than it otherwise would have paid normally (something it was not required to do under the Choice of Accommodation Directions in LAC(92)27): it would 'simply be paying what the law required'. He also referred to guidance (LAC(92)15) on adults with learning disabilities, which states that services should be arranged on an individual basis (and which goes on: 'taking account of **age**, needs, degree of **disability**, the personal preferences of the individual and his or her parents or **carers, culture,** race and gender').

The judge found that it was **unlawful** for the council to disregard the recommendation of the review panel without a substantial reason, given the weight of evidence informing the panel's findings.

BALANCING EXERCISE

When the *Gloucestershire* case reached the High Court, the court stated that in assessing a disabled person's **needs** under s.2 of the *CSDPA 1970*, the local authority had to weigh three factors in the balance: (a) the individual's needs, (b) the needs of other people, and (c) the resources available.

Such a balancing exercise therefore allowed resources to be taken into account. Although the Court of Appeal disagreed, the House of Lords reinstated the High Court's decision. It did not refer explicitly to the term 'balancing exercise', but ruled that the setting of **criteria of eligibility** to determine people's needs **may** – although it does not have to – be influenced by the availability of resources, and that 'relative cost will be balanced against relative benefit and relative need for that benefit'.

Indeed, in exercising their **discretion** generally (whether in community care or under other functions), local authorities are continually performing a balancing exercise when they weigh up the various **relevant** factors, before reaching an overall decision. In both the *McMillan* and *Bucke* cases, the court found that in deciding to alter or reduce services, the local authorities had carried out the correct balancing exercise.

BALANCING THE EQUATION

It would be easy to suppose that if local authorities and their staff planned carefully, spent money effectively and knew the **legislation** thoroughly, then the community care equation would balance. In other words, authorities could meet people's **needs**, and yet stay within both **resources** and the **law**.

However, it is open to question whether this can be achieved easily or at all, since it seems clear that resources are simply not matching people's needs or **expectations**. Certainly, provision might work better in some localities than others, and it helps if staff and managers adopt an approach of saying 'yes', rather than 'no' to people, ensure **co-operation** between different agencies, explore different solutions (the optimum ones are not always the most expensive) and sources of funding, and adopt efficient working procedures.

Nevertheless, even positive and creative approaches can only achieve so much. Lord Lloyd, at the House of Lords stage of the *Gloucestershire* case, summed up the problem when he referred to the 'truly impossible' and 'wretched' position the local authority found itself in owing to the apparently inexorable shortage of resources caused by the **policies** of **central government**. Hence the authority had sought an escape route by raising its **threshold of need** in response to diminishing resources.

BATH

Facilitating access to a bath by a **disabled occupant**, and provision of the bath for and facilitation of its use by the disabled occupant, is one of the statutory purposes for which a housing authority has a duty to approve an application for a **disabled facilities grant** – assuming various other conditions are also met (*Housing Grants, Construction and Regeneration Act 1996*, s.23).

BATHING SERVICES AND EQUIPMENT

The question of bathing remains a contentious issue within community care.

(1) **Migration of services from the NHS to social services.** Some bathing services formerly provided free of charge by NHS district nurses are now arranged and charged for by local authorities. This illustrates the flexibility and uncertainties afforded by **grey areas** of responsibility between statutory services, and the fact that services migrate more easily from the NHS to local authorities than in the opposite direction.

(2) **Lifting and handling.** There is increased awareness of the risk of back injury and the operation of the Manual Handling Operations Regulations 1992, which place a duty on employers to minimise the risk of injury to their staff in relation to **lifting and handling** at work: for instance, when they are helping people in and out of baths.

(3) **Low priority of bathing needs.** Many local authorities apparently regard access to **bath** or **shower**, in isolation from other **needs**, as a low **priority**. For instance, they might reduce the provision of bathing **equipment** such as grab rails, electric bath-seats,

bath-boards, bath-mats, etc., to at least some groups of **elderly people** and **disabled people**, and instead maintain that a **strip wash** meets the need to keep clean.

However, if authorities operate **rigid policies**, without really assessing the **individual needs** of people, they might run the risk of being found by the law courts **(judicial review)** or the **local ombudsmen** to have **fettered their discretion**; or possibly even to have operated a **policy** which is **illegal** under the *CSDPA 1970*, s.2 (e.g. if they fail even to consider **home adaptations** or **additional facilities** for greater **safety, comfort or convenience**). For instance, a rigid policy might not to be able to take account of a person's special needs for bathing facilities on **medical**, religious or **cultural** grounds.

(4) **Disabled facilities grants.** The low priority sometimes given by social services departments to bathing for disabled people does not accord with housing **legislation** governing **disabled facilities grants**, recently modified so as to emphasise further the importance of access to a bath or shower. (Compare the wording of the *Housing Grants, Construction and Regeneration Act 1996* with its previous incarnation in the *Local Government and Housing Act 1989*.) Indeed, **guidance** explains this change: it is to 'clarify that a disabled person should have access to a washhand basin, a WC and a shower or bath (or, if more appropriate, both a shower and a bath)' (DoE 17/96). However, some confusion arises because it is precisely social services departments which (a) are consulted by housing authorities about whether the proposed works are **necessary and appropriate** for the housing authorities to award a grant for; but (b) are also wary about how they respond, for fear of incurring the duty themselves to provide the **home adaptations** if housing authorities fail to assist for some reason.

■ BECKWITH CASE

This case illustrates how the law courts sometimes diminish the stature of **guidance** from the Department of Health.

At issue was whether certain wording in s.26 of the *National Assistance Act 1948* meant that a local authority was not obliged to make any direct provision of **residential accommodation** under s.21 of the Act. In other words, could it **make arrangements** for provision entirely with the independent sector, and so shed all its own **residential homes**? The court ruled that it could, and that Department of Health guidance on the matter, advising the opposite (in LAC(93)10), was 'entitled to respect' but was 'simply wrong'.

■ BECKWITH (NO.2) CASE

A separate issue in the *Beckwith* case was whether **consultation** about the closure of the authority's **residential homes** had been adequate. The court's ruling that it had not, reinforced an earlier judgment (the *Durham* case) about the need for proper consultation with residents. It also went a little further, because the judge held that in the circumstances, 'proper consultation' should have been extended not only to the residents of the particular home in issue (George Potter House), but also to those 'properly interested at the Council's other homes'.

■ BEDFORDSHIRE CASE

A case in which the House of Lords considered in detail the circumstances in which **private law** claims in **damages** might, in principle, succeed against local authorities in respect of their **social services functions**, in **negligence** or breach of **statutory duty.**

(1) Background. In fact, several cases were heard together, but those concerning social services and child care were as follows. In the first, five **children** were living in appalling circumstances, and yet despite reports being made over a period of years to the local authority – by relatives, neighbours, police, the **general practitioner**, a headteacher, the National Society for the Prevention of Cruelty to Children (NSPCC), a social worker and a health visitor – none of the children were placed on the child protection register, nor any court orders made.

In the second case, a social worker and psychiatrist assumed that the name given by a child – who was suspected to be the subject of sexual abuse – was that of her mother's boyfriend. The child was removed and the mother barred her boyfriend from her home. It later transpired that the child had referred not to the boyfriend but to a cousin with the same first-name.

(2) Negligence. As far as negligence in respect of social services (child care) went, the court basically ruled that the authorities would neither be directly, nor vicariously (i.e. on behalf of its staff) liable. The authorities could not be directly liable because the decisions challenged might be (a) 'non-justiciable' (ie the courts could not interfere) because they were related to resources or general policy; or (b) 'operational' (i.e. not related to policy) but stemming from power conferred by **Parliament** on the local authority (eg to remove children).

Even if the decisions challenged fell into neither of these categories, the court stated that the authority would still not be liable because, applying the ordinary test for negligence, it would not be 'just and reasonable' to impose liability – for a number of reasons. These included (a) the complex statutory system for the protection of children at risk; (b) the 'extraordinarily delicate' task facing local authorities in relation to children; (c) the danger of legal liability provoking local authorities into defensive approaches to their duties; (d) the danger of encouraging 'hopeless', 'vexatious and costly' ligitation; and (e) the fact that there were other remedies available, such as **complaints procedures** and the **local ombudsman.**

The local authority staff – and therefore the authority also vicariously – would not be liable because the staff owed a **duty of care** to the local authority and not to the children. But, the court went on, even if they did owe a duty of care to the children, it would still not be just and reasonable to impose a duty of care – for the same reasons as applied in the case of direct liability of the authority (immediately above).

(3) Breach of statutory duty. As for breach of statutory duty, the court stated that a cause of action could only arise if it could be shown that the particular **legislation** in question both created a **duty** to protect a 'limited class of the public' and also conferred on members of that class private law rights – i.e. a right to sue for damages. In order to decide this question, the legislation had to be examined for 'indicators'. For instance, if the legislation provided no other remedy for breach of duty (e.g. appeal to the Secretary of State), then this would normally indicate that private legal actions were not contemplated by Parliament. However, the existence of such **alternative remedies** might not necessarily deprive people of private law remedies: each case depended on the interpretation of the legislation in question. The court pointed out that:

> 'it is significant that your Lordships were not referred to any case where it had been held that statutory provisions establishing a regulatory system or a scheme of social welfare for the benefit of the public at large had been held to give rise to a private right of action for damages for breach of statutory duty. Although regulatory or welfare legislation affecting a particular area of activity does in fact provide protection to those individuals particularly affected by that activity, the legislation is not to be treated as being passed for the benefit of those individuals but for the benefit of society in general'.

The court concluded that although the relevant child care legislation was for the protection of a limited class – i.e. children at risk – nevertheless the duties contained in it were 'dependent upon the subjective judgement of the local authority'. For instance, there were phrases such as 'where it appears to the local authority', 'such inquiries as they consider necessary', 'take reasonable steps'. Such duties could not give rise to private law rights. In addition, s.17 of the *Children Act 1989* imported a general duty to safeguard children in need and, so far as was consistent with that, to promote their upbringing by their **families**. The court found it:

> 'impossible to construe such a statutory provision as demonstrating an intention that even where there is no carelessness by the authority it should be liable in damages if a court subsequently decided with hindsight that the removal, or failure to remove, the child from the family either was or was not 'consistent with' the duty to safeguard the child'.

■ BEDMAKING

Bedmaking might be part of **home help** or **practical assistance in the home**.

■ **BEDROOM:** see **Sleeping room;** and generally **Home adaptations**

■ BERKSHIRE CASE

This case illustrates the **contortions** authorities sometimes go through in attempting to mould legal requirements to available **resources**. It also confirmed that local authorities should assess people for **community care services** which could be provided *in principle*, even if *in practice* the authority happened not to be providing them at the time of the assessment.

(1) **Background: assessment.** The case concerned a seriously disabled man suffering from viral brain damage and epilepsy, who was resident at the British Home and Hospital for Incurables, but whose mother felt that he required different types and levels of care not available at the hospital. She had solicitors write to a social services department requesting a community care **assessment**. Before the court, the authority produced a document purporting to record the results of the assessment. However, the mother claimed that it was not a lawful assessment, since it merely described the services her son was receiving, and did not identify his **needs**. This issue was not decided in court, although the authority did appear to admit that the document had not been drawn up in accordance with **good practice**.

(2) **Assessing for discretionary services.** The hub of the case was whether the authority had a **duty** to make an assessment at all, because – it claimed – the man was not **ordinarily resident** within its area. The authority argued that the effect of s.29 of the *National Assistance Act 1948* (together with Directions and Approvals contained in LAC(93)10) was that authorities had a **power** to **make arrangements** generally to provide for those not ordinarily resident, but did not have a power in relation to *specific* services. Therefore, it maintained, if no relevant services were physically available, then the duty to assess would not arise at all in the case of somebody not ordinarily resident. The judge rejected this argument, and also expressed 'a degree of judicial unease' at reliance on the Department of Health's **guidance** to ascertain the meaning of **legislation** – even if it did contain **Directions** and **Approvals**.

■ BEXLEY CASE

A case involving the inter-relationship between s.17 of the *Children Act 1989* and s.2 of the *CSDPA 1970*, and exposing the apparent tendency of some authorities to ignore the 1970 Act in respect of disabled **children**.

(1) **Ignoring the CSDPA 1970?** It was common ground that the **specific duty** under the *CSDPA 1970* in relation to **practical assistance in the home**, was stronger than the **general duty** to provide services for children in need under s.17 of the *Children Act 1989*. However, the authority argued that since no request had been made (under s.4 of the *Disabled Persons, Services, Consultation and Representation Act 1986*), it had no duty to make an **assessment** for *CSDPA* services. The judge said in effect that the authority should not put its head in the sand by ignoring the 1970 Act, since provision for the child under it was the 'only conclusion which a reasonable authority could reach'. Furthermore, the circumstances were such that the authority had, in reality, been 'satisfied that it was necessary to provide practical assistance for him in the house'. The authority had therefore failed to 'apply their minds to the true position' and to 'take into account a material consideration'.

(2) **Availability of damages?** The judge also considered whether financial **damages** might be available if an authority breaches its specific duty under s.2 of the *CSDPA*. Cautiously, he suggested that the duty might be capable of giving rise to a claim for damages for the tort of **breach of statutory duty** (the caution was justified: see the subsequent *O'Rourke* judgment by the House of Lords).

BIRMINGHAM CASE

This case illustrates the reluctance of the courts to deal with cases which are solely about **delay**, without other points of **law** or fact involved.

(1) **Delay in foster placement.** The case concerned a child who had entered a psychiatric unit for **assessment**, where her doctor decided that a special foster placement was required as soon as possible. This had proved difficult and the child was still, nearly a year later, in the unit.

(2) **Judicial review inappropriate.** The judge held that if neither facts nor law were in dispute and the chief ground for **complaint** was that the authority had delayed in carrying out its **duty** (to provide **accommodation** under s.20 of the *Children Act 1989*), then **judicial review** was not the appropriate avenue, since delay did not amount inevitably to an error in law. He stated that in cases of delay it was necessary to know the precise circumstances, and these could not be investigated properly in a judicial review hearing. Therefore, the correct approach was not via judicial review but through the local authority's **complaints** procedure under s.26 of the *Children Act 1989*.

BLANKET POLICIES

Blanket **policies** should be treated with caution by local authorities. *First*, if a policy cannot cater for **exceptions** – a particularly important consideration given that community care **assessment** is supposed to be about people's **individual needs** – it puts authorities at risk of **judicial review** on the ground of **fettering of discretion**. *Second*, some blanket policies, snatched at hastily by authorities, can all too easily bear the marks of **illegality** when they contravene the wording of legislation; as happened in the *Leaman* and *Hargreaves (no 2)* cases, concerning **holidays** provided under the *CSDPA 1970*, s.2.

BLIND

People who are blind are eligible for **welfare services** under s.29 of the *National Assistance Act 1948*, under s.2 of the *CSDPA 1970*, Part 3 of the *Children Act 1989*, and for provision of **disabled facilities grants** under the *Housing Grants, Construction and Regeneration Act 1996* (s.100). See also: **Disability**

■ **BOARD:** see **Residential accommodation**

■ BRADFORD CASE

An education case illustrating an attempt to enforce a **general duty** to publish **information**. The education authority was under a duty in s.8 of the Education Act 1980 to publish information about its admissions policy. The adequacy of the information was challenged. The court stated that:

> 'The statutory requirement is to publish information about the policy to be followed in deciding submissions. That does not require that every nut and bolt of what is to be done has to be spelt out in the information to be provided. [It was claimed] that the applicant did not know whether he was in a traditional catchment area or not and that the failure to inform him of that meant that it was really an unexpressed policy. I am afraid I do not agree. It seems to me that the policy was quite adequately set out in the booklet when one adds to it the information which the booklet said was available at various places. It was open to the applicant to ask questions about the admissions and catchment areas in relation to traditional areas. It does not seem to me that the applicant was underinformed or misled.'

■ **BREACH OF STATUTORY DUTY:** see **Statutory duty**

■ BRISTOL CASE

A case illustrating that the courts are prepared to consider whether an authority is **fettering its discretion**, even in the case of a **power**, rather than a **duty**, to do something.

(1) Discretionary renovation grants. The case concerned the provision of **discretionary renovation grants**. The judge held that a letter which stated, in effect, that no discretionary grants were available, would have amounted to an unlawful fettering of discretion had it truly represented the council's **policy**. In fact, it did not; and the policy did *in practice* allow for the giving of discretionary grants on individual merits, as well as for other discretionary assistance in the form of **minor works assistance** and other assistance. At the same time, the authority had been justified in adopting its restrictive policy, given the lack of **resources**.

(2) Giving reasons. The judge's additional ruling, that the council had no duty to give **reasons** either under the **legislation** or under the general banner of **fairness,** has now been overtaken by legislative change in s.34 of the *Housing Grants, Construction Act 1996* which imposes a duty to give reasons in this particular context.

■ BRITISH OXYGEN CASE

Like the *Bristol* case (immediately above), this case shows that even in respect of a **power** – not just a **duty** – to do something (e.g. provide **discretionary disabled facilities grants, home repair assistance,** or **direct payments**), authorities should beware of **fettering their discretion** through excessively **rigid policies**.

Policy about items costing under £20 each. Under the Industrial Development Act 1966, the Board of Trade had the power to give grants towards approved capital expenditure for particular purposes. British Oxygen applied for grants for various items, including metal cylinders for pressurised gases costing just under £20 each, and on which it was spending a total of over £4 million: hence its interest in obtaining grants. The Board of

Trade denied that the various items were eligible for grants, and that in the case of the cylinders – even if they were potentially eligible – it had a policy not to give grants for items costing under £25. In respect of the cylinders, the House of Lords ruled that the Board was entitled to have a policy, but should not shut its ears to applications. Thus, a:

> 'large authority may have had to deal already with a multitude of similar applications and then they will almost certainly have evolved a policy so precise that it could well be called a rule. There can be no objection to that, provided the authority is always willing to listen to anyone with something new to say.'

■ BRUCE CASE

This illustrates how the courts sometimes apply strictly the concept of **unreasonableness** in **judicial review**, thus making it difficult to show that an authority has behaved unreasonably or **irrationally**.

Difficulty of showing unreasonableness under the CSDPA 1970. A challenge was made against West Sussex County Council for breach of its duty in providing **practical assistance in the home** under s.2 of the *CSDPA 1970*, and against the Secretary of State for failing to exercise his **default powers** against the Council. The judge found against the applicant, and set out with some emphasis the hurdles to be surmounted.

First the applicant would have to establish (a) the specific **need**, (b) the specific **arrangements** required to meet it, (c) that an express request had been made to the local authority to meet the need, and (d) that the authority had clearly failed to satisfy the request. *Second*, the applicant would have then to show – 'and no doubt it would be yet more difficult' – that 'the refusal to meet the identified need or contended for need was **irrational**...that no local authority, properly discharging their duty and having regard to the facts before them, would have declined that request'.

■ BUCK-PASSING AND COST-SHUNTING

The existence of **grey areas** – uncertain divisions of statutory responsibility – allow at best for flexibility of provision, and at worst for buck-passing between statutory services. The latter course can lead to delay in provision or even non-provision of services, and, as the judge put it in one of the *Harrow* cases, to an 'unhappy state of affairs' when **disabled people** go without.

(1) Primary purpose, resources and strength of legislation. In principle, a division exists in terms of the primary purpose of a particular service or item of equipment. However, this might not always be clear; for instance, is the primary purpose of a child's wheelchair educational, health-related, or social? In the first case, the education authority might provide, in the second the NHS, and in the third perhaps nobody. Unfortunately, arguments between authorities are only too frequent when **resources** are scarce. In practice, the decisive factor might not be the primary purpose – which is, in any case, hard to discern sometimes – but the availability of resources and the relative strengths of the duties involved.

The question of who should be taking responsibility and paying – the NHS, local authorities or people themselves – for **continuing care** is a particularly sensitive example of **buck-passing**. For instance, the **Leeds investigation** of the **health service ombudsman** showed that the health authority was attempting to deny responsibility for caring for a severely disabled and ill person, leaving his wife to pay for **nursing home** care.

(2) Example: who provides therapies for a child? In the *Harrow* cases a child and parent sought **judicial review** of the education authority for failing to provide various **therapies**, while the education authority sought it of the health authority on the grounds of the latter's failure to provide the same. The outcome of this type of case shows how a **general duty** in NHS legislation (*NHS Act 1977*, s.3) is more difficult to enforce than a **specific duty** in education or social services legislation (e.g. under the *CSDPA 1970*, s.2). See also the *Oxfordshire* and *M* cases, involving disputes over responsibility for speech and language therapy.

BUCKE CASE

The case was essentially about how a local authority can take **resources** into account when **assessing** and **reassessing** people's **needs** under s.2 of the *CSDPA 1970* by performing a **balancing exercise**.

(1) **Review of care arrangements.** The applicant was a fifty-year-old man with **learning disabilities**, poor eyesight and requiring assistance in looking after himself. In order to save money, the local authority was conducting a review of its care arrangements, and transferring the provision of care for some people to cheaper providers. The social worker 'was supposed to go down the list, starting with the cheapest, until he or she found a provider who was able to provide the care that was needed'. This entailed a change of provider for the applicant, from a male support worker to a female carer: a change he did not want. The authority was accused of **fettering its discretion** in only making exceptions where the change in provision would be 'significantly detrimental', and of making resources the prevailing or predominant consideration.

(2) **Balancing of needs and resources.** The judge did not find a fettering of discretion, and stated that the authority could take account of resources 'provided that it never forgets that the needs of the user are to be regarded as of greater importance than the need to save money'. The judge accepted that the changes were resource-led in that they would not have been made unless there was a need to cut costs; but they were not on that account **unlawful**, so long as the 'correct balancing exercise' had been carried out in reassessing individual needs. The reassessment exercise had in fact resulted in 7 out of 13 users remaining with the more expensive care agency. Consequently, there was nothing 'to indicate that resources were regarded as paramount or that the Council manifestly got the balance wrong'.

C CASE

An education case, involving a gifted child with certain difficulties, and illustrating the scope the courts allow public bodies to arrive at **inconsistent** decisions.

The Secretary of State had become involved and reached two separate decisions about the same child on the basis of 'substantially the same material'. The court decided that 'there is nothing on the face of it irrational even in the same person [let alone two different people] reaching a different conclusion when he re-examines the same facts'.

CADDELL CASE

A dispute between two local authorities about which of them was responsible for continuing to provide advice, assistance and support for a child who had reached the age of 18 years. The child had been placed by Lambeth with a foster mother in Kent, before, at the age of 18, moving into independent accommodation. Referring to s.24 of the *Children Act 1989*, the court ruled that the authority, within whose area the child was living at the time, bore the responsibility: ie Kent.

■ CAKE-CUTTING

At the High Court stage of the *Gloucestershire* case, the judge acknowledged the **impossible** task facing local authorities unless they take account of **resources** when assessing the needs of **disabled people** under s.2 of the *CSDPA 1970*: i.e. 'unless they can have regard to the size of the cake so that in turn they know how fairest and best to cut it'.

■ CALL FOR

When **having regard** to its **assessment** of a person's **needs** for **community care services**, a local authority must decide whether those needs call for the provision of services by it (*NHS and Community Care Act 1990*, s.47).

The upshot of the *Gloucestershire* case seems to be that the terms 'having regard to' and 'called for' mean that an authority has some **discretion** in deciding whether to meet the person's needs and can take **resources** into account in respect of most, but not all, community care services. This would appear to follow simply from the fact that the provision of community care services is governed variously by **duties** of different strengths and by **powers**. Therefore, in respect of any one service, an authority will have greater or lesser discretion following the s.47 assessment of need, depending on which **legislation** is applicable.

■ CAMBRIDGE CASE

This case illustrates how reluctant the law courts are to intervene when the **NHS rations** its services.

(1) **Tolling the bell of tight resources: High Court.** The case concerned the refusal by a health authority to provide possibly lifesaving treatment for a 10-year-old child suffering from leukaemia. One of the grounds for the refusal was that the proposed treatment would not be an effective use of **resources**. In the High Court, the judge ruled against the authority on various grounds. On the resources issue, he stated that the authority's evidence about money consisted only of 'grave and well-rounded generalities' and that the authority should 'do more than toll the bell of tight resources'.

(2) **Agonising judgements: Court of Appeal.** The Court of Appeal immediately overturned the High Court's decision. On the question of resources, it stated that it was:

> 'common knowledge that health authorities cannot make ends meet. They cannot pay their nurses as much as they would like; they cannot provide all the treatments they would like; they cannot purchase all the extremely expensive equipment they would like... Difficult and agonising judgements have to be made as to how a limited budget is best allocated to the maximum advantage of the maximum number of patients. That is not a judgement which the court can make...it would be totally unrealistic to require the authority to come to the court with its accounts and seek to demonstrate that if this treatment were provided for B then there would be a patient, C, who would have to go without treatment. No major authority could run its financial affairs in a way which would permit such a demonstration.'

■ CARE AND ATTENTION

In order to qualify for the provision of **residential accommodation**, people must be at least 18 years old and in **need** of care and attention – because of **age, illness, disability** or any **other circumstances** – which is not **otherwise available** to them (Direction under *National Assistance Act 1948*, s.21).

In the *Hammersmith and Fulham* case, the Court of Appeal ruled that asylum-seekers might be eligible, on the basis that a lack of food and accommodation – together with their inability to speak the language, their ignorance of this country, and the stress they were under – could bring about illness or disability and consequent need for care and attention. However, a need for food alone, but not for accommodation as well, would be insufficient to trigger the **duty** (*Gorenkin* case).

CARE FOR A PERSON: HOME ADAPTATIONS

Enabling a disabled occupant to care for another person, by facilitating access and movement around the dwelling, is one of the statutory purposes for which a housing authority has a **duty** to approve an application for a **disabled facilities grant**, assuming various other conditions are also met (*Housing Grants, Construction and Regeneration Act 1996*, s.23).

CARE MANAGEMENT

Care management is a term not found in **legislation**, but highlighted and elaborated upon by community care **guidance** (DH 1990, SSI/SWSG 1991a). The term evolved from 'case management' in the 1989 community care White Paper (DH 1989). Depending on the reader's point of view, the guidance sets out a thoughtful system for **assessment** and decisions about services; or alternatively, it places a daunting and bureaucratic obstacle course in the way of both service users and local authority practitioners. The guidance envisages roughly the following:

(1) **Screening.** A **screening** process is required to determine whether or not a person **appears** to be in **need** of **community care services** at all. If he or she does not appear to be, then the duty of assessment does not arise.

(2) **Urgency and level of assessment.** A set of **criteria of eligibility** are required in order to identify the **urgency** of the case, the level of assessment and its complexity. So, there are two separable decisions to be made at this stage, over the speed of response and the level or depth of assessment.

(3) **Eligibility for services.** Once the assessment has been carried out, the authority should determine, through **criteria of eligibility**, whether it will provide services.

(4) **Priorities for services.** Having determined that eligibility, there is a further decision to be made about the relative **priorities** of the **needs** which have been assessed.

(5) **Objectives.** Objectives to be met for each of the prioritised needs should be agreed.

(6) **Care plans.** The assessment should be **recorded** and given, normally in writing – together with the **care plan** – to the user. A care plan should be formulated by looking at a variety of options and alternatives which will meet the identified needs.

(7) **Charges.** If **charges** are to be made, then the user's financial **resources** should be assessed and a decision taken about what to charge.

(8) **Preferences and resources.** The **preferences** of users should be reconciled with available **resources**, perhaps according to guidelines about the level of expenditure appropriate to particular types of need.

(9) **Unmet need. Unmet need** should be identified and prioritised: for example, it is suggested that unmet need under the *CSDPA 1970* in particular would be a priority –

unsurprisingly since unmet need (i.e. need which the authority accepts it is **necessary** for it to meet) is not legally permissible under this Act (see *Gloucestershire* case, House of Lords).

(10) **Review.** Review should consist of **reassessment** of the person's needs and preferences, and a reappraisal of eligibility for assistance – which may be increased, reduced or **withdrawn**, not only because of the user's changing needs but also in the light of the authority's changing **policies** and eligibility criteria.

■ CARE OF PEOPLE WHO ARE SUFFERING FROM ILLNESS

This phrase, or similar, recurs in the **legislation**: see **Illness**

■ CARE PLANS

A term not found in **legislation**, but nevertheless a key element in community care **guidance**. Policy guidance envisages that once a person's **needs** have been **assessed**, any services to be provided should be **recorded** in a care plan (DH 1990). Practice guidance adds that, normally, service users should receive a written copy of the **assessment** and the care plan (SSI/SWSG 1991a). In the *Rixon* case, for example, the court judged the **unlawfulness** of an authority's decisions and actions by measuring them against the detailed aspects of care plans envisaged by the guidance.

■ CARE PROGRAMME APPROACH

Not referred to in **legislation**, the Care Programme Approach has been advocated by Department of Health **guidance** as a means of providing care in the community for people who suffer from **mental illness**. Key elements of the Care Programme Approach include systematic **assessment** of patients in relation to their **health care** and **social care needs**, and effective systems for ensuring that health and social care services are provided for people who can be treated in the community (HC(90)23).

■ CARE SERVICES: MENTAL DISORDER

For the prevention of **mental disorder**, or for people who are – or have been – suffering from mental disorder, local authorities have a **duty** to **make arrangements** for the provision of **social work** and related services to provide **domiciliary services** and care services for people living in their homes or elsewhere (Direction under *NHS Act 1977*, schedule 8).

■ CARERS

The importance of informal care provided by parents, **children**, relatives, friends and neighbours for sick or **disabled people** is recognised explicitly in the *Carers (Recognition and Services) Act 1995*, in the *Disabled Persons (Services, Consultation and Representation) Act 1986*, and in accompanying **guidance**.

Carers: assessment. Under the *Carers (Recognition and Services) Act 1995*, local authorities have a **duty** to assess a **carer** who requests an **assessment** when an assessment is already being provided for an adult under s.47 of the *NHS and Community Care Act 1990* – or for a child under s.2 of the *CSDPA 1970* or Part 3 of the *Children Act 1989*. The Act applies both to adult and child carers.

The assessment of the carer must determine the carer's ability to 'provide and to continue to provide' care. The authority must then 'take into account the results of that assessment' when deciding what services are **called for**, for the person being cared for. There are several points to note.

(1) **Substantial and regular care.** Entitlement to assessment depends on the carer either providing, or intending to provide a 'substantial amount of care on a regular basis'. Policy **guidance** (DH 1996) points out that the words 'regular' and 'substantial' are to be taken in their everyday sense, and that it is for authorities to make **judgements** about the circumstances in which they apply.

(2) **Request and information.** The right to an assessment depends on a request for it; although policy guidance states that authorities should ensure that carers have access to **information** about their rights under the Act, and that procedures are sufficiently clear for them to know what is happening (DH 1996). Indeed, a failure to let people know of their right to request an assessment might be regarded by the local ombudsman as **maladministration**, or even as **unlawful** by the law courts, since it could have the effect of denying people a statutory entitlement.

(3) **Commercial carers.** The Act does not apply to people who are caring by contract (i.e. commercial carers), or to volunteer carers from voluntary organisations.

(4) **Entitlement to services.** The Act gives no explicit entitlement to services for carers (as pointed out in the *Good* case). However, (a) the assessment of the carer might influence the decision about services for the person being cared for, and (b) services provided will often benefit both carer and cared for. For example, provision of an electric bath-seat helps both the **disabled person** and the carer (who no longer has to lift the person in and out of the bath-tub).

(5) **Carer's own needs.** The carer might have needs of his or her own under community care **legislation** or the *Children Act 1989*, and so be entitled to an assessment in his or her own right as a person in need.

Carers: having regard to their ability. When **assessing** the needs of a **disabled person** for **community care services** or for services under Part 3 of the *Children Act 1989*, the local authority must have regard to the ability of a carer – who is providing a 'substantial amount of care on a regular basis' – 'to continue to provide such care on a regular basis' (*Disabled Persons (Services, Consultation and Representation) Act 1986*, s.8). This **duty** does not apply if an authority is carrying out an assessment of a carer under the *Carers (Recognition and Services) Act 1995*.

Carers: other legislation. Carers might in some circumstances be able to obtain direct assistance in their own right (rather than via the person being cared for) under **legislation** other than that already mentioned immediately above.

Households, families etc. For example, the provision of **home help** and **laundry facilities** by local authorities – under the *NHS Act 1977*, schedule 8 – is expressed to be toward 'households' which **require** help because of the presence of somebody who is **ill, aged, disabled** or lying-in, or who is an **expectant mother**. And local authorities are expressly empowered to provide services for the **family** generally, or any particular member of the family, of **children in need** (*Children Act 1989*, s.17). Policy **guidance** suggests that services such as **information** and carer support groups could be provided through the **power** to provide services for the prevention of **illness**, the care of people who are ill and **after-care**, under the *NHS Act 1977*, schedule 8, supplemented by the *Local Government Act 1972*, s.111 (DH 1996).

Less explicitly, the **social work** service, **advice** and **support** which authorities **may** provide for **disabled people** might in practice be indivisible from giving the same to family members and carers (Approval under *National Assistance Act 1948*, s.29). Even under s.2 of the *CSDPA 1970*, the **duty** to provide **home adaptations** is not expressed as being only 'for the disabled person', but rather as being to meet his her **needs**.

■ CARERS (RECOGNITION AND SERVICES) ACT 1995

This Act gives carers a right to **assessment**. The Department of Health has issued both policy (DH 1996), and practice **guidance** (SSI 1996). See: **Carers**.

■ CARROLL CASE

A housing case, illustrating that when an authority has a **duty** to make a decision, it must ensure that (a) it, and nobody else, makes it (e.g. makes a community care **assessment** and decision about services under s.47 of the *NHS and Community Care Act 1990*); and (b) it takes account of **relevant** factors.

Over-reliance on medical opinion. In deciding about a person's vulnerability in relation to priority need for **accommodation** under the *Housing Act 1985* (the relevant provisions have since been superseded by the *Housing Act 1996* and by SI 1996/3205), the housing authority had relied on the **medical opinion** of a doctor. The court found the decision **unlawful** because it had not enquired into housing or social welfare matters which were also **relevant** to the decision. The:

> 'authority should always bear in mind that it is its function and no one else's to decide whether an applicant is vulnerable or not and that it is their duty, in order to enable it [sic] to satisfy themselves whether a homeless person has priority need to make all necessary enquiries.'

■ **CASH PAYMENTS:** see **Direct payments**

■ CCSU CASE

The House of Lords case concerned with the Prime Minister's (as Minister for the Civil Service) successful attempt to deny trade union membership to staff at Government Communications Headquarters (GCHQ). Lord Diplock formulated the legal meaning of **irrationality.**

■ CENTRAL GOVERNMENT

Central government is a link in the **community care chain**, in the form of the Department of Health and, behind it, the Treasury; which together determine **policy, legislation** and funding.

The Department of Health's role, underlying community care, was referred to by the House of Lords in the *Gloucestershire* case. Lord Lloyd, in the minority, expressed his satisfaction that the Department had participated in the case; since central government was, in his view, responsible for the 'truly impossible' situation in which the local authority found itself. It had departed from the 'fine words' of its community care White Paper (DH 1989), failed 'to supply the funds necessary to enable the Council to carry out...their **statutory duty**', and prevented, through the **rate-capping** system, the authority from raising extra money to meet its obligations.

Central government itself sometimes hints publicly, and doubtless more often privately, that judges are now exercising increased control over law and policy and are usurping the will of **Parliament**. However, in the area of community care at least, such complaints ring hollow, due to (a) the **impossible position** authorities have been placed in financially by central government, and the disputes inevitably arising; (b) the complex and confusing community care legislation (requiring constant clarification) of which central government is the author; and (c) the important constitutional role of the judiciary in balancing the power of the executive (i.e. government).

■ **CENTRAL HEATING:** see **Heating**

■ CERTIORARI

Certiorari is a remedy the courts can order in **judicial review** to quash the decision of a local authority.

■ CHARGES

The following paragraphs explain the basis in legislation for various charges.

Charges: assessment. Community care **legislation** – the *National Assistance Act 1948*, s.22 **(residential accommodation)**, and the *HASSASSA 1983*, s.17 (non-residential **welfare services**) – appears not to give authorities the **power** to make charges for **assessment** or **care management**. That assessment cannot be charged for has been emphasised both by the community care White Paper (DH 1989), and by an 'advice note' from the Social Services Inspectorate (SSI 1994). Nevertheless, sometimes local authorities contemplate making charges for assessment: either directly, or by including an element for assessment in the overall charge made for services provided subsequent to the assessment. Such charging **policies** run the risk of being **unlawful**.

Charges: housing services. Housing authorities have the **power** to provide, and to make charges for, 'professional, technical and administrative services' to assist people to carry out work, including **home adaptations**, to their homes (*Local Government and Housing Act 1989*, s.169).

Charges: non-residential services. Local authorities have the **power** to make such charges for non-residential **community care services** as they consider **reasonable**. The *Hooper* case confirms that a local authority must be prepared to justify the reasonableness of making a change in the light of all the relevant circumstances. However, local authorities cannot require service users to pay more than it is **reasonably practicable** – in the authority's opinion – for them to pay (*HASSASSA 1983*, s.17). There are a number of points to make.

(1) **What community care services can be charged for?** The 1983 Act states that charges **may** be made for (a) **welfare services** for **disabled people** (*National Assistance Act 1948*, Part 3); (b) welfare services for **elderly people** (*Health Services and Public Health Act 1968*, s.45); and (c) prevention of **illness**, care, **after-care, home help, laundry facilities** etc.

(*NHS Act 1977*, schedule 8). However, after-care services provided under s.117 of the *Mental Health Act 1983* are not listed in the Act as services which can be charged for.

(2) Charges under s.2 of the CSDPA 1970. In addition, it has been assumed by many local authorities and the Department of Health that charges can be made under s.2 of the *CSDPA Act 1970*, because although the *CSDPA* is not mentioned in the 1983 Act, it appears to be 'part and parcel' of s.29 of the *National Assistance Act 1948*. The argument runs that if charges can be made under the 1948 Act, so too can they be made under the 1970 Act. This particular assumption has not been explicitly tested in the courts, although, at the time of writing, judgment is awaited of a **judicial review** case to test the point (*Powys* case).

(3) Trends in charging. The onset of mainstream community care from April 1993 onwards, has seen increased emphasis on charging for non-residential services. For example, **guidance** encourages authorities to make charges, warning that failure to do so places an extra burden on the local population or foregoes **resources** which could otherwise benefit the service (LAC(94)1).

(4) Setting and collecting charges. The **legislation** has been fleshed out by an 'advice note' issued by the Social Services Inspectorate (SSI 1994). Of somewhat indeterminate status, with a confusing title, and not made under s.7(1) of the *Local Authority Social Services Act 1970*, this guidance bears all the hallmarks of policy slipping out through the back door.

The note makes various points. Authorities should take account of the full cost of providing the service, including overheads directly related to service provision, but not costs associated with purchasing or with operating the charging system. Charges cannot be set by an independent provider contracted to the authority, although arrangements may be made for collection by the provider.

It also states that any means-test should be restricted to the means of the user, and that normally only the user can be charged. However, it then suggests somewhat confusingly that in the case of couples (married or unmarried) the authority might sometimes wish to consider the resources of the spouse or partner as well. Automatic exemption from charges for people on social security benefits (except the mobility component of disability living allowance) is not recommended, although the situation of people in receipt of benefits, receiving a low income or incurring extra costs because of **disability** or frailty, should be viewed sympathetically. If people refuse to pay, authorities should not **withdraw** services, but instead consider pursuing the debt through the courts (SSI 1994).

This last bit of advice is given in the light of the legislation itself which states that a charge 'may, without prejudice to any other method of recovery, be recovered summarily as a civil debt' (*HASSASSA 1983*, s.17): there is no mention of withdrawing services.

Charges: residential accommodation. Local authorities have a **duty** to charge (or at least apply a test of **resources**) to each person for whom they **make arrangements** for the provision of **residential accommodation**.

(1) Overall charging scheme. If the authority is providing the accommodation directly, then the charge should be at a standard rate and represent the full cost of provision. However, if the authority is **satisfied**, according to the statutory test of resources (see below), that a person cannot afford to pay at the standard rate, then it must assess the person's ability to pay, and charge a lower rate accordingly. In calculating the weekly amount payable by a resident, the authority must assume that he or she will require a certain amount of money for personal requirements: the personal expenses allowance (PEA) (*National Assistance Act 1948*, s.22). The amount of this is determined by **regulations** and is currently £14.10 per week (SI 1997/486). Its purpose is to cover stationery, personal toiletries, treats and small presents for friends and relatives. Nevertheless, the amount can be varied: for instance, in the case of less dependent residents (see below), where the person in the residential accommodation has a dependent child; or where the resident is paying half of an occupational pension to a spouse, etc. **(CRAG)**.

(2) **Independent providers.** Where arrangements are made with independent providers, the charging procedure is more or less the same: the local authority pays the provider the cost of the place, and the resident repays the authority the amount he or she has been **assessed** to pay (*National Assistance Act 1948*, s.26).

Charges: residential accommodation (details). The details of the **assessment** of a person's ability to pay for **residential accommodation** are governed by **regulations** (SI 1992/2977), and by looseleaf, regularly updated **guidance**, issued by the Secretary of State under s.7(1) of the *Local Authority Social Services Act 1970* and known as the **Charging for Residential Accommodation Guide (CRAG)**.

The rules for charging are complicated and it is beyond the scope of this book to explain them in detail. The reader should consult the Act, regulations and guidance, and seek professional advice as appropriate. However, the following covers some of the main points:

(1) **Assessment of income.** If a person has capital worth more than £16,000, then he or she is liable to pay the full cost of any residential accommodation arranged for the person by the local authority. If the capital is, or drops below, that figure, then the person's contribution is based on (a) both *normal income* (including *notional income*), and (b) *tariff income* – i.e. income calculated on the amount of capital valued between £10,000 and £16,000. If the capital is, or drops to, less than £10,000, then it is not taken into account, but is disregarded. Some income is either partly or fully ignored in the calculation; for example, some social security benefits or charitable payments (SI 1992/2977). Notional income could consist of, for example, payments made by a third party such as a relative towards the cost of the residential accommodation.

(2) **Deprivation of capital or income.** Residents might be deemed to have notional capital if, for example, they have deprived themselves of capital assets in order to reduce the charges they have to pay (SI 1992/2977). The local authority must decide whether avoiding payment of charges was a significant – if not the only – purpose of the deprivation. It must decide similarly in the case of any deprivation of income (CRAG).

(3) **Disregarding of property.** In some circumstances, local authorities have a **duty** to disregard (i.e. ignore) the value of the person's property as a capital asset: for example, when the resident's stay might be only temporary, since he or she is intending to return home.

The duty to disregard property applies also when – although the resident will not be returning to his or her own home – the dwelling is occupied by the resident's partner or former partner (except in the case of divorce or estrangement), or by a relative or other member of the family for whom the resident is responsible who is aged 60 or over, is aged under 16 or is incapacitated (SI 1992/2977). The local authority **may** also, but does not have to, disregard the value of property in which any other third party continues to live; for example, where the third party has given up his or her own home in order to care for the resident (SI 1992/2977, and CRAG). Exercise of this power was disputed in the *Harcombe* case.

(4) **Liability of spouses.** Spouses are liable to maintain each other (*National Assistance Act 1948*, s.42). However, guidance states that authorities cannot demand that the spouse provide details of his or her financial resources, and that they should not use the

assessment forms aimed at the resident in order to gather information about the means of the spouse as well. Nevertheless, the guidance envisages that in some circumstances, authorities will request that the spouse refund part or all of the local authority's expenditure on the residential accommodation **(CRAG)**.

(5) Less-dependent residents. Where local authorities are supporting less-dependent residents, they have a power not to exact the full charges normally applicable, 'if they consider it **reasonable** in the circumstances not to do so'. This is so that such residents will be left with more than the standard personal expenses allowance (see above). Less-dependent residents are people who live in independently-provided accommodation which does need to be registered under the *Residential Homes Act 1984*, or in local authority accommodation which does not provide board (SI 1992/2977). See also: **Residential accommodation: different types.**

(6) Short stays. Authorities have a **power** to charge what they think is reasonable for a person to pay, irrespective of his or her means, for temporary stays (e.g. for **respite care**) of no longer than eight weeks' duration (*National Assistance Act 1948*, s.22). In practice, the level of charges made is likely to vary locally.

(7) Creating a charge on the property. If a resident's contribution to residential accommodation has been assessed on the basis of property, he or she will not be able to make payments to the local authority while the property remains unsold. In such a situation, the local authority has the power to create a charge on the property; though interest cannot be charged until the person dies, after which time it must be charged (*HASSASSA 1983*, ss.22,24). Guidance adds that the Department of Health's view is that local authorities cannot use s.111 of the *Local Government Act 1972* (instead of the 1983 Act) to create a charge on which interest could accrue during the person's lifetime as well **(CRAG)**.

(8) Recovering assets disposed of by residents to third parties. Local authorities have the power to recover assets from third parties who have received assets from the resident. The resident must have deprived himself or herself of assets no more than six months before entering residential accommodation, and have received in return either no consideration (e.g. payment) or less than the value of the asset. This must have been done 'knowingly and with the intention of avoiding charges for the accommodation' (*HASSASSA 1983*, s.21). If the transfer was over six months before entry, certain provisions of the Insolvency Act 1986 may apply.

Charges: children's services. Local authorities have the **power** to make various charges for services, including those provided for **children in need** under the *Children Act 1989*, s.17. The charges should be **'reasonable'** ones, which it is **reasonably practicable** for the person – the child (if 16 years old or over), the parents, or another member of the **family** (for whom a service is being provided) – to pay. However, charges cannot be made for **'advice, guidance** or **counselling'** – nor can they be made if the person is receiving income support, family credit or disability working allowance (*Children Act 1989*, s.29). Presumably, **assessment** too cannot be charged for, since it is not listed as a service provided under s.17.

In addition, authorities have the power to impose conditions as to repayment of any assistance given to children in need; but before giving assistance or imposing any repayment conditions, the authority must 'have regard to the means of the child concerned and of each of his parents'; and no repayment can be obtained from a person receiving income support or family credit

(*Children Act 1989*, s.17). This carries the implication that parents or children with sufficient **resources** of their own might have to pay for services.

Charges: NHS services. Charges cannot be made for any NHS services, except where **legislation** specifies otherwise (*NHS Act 1977*, s.1). Items so specified via **regulations**, and thus attracting prescription charges (subject to various exemptions and reductions according to a patient's age, financial status, medical condition), are wigs, elastic hosiery, spinal supports, surgical brassieres and items (drugs and appliances) listed in the Drug Tariff (published monthly by the Stationery Office)..

In addition, other services can be sold to patients under income generation schemes. Such schemes must not interfere with the provision of NHS services, and charges must be made on an '**appropriate** commercial basis' (Health and Medicines Act 1988, s.7).

This seemingly clear statement of the law has not prevented, from time to time, health authorities or NHS Trusts making **illegal** charges; for example, for orthotic footwear. An issue which surfaces sometimes in the Press and in **Parliament, illegal** charging is probably due to over-enthusiasm and ignorance of legislation on the part of managers who, faced with a shortage of **resources**, attempt in good faith to find ways of adequately funding services.

Charges: not specifically authorised by legislation. In addition, local authorities are sometimes tempted to make charges for services which are not otherwise authorised in **legislation** under s.111 of the *Local Government Act 1972*. Basically, the 1972 Act allows authorities to provide services incidental to their functions under other legislation. However, the House of Lords has ruled that s.111 does not in fact give authorities a **power** to make charges (*Richmond* case).

Charges for Residential Accommodation Guide (CRAG). This **guidance** is issued and regularly updated by the Department of Health under s.7(1) of the *Local Authority Social Services Act 1970*. In looseleaf form, it sets out 'rules' (which explain and complement **legislation**) for charging people for **residential accommodation** arranged by local authorities.

■ CHILDREN

Most services legally defined as **community care services** are available only to people aged 18 years or over. Comparable legal provisions for children lie in Part 3 of the *Children Act 1989* which covers **children in need**, including **disabled children**. However, it should be noted that s.2 of the *CSDPA 1970* continues to apply to both adults and children as does part of schedule 8 of the *NHS Act 1977* (duty and power to provide home help and laundry facilities respectively).

Children: disabled. Local authorities have a **duty** to keep a **register** of disabled children. If it **appears** to an authority that a child is in need, then the authority has the power to **assess** his or her needs under the *Children Act 1989*, at the same time as assessing them under the *CSDPA 1970*, s.2 (see *Children Act 1989*, schedule 2).

Authorities have a **duty** to provide services 'designed to minimise the effect on disabled children of their disabilities and to give such children the opportunity to lead lives which are as normal as possible' (*Children Act 1989*, schedule 2). A disabled child is defined in substantially the same way under Part 3 of the *Children Act 1989* as an adult is under s.29 of the *National Assistance Act 1948*. Department of Health **guidance** about disabled children was issued under s.7(1) of the *Local Authority Social Services Act 1990* (DH 1991).

Children: in need. Part 3 of the *Children Act 1989* covers children 'in need' including disabled children.

(1) **Children in need: definition.** A child in need might be disabled (see immediately above). Otherwise, he or she is *either* 'unlikely to achieve or maintain, or to have the opportunity of achieving or maintaining, a reasonable standard of health or development without the provision for him of services by a local authority' *or* 'his health or development is likely to be significantly impaired, or further impaired, without the provision for him of such services' (*Children Act 1989*, s.17).

(2) **Welfare.** Local authorities have a **duty** 'to safeguard and promote the **welfare** of children within their area who are in need' by providing a range of **'appropriate'** services. A service **may** be provided for the **family** as a whole, or for any particular member of the family, 'if it is provided with a view to safeguarding or promoting the child's welfare'.

(3) **Children living with families: services.** For children in need who are living with their families, local authorities have a duty to make 'such provision as they consider appropriate' for various services including **advice, guidance** and **counselling; occupational, social, cultural** or **recreational activities; home help** (which may include **laundry facilities**); 'facilities for, or assistance with, **travelling** to and from home for the purpose of taking advantage of any other service' either provided under the 1989 Act or similar services; and assistance for the child and his or her family to have a **holiday** (*Children Act 1989*, schedule 2).

(4) **Accommodation for children looked after.** Local authorities have a duty toward 'any child' in need in their area to provide **accommodation** in certain circumstances. For children 'looked after' by an authority, there is a also a duty toward 'any child' to safeguard and promote the child's welfare (*Children Act 1989*, ss.,20,22).

(5) **Extent of need and information.** Local authorities also have a duty to 'take **reasonable** steps' to identify the extent to which there are children in need in their area, to publish **information** about services they provide and, where they consider it appropriate, about services which they have the **power** to provide themselves, but which are in fact provided by other bodies (in particular voluntary organisations). Authorities must take reasonably practicable steps to ensure that those who might benefit from services receive relevant information (*Children Act 1989*, schedule 2).

Children: NHS. To 'such extent as he **considers necessary** to meet all **reasonable requirements**', the Secretary of State has a **duty**, exercised by health authorities, to provide 'such other' facilities for the care of young people 'as he considers are **appropriate** as part of the health service' (*NHS Act 1977*, s.3).

This represents a vague duty, difficult to enforce in the law courts because of the wide discretion it confers on authorities. This difficulty has been confirmed in, for instance, the *Cambridge* and *Hincks* cases.

Children Act 1989. Part 3 of this Act applies to **children in need**, including **disabled children**. Amongst a mass of **guidance** there is one volume specifically covering disabled children (DH 1991).

Children's shoes. This was one of the hypothetical examples discussed in the House of Lords during the *Gloucestershire* case in the minority judgment of Lord Lloyd: 'Every child needs a new pair of shoes from time to time. The need is not the less because his parents cannot afford them'. This argument did not find favour with the majority.

■ CHIROPODY

Chiropody is a specific example of an **NHS continuing care** service which, **guidance** explains, people – in **nursing homes, residential homes** or in their own homes – might **require**, and for which **criteria of eligibility** and **priorities** should be set within available **resources** (HSG(95)8). Chiropody services are provided under the *NHS Act 1977*.

■ CHOICE

Much lauded in community care **guidance**, choice is nevertheless a term absent from **legislation** and is hedged around with various limitations.

(1) **Final decisions.** Legislation makes it quite clear that it is for local authorities to make final decisions about people's **needs** and about service provision – not the people themselves, or even independent expert assessors. Policy **guidance** states that agreement between all parties will not always be possible (DH 1990), and practice guidance emphasises that in case of conflict it is, ultimately, for assessing practitioners to decide (SSI/SWSG 1991a).

(2) **Preferences.** Nevertheless, the policy guidance does allude to the exercising of 'genuine choice' and the participation of users and carers in the **assessment** process. It also refers to the securing of a cost-effective package of services which meets a person's needs, but which also takes account of **preferences** (DH 1990). So, in practice, while an authority eventually might not meet what it calls preferences, it should at least identify and pay some attention to them.

(3) **Choice of accommodation. Directions** issued by the Secretary of State state that – subject to cost, suitability and availability (i.e. the authority does not have to pay more than it would usually do for a particular level or type of assessed need) – local authorities should **make arrangements** in line with people's preferred choice of **residential accommodation** (Direction in LAC(92)27). Nevertheless, the *Lancashire* case exposed limits to such choice, when the Court of Appeal held that so long as the authority met the needs of an elderly woman for 24-hour care, it could do so by providing the cheaper option (**nursing home** care) rather than the woman's preferred option (care in her own home).

■ **CHRONICALLY SICK AND DISABLED PERSONS:** see **Disability**

■ CHRONICALLY SICK AND DISABLED PERSONS ACT 1970

(Abbreviated elsewhere to *CSDPA 1970*). **Guidance** on the Act is to be found in a Circular (DHSS 12/70), and also within community care policy guidance (DH 1990), and practice guidance (SSI/SWSG 1991a).

Chronically Sick and Disabled Persons Act 1970: housing authorities and disabled people. In discharging their **duty** under s.8 of the *Housing Act 1985*, to consider housing needs within the district, housing authorities must 'have regard to the special needs of **chronically sick or disabled persons**' (s.3).

Chronically Sick and Disabled Persons Act 1970: information and scale of need. Local authorities have a duty to identify local needs, and two **duties** to provide information, one **general**, one **specific** (s.1).

(1) **Scale of need.** Authorities have a duty to inform themselves of the numbers of **disabled people** in their area to whom s.29 of the *National Assistance Act 1948* applies and of the need for the authority to **make arrangements** under that section.

(2) **Publishing information.** Local authorities have a duty to 'cause to be published from time to time at such times and in such manner as they consider appropriate general **information** as to the services provided under arrangements made by the authority under [s.29 of the 1948 Act]...which are for the time being available in their area'.

(3) **Informing individual people.** In addition, there is a duty to **inform any person** who uses the authority's services 'of any other of those services which in the opinion of the authority is relevant to his needs and of any service provided by any other authority or organisation which in the opinion of the authority is so relevant and of which particulars are in the authority's possession'.

Chronically Sick and Disabled Persons Act 1970: welfare services. Under s.2 of the *CSDPA 1970*, Local authorities have a **duty** towards individual **disabled people** to **make arrangements** for the provision of various **welfare services**, if certain conditions are met.

This is a key provision within community care, because it contains a strong, **specific duty** towards individual **disabled people** (adults and children) to **make arrangements** for providing a range of **welfare services**. It is the strength of the duty that has made the Act the natural focus and centre-piece of **judicial review** cases such as the *Gloucestershire* case, and a battleground for the conflict between people's **needs** and available **resources**. The duty under s.2 of the *CSDPA* is as follows:

(1) **Establishing the need and the necessity to meet it.** The person in question must be (a) disabled under the definition given in s.29 of the *National Assistance Act 1948*, and (b) **ordinarily resident** in the local authority's area. The authority must be **satisfied** that in order to meet the **needs** of the person, it is **necessary** for it to **make arrangements** for all or any of a number of welfare services listed in the Act. Having established all this, the authority comes under a duty to make those arrangements.

(2) **Services.** The services, for some or all of which authorities must make arrangements are as follows:

'(a)the provision of **practical assistance** for that person in his home;

(b)the provision for that person of, or assistance to that person in obtaining, **wireless, television, library** or similar **recreational facilities;**

(c)the provision for that person of **lectures, games, outings** or other recreational facilities outside his home or assistance to that person in taking advantage of **educational facilities** available to him;

(d)the provision for that person of facilities for, or assistance in, **travelling** to and from his home for the purpose of participating in any services provided under arrangements made by the authority under the said section 29 or, with the approval of the

authority, in any services provided otherwise than as aforesaid which are similar to services which could be provided under such arrangements;
(e)the provision of assistance for that person in arranging for the carrying out of any works of **adaptation** in his home or the provision of any **additional facilities** designed to secure his greater **safety, comfort or convenience;**
(f)**facilitating** the taking of **holidays** by that person, whether at holiday homes or

otherwise and whether provided under arrangements made by the authority or otherwise;
(g)the provision of **meals** for that person whether in his home or elsewhere;
(h)the provision for that person of, or assistance to that person, in obtaining, a **telephone** and any special equipment necessary to enable him to use a telephone'.

CIRCULARS

Central government Circulars are a typical vehicle for carrying **guidance**, and sometimes **Directions** and **Approvals**.

CIVILISED SOCIETY

In the *Gloucestershire* case at the House of Lords stage, Lord Lloyd, in the minority, felt that the **yardstick** against which the **needs of disabled people** were to be measured under s.2 of the *CSDPA 1970* was the 'standards of a civilised society'. However, the majority felt that money and **resources** supplied a far more realistic and tangible measure.

CLEANING

Cleaning might be part of **home help** or **practical assistance in the home**.

CLEVELAND CASE

This case illustrates how the courts sometimes use the concept of **unreasonableness** to strike down the decisions of local authorities as **unlawful**.

(1) **Contractual terms.** An association of residential home owners (and others) challenged the contractual terms on which the local authority was prepared to enter contracts with the homes, in fulfilling its community care obligations to **make arrangements** to provide **residential accommodation** for people in **need** of it. The challenge rested on a number of grounds: (a) that the authority had failed to **consult** with the association as required by community care **legislation**, or, alternatively, that the association had a freestanding **legitimate expectation** to be consulted; (b) that contractual terms going beyond the statutory requirements imposed by the *Registered Homes Act 1984* were unlawful; and (c) that the contract terms were unlawful on grounds of unreasonableness.

(2) **Unreasonableness.** The judge found in favour of the association, on ground (c), unreasonableness, because he was satisfied that the effect of the contract terms would have been to **frustrate the purpose of** the *NHS and Community Care Act 1990*, by threatening the very existence of the private homes, and thus the **choice** of potential residents.

CLINICAL JUDGEMENT

Clinical judgements made by NHS staff determine the care and treatment of patients. In general, the law courts will not interfere with such judgements (e.g. *Re*

J case). (Although of course, in medical negligence cases, clinical judgements are 'on trial' in retrospect and expert evidence is heard to determine their competence.)

Since April 1996, the **health service ombudsman** is empowered to consider complaints about clinical judgement, as well as **maladministration**, and failure to provide – or failure within – a service. However, even before this recent extension of his powers, he sometimes found ways to undermine clinical decisions. For example, the clinical decision to discharge a patient might be administratively flawed if it is taken on clearly inadequate **information** (such as missing notes or notes which are not up-to-date about the patient's condition).

CLINICAL NEED

The term 'clinical need', in relation to people's entitlement to treatment for NHS services, sometimes gives rise to considerable confusion. Unlike **legislation** governing the provision of some **community care services**, the *NHS Act 1977* (ss.1 and 3) does not include the actual word **'need'**, but does refer to the provision of services to meet 'all **reasonable requirements**'.

(1) **Relative nature of clinical need. Central government** has in the past tended to imply – for example, in carefully and sometimes misleadingly (or at least elliptically) worded, replies in **Parliament** – that if a person has a clinical need, then he or she will as a matter of course gain timely access to **appropriate** NHS services. However, this is not necessarily the case, since the law courts (for example, in the *Hincks* and *Cambridge* cases) have accepted that NHS provision in any locality is subject to **resources** and **priorities**. Consequently, a person's access at any one time to care and treatment might depend on how many people are judged to be in greater clinical need, and on the availability of resources. The **health service ombudsman**, too, has on occasion elicited, and accepted, clear statements precisely to this effect from the NHS Executive.

(2) **Professional integrity.** There is some concern that professional integrity should be safeguarded, and clinical decision-making should remain separate from decisions based on resources. Thus, it might be preferable, for example, for a hospital **physiotherapist** to state that 'this woman needs two weeks' **rehabilitation** in hospital, but she will be discharged because of pressure on beds'; rather than simply to say, with the hospital's bed **policy** and her own overwhelming caseload in mind: 'this woman does not need rehabilitation'. Of course, from the point of view of avoiding controversy and dispute, rather than on professional integrity, the latter course is the easy option sometimes adopted in practice.

COCKS CASE

A case in which the House of Lords stated that claims for **damages** for **breach of statutory duty** are possible in the **homelessness** context, so long as **private law** rights and obligations have arisen after a **public law** decision has been made first and separately. Basically, the court was stating that the existence of *executive*, as opposed to *decision-making* functions, was sufficient to create a duty enforceable in private law.

This case greatly limited the circumstances in which such claims would be possible: for instance, in the community care context, claims might be limited to the situation where a local authority fails to meet a person's **needs**, which it had already accepted it was **necessary** for it to meet under s.2 of the *CSDPA 1970* (see e.g. comments in *Bexley* case). However, the *Cocks* case must now be read in the light of the *O'Rourke* case (June 1997), in which the House of Lords appears to have restricted further still the possibility of such actions for breach of social welfare duties.

■ COLLYMORE CASE

A case illustrating (a) that even in the case of a **power**, rather than a **duty**, authorities should beware of operating excessively rigid **policies**, and (b) that the courts are prepared to consider whether policies which appear to be lawful *in theory* are in fact **shams** *in practice.*

It concerned **discretionary** grants which the education authority had a power, but not a duty, to award. The authority operated a policy of refusing all awards, but then of inviting appeals when exceptional circumstances were being claimed. On the face of it this saved the policy from being over-rigid and **fettering the discretion** of the authority. However, in practice, of 300 appeals made over a period of three years, all had been rejected. The judge could only conclude that the policy had been implemented too rigidly, albeit in good faith. In addition, he also doubted, but did not strike down, the aspect of the authority's policy which stated that only in the 'most extraordinary circumstances' would an exception be made. This came very close to being a **blanket policy** – which would have been **unlawful**.

■ **COMFORT:** see **Safety, comfort or convenience**

■ COMMUNICATION

Local authorities have a **duty** to **make arrangements** to provide, whether at centres or elsewhere, facilities for **social rehabilitation** and **adjustment to disability**, including assistance in overcoming communication limitations, for **disabled people** who are **ordinarily resident** in the area. In respect of those not ordinarily resident, there is only a **power** (Direction and Approval under *National Assistance Act 1948*, s.29). Amongst other things, assistance with communication might in principle include provision of **speech and language therapy**, **communication aids**, provision of interpreters for deaf people etc.

Communication aids. A type of **disability equipment**, notoriously falling into the **grey area** between the NHS (*NHS Act 1977*), education authorities (Education Act 1996), and sometimes social services departments (*National Assistance Act 1948*, s.29 or *CSDPA 1970*, s.2). Communication aids range from cheap and simple (e.g. symbol charts), to highly sophisticated, multi-functional (combining speech and writing facilities), and expensive electronic equipment.

■ COMMUNITY CARE CHAIN

The people and organisations making up community care form a long chain, the links of which come under strain when things go wrong.

(1) **Parliament.** The electorate votes in **Parliament** (e.g. on a platform of limited taxation and public expenditure).

(2) **Treasury.** Within **central government** the Treasury attempts to control spending and generally abhors 'demand-led' provision of services.

(3) **Department of Health.** The Department of Health attempts to promote good practice in community care despite confusing **legislation**, lack of **resources**, pressure from the Treasury and the myopic tendencies of civil servants.

(4) **Local authorities.** Local authorities find themselves in an **impossible position**, caught between providing effective services for the local population and the demands and restrictions imposed by central government.

(5) **Staff.** Local authority staff similarly become wedged between their desire to help people, people's **needs** and **expectations**, the restrictive **policies** dictated by resources, and a culture of **complaint**.

(6) **Service users.** A proportion of the needs or expectations of service users remains unmet.

(7) **Lawyers.** Solicitors and barristers increasingly get involved from a variety of motives.

(8) **Law courts.** The law courts have to make difficult decisions about people's welfare and about the meaning of particular words and phrases scattered around the legislation. Some of those decisions might attract adverse publicity and bring calls for **law reform**. However, central government might be tempted to let things drift, watching with both interest and disapproval as the judges attempt to bring some sort of order to the uncertainty, and even chaos, characterising some aspects of community care.

■ COMMUNITY CARE CHARTERS

Unlike the Patient's Charter (DH 1997c), which covers the NHS, no national charter covers the provision of **community care services**. Instead, Department of Health **guidance** suggests a framework, within which local authorities should develop their own charters (LAC(94)24).

Such local charters do not therefore have the force of law, but could form one strand of evidence called on by, for example, the **local ombudsman** in investigations of **maladministration**. Indeed, the guidance suggests that detailed, quantifiable **standards** should be included in charters. However, given that resources are in unpredictable and short supply, it is scarcely surprising that some local authorities – in order to avoid being hoist with their own petard – prefer generality to detail.

■ COMMUNITY CARE (DIRECT PAYMENTS) ACT 1996

The Act gives authorities, from April 1997, the **power** to make **direct payments** to certain groups of people, so that they can purchase their own **community care services. Regulations** (SI 1997/734), Circular **guidance** (LAC(97)11 and LASSL(97)9), and both policy and practice guidance (DH 1997) has been issued. See: **Direct payments**

■ COMMUNITY CARE PLANS

Local authorities have a **duty** to **consult** the relevant local health authorities, housing authorities and voluntary organisations about their community care plans (*NHS and Community Care Act 1990*, s.46).

Directions impose various duties in relation to the preparation and publication of plans, publication of details about purchasing non-residential services from the independent sector, and publication about how the authority proposes to consult in the next round of planning (these Directions are contained in LAC(91)6, LAC(94)12 and LAC(93)4).

COMMUNITY CARE SERVICES

Community care services are legally defined in s.46 of the *NHS and Community Care Act 1990* and cover the provision by social services departments of (a) **residential accommodation** (*National Assistance Act 1948*, s.21); (b) various **welfare services** (under s.29 of the 1948 Act and the *NHS Act 1977*, schedule 8); (c) **after-care** services for people with a **mental disorder** (*Mental Health Act 1983*, s.117); and (d) services to promote the welfare of **elderly people** (*Health Services and Public Health Act 1968*, s.45).

(1) ***CSDPA 1970*: community care services?** Unhelpfully, the definition of community care services does not explicitly include services provided under sections 1 and 2 of the *CSDPA 1970*. This has caused some uncertainty about whether these services, although certainly part of the wider community care regime, are actually community care services in a legal sense (i.e. an integral part of the *National Assistance Act 1948*, s.29).

The question is not necessarily academic, since if they are not in fact community care services, then local authorities might not have the **power** to make **charges** for services under the 1970 Act, nor to make **direct payments** in connection with it. Indeed, some judicial comments appear to throw into doubt the claim that the 1948 and 1970 Acts are inseparable. For instance, in the *Gloucestershire* case, the High Court stated that 'what is authorising the local authority to make arrangements under s.2 is s.2', and not s.29 of the 1948 Act. And even the House of Lords, whilst accepting that *CSDPA* services are part of the 'community care regime' did not actually refer to them as 'community care services'. On the other hand, the judge in the *Hargreaves (no.2)* case explicitly stated that services under the *CSDPA 1970* are community care services as defined in the *NHS and Communtiy Care Act 1990*.

(2) **Restrictions.** Community care does not, legally at least, embrace either housing or NHS services. In practice of course, both are an essential part of care in the community. Furthermore, community care services are available, in the main, to adults only (those of at least 18 years of age), although **children** do not appear to be excluded in relation to provision of **home help** and **laundry facilities** under schedule 8 of the *NHS Act 1977*. The *CSDPA 1970*, s.2, applies to children as well as adults.

COMMUNITY HEALTH SERVICES

Community health services are listed in **guidance** as NHS **continuing care** services for people in their own homes, **residential** or **nursing homes**; for which **criteria of eligibility** and **priorities** should be set within available **resources** (HSG(95)8). Community health services are provided under the *NHS Act 1977*.

COMPLAINTS

The introduction and publicising of statutory complaints procedures for social services departments, together with wider **publicity** about what services are available and the raising of people's **expectations** – all at a time of limited **resources** – has led to a predictable proliferation of complaints. This is a mixed blessing.

Benefits are that individuals are provided with what should, if it works well, be a speedy and informal procedure to resolve disputes. In addition, local authorities can use complaints in order to identify weaknesses in, and to improve, their services. These are substantial benefits but are not the whole picture, as the following points suggest:

(1) **Staff resources.** An escalation of complaints demands staff-time for handling them, and can also lead to defensive practices. Both of these might be at the expense of providing services.

(2) **Solubility.** At least one major study has concluded that up to 50 per cent of complaints are at root about a lack of resources: matters which might simply not be open to solution. Indeed, to raise people's expectations with **information** about **community care services**, but to provide insufficient resources is, arguably, to invite insoluble contention, dispute and complaint – as well as a general undermining of social services departments.

(3) **Scope.** Some local authorities utilise their complaints procedures narrowly and refuse to investigate **policies** underlying, or the merits of, decisions; instead scrutinising only whether procedures have been followed. This is markedly unhelpful if a policy is excessively stringent or even **illegal**.

(4) **Shouting loudest.** One aim underlying the Citizen's Charter (Prime Minister 1991) and its offshoots (such as local authority complaints procedures) is to allow ordinary, rather than vexatious and troublesome, people to complain. Nevertheless, complaints procedures might, to some extent, be utilised by those who **shout loudest**, and not necessarily by those in the greatest **need** or with greatest cause for complaint.

(5) **Diversion from the law courts.** Complaints procedures are designed to defuse complaints before they get as far as the **local ombudsmen** or the law courts. However, it is likely that a proportion will spill over: either because the complainants are simply not satisfied, or because the complaints procedure is unsuitable for certain types of dispute; for example, when uncertain and developing points of **law** are in issue and **judicial review** is more appropriate (e.g. the *Tucker* and *Gloucestershire (no.2)* cases).

(6) **Review panel's recommendations.** The **legislation** does not oblige local authorities to follow the recommendations of complaints procedure review panels, which are convened at the final stage of a complaint. The courts might (*Avon* case), or might not (*Hargreaves* case), suggest that authorities should normally follow recommendations. In the *Rixon* case, the judge stated that: 'a failure to comply with a review panel's recommendations is not by itself a breach of the law; but the greater departure, the greater the need for cogent articulated reasons if the court is not to infer that the panel's recommendations have been overlooked'.

Complaints: adults. The Secretary of State has the **power** to order local authorities to establish **complaints** procedures for all those people for whom there is a power or **duty** to provide services (*Local Authority Social Services Act 1970*, s.7B). **Regulations** place a duty on authorities to do so (SI 1990/2444). Details of the form complaints procedures should take are contained in **Directions** (in DH 1990). There is also both policy **guidance** (in DH 1990) and practice guidance (SSI 1991).

(1) **Informal and formal stages.** The local authority must appoint an officer to assist in co-ordinating all aspects of complaints. Three stages are laid down: the informal, formal and review stages. If informal resolution is not achieved, the authority must send the complainant an explanation of the procedure (as set out in the Directions) and ask him or her to submit a formal written complaint (although the practice guidance states that many people will need help in doing this). The authority must normally respond within 28 days (and if this is not possible it must explain why) and in any case within three months. The authority must communicate its decision by writing to the complainant, the person on behalf of whom the complaint was made (unless the authority believes that the person would not understand or would be caused distress), and any other person the authority **considers** has sufficient interest (Directions).

(2) **Review panel.** If the complainant is still not satisfied, then if he or she informs the local authority within 28 days, the authority must appoint a review panel containing an independent person. The panel must sit within 28 days of the complainant's notification of continued dissatisfaction, and consider any written and oral evidence submitted by the complainant or by the authority.

Within 24 hours of the panel's meeting, it must **record** its recommendations in writing, and send copies to the local authority, the complainant, (if **appropriate**) the person on whose behalf the complaint was made, and any other person the authority **considers** has sufficient interest. The panel must also record the reasons for its recommendations in writing. The local authority must then decide what to do and write to the same people explaining its decision and the underlying reasons within 28 days of the panel's decision (Directions).

(3) **Availability of procedure.** Policy guidance suggests that the procedure will not be available where the complaints are anonymous or of a general nature, although authorities will still have the discretion to allow the procedure to be used. It also suggests (a) that, exceptionally, the earlier stages of the complaints process could be omitted; and (b) that complainants should not be accompanied to review panel hearings by a lawyer acting in a professional capacity (DH 1990).

Complaints: children. Local authorities have a **duty** to establish complaints procedures. Complainants can include **children**, parents, people with parental responsibility and anybody else the authority thinks has sufficient interest. A significant difference between adult and children's procedures is that in the latter, an independent person must be involved from the start (*Children Act 1989*, s.26). Otherwise, children's complaints procedures are described by Department of Health guidance as broadly compatible with adult procedures, thus allowing common administrative structures (DH 1991a).

Complaints: NHS. A new NHS complaints procedure, operative from April 1996, emphasises informal resolution of disputes. Failing this, an independent review panel is set up, including a lay chairman, a panel convener and a purchaser. Independent clinical assessors advise the panel in case of complaints about clinical matters. If complainants are still not satisfied, they can refer the dispute to the **health service ombudsman** (DH 1996b).

■ **COMPREHENSIVE ASSESSMENT:** see **Assessment level**

■ COMPREHENSIVE HEALTH SERVICE

The Secretary of State has a **duty** to provide a comprehensive health service (*NHS Act 1977*, s.1). This represents a vague duty, the enforcement of which is difficult: as illustrated by the *Hincks* case.

■ CONFLICTS BETWEEN AUTHORITIES

Lack of **resources, grey areas** of responsibility and **buck-passing** all contribute to the unedifying sight of public bodies going to the law courts over who is going to pay for somebody's care: see eg the *Harrow, Hooper, M, Oxfordshire, Quinn* and *Steane* cases.

■ **CONGENITAL DEFORMITY:** see **Disability**

CONNICK CASE

A Social Fund case illustrating well the confusion surrounding **duplication** of provision, **grey areas** of statutory responsibility and **buck-passing**.

What is a medical item as opposed to an everyday item? On the basis that **incontinence pads** were medical items provided by the NHS, a Social Fund officer had denied a 26-week supply of pads to a woman who was incontinent, arthritic and had asthma. The relevant health authority did provide free incontinence pads *in principle*, but *in practice* its criteria were so stringent – regular double incontinence or terminal illness – that the woman did not qualify. The judge found that the decision of the Social Fund officer, that the pads were medical items and thus excluded, was wrong. She had asked whether the pads were needed for a medical problem, but:

> 'It is quite clear that a handkerchief might not be needed, but for a severe attack of a runny nose in a heavy cold. It is quite clear that a bowl might not be needed unless there was a medical problem of a severe bout of vomiting but nobody would think of those articles, the handkerchief or the bowl, as medical items.'

CONSIDERS

Along with terms such as **'satisfied'** or **'appears to'**, the term 'considers' leaves much to the **subjective** opinion of an authority.

Considers: NHS provision. To 'such extent as he **considers necessary** to meet all **reasonable requirements**', the Secretary of State has a **duty** (exercised by health authorities) **to provide various services** (*NHS Act 1977*, s.3). The term 'considers' contributes to the vagueness of the duty, which is difficult to enforce in the law courts because of the wide discretion it confers on authorities, as confirmed in cases such as *Hincks*.

■ CONSISTENCY: see **Inconsistency**

CONSULTATION

When drawing up its **community care plan**, a local authority has a **duty** to consult any health authorities and housing authorities lying wholly or partly within its area. In addition, it has a duty to consult voluntary organisations which represent the interests of service users or of **carers**. (*NHS and Community Care Act 1990*, s.46). **Directions** extend the duty of consultation to include the independent (private) sector (Directions in: LAC(93)4).

Apart from **legislation**, the common law concept of **legitimate expectation** employed in **judicial review** is sometimes used to challenge the failure of authorities even to consult service users before **withdrawing** or reducing services. Successful challenges have been made on this basis in, for example, the *Beckwith* and *Durham* cases, both involving the closure of **residential accommodation**. However, in the context of non-residential services such as **home help**, it could be argued that **reassessment** will satisfy people's legitimate expectations.

■ CONTINENCE ADVICE: see **Incontinence**

CONTINUING CARE

By 1994, the NHS was facing sustained criticism that it was attempting to discard various continuing care responsibilities. A combination of vague **legislation** (*NHS*

Act 1977, ss.1 and 3) and tight budgeting had apparently brought this about. The publication by the **health service ombudsman** of his **Leeds investigation**, about the refusal of a health authority to care for a severely disabled man, brought matters to a head. In response to this adverse publicity for its **policies**, the Department of Health issued **guidance**. This was designed to clarify the situation, and to discourage the wholesale off-loading of financial responsibility for continuing care onto local authorities and onto patients and their relatives. However, even this guidance conceded that authorities had to set **priorities** within available **resources** (HSG(95)8).

(1) **Status of the continuing care guidance.** The status and strength of the **guidance** is not formally indicated. However, some of the language is of the strong variety – for example, telling health authorities that they 'must' provide certain services – even though the subsequent list of services goes well beyond anything to be found in **legislation**. (Note: it is not always clear what the Department of Health intends in its guidance, and the courts have on occasion – for example, in the *Manchester* case – found that the peremptory nature of language in what appears to be guidance actually amounts to a **Direction**.) In summary, the guidance deals with the following:

(2) **Co-operation and eligibility.** The approach of the guidance is to stress the importance of **co-operation** between health authorities and social services departments, so that clear agreements and **procedures** are in place to decide **eligibility** either for continuing NHS care, or for services arranged by social services departments.

(3) **List of continuing care services.** The guidance lists a range of continuing care services which all health authorities (and GP fundholders in respect of certain services) must arrange and fund to meet the needs of the population 'within the resources available to them'. Listed are: specialist **medical and nursing assessment, rehabilitation and recovery, palliative health care, continuing inpatient care** in hospital or **nursing homes, respite health care,** specialist **health care support** for people in nursing or residential care homes or in their own homes, **community health services** for people in their own homes or in residential care, **primary health care**, and specialist **transport** services.

(4) **Examples of specialist and community health services.** An annex to the guidance emphasises the importance of rehabilitation and recovery, and health authorities are warned against the 'risk of premature discharge' of people from hospital. It also states that access to specialist NHS medical, nursing or other community health services might be required by patients in nursing homes, as well as in **residential homes** and in their own homes. Health authorities, in consultation with GP fundholders, local authorities and the independent sector, should set **criteria of eligibility**. The guidance states that provision **may** include:

> 'occasional continuing specialist **medical advice or treatment**, specialist palliative care, specialist **nursing care** such as **continence advice, stoma care** or **diabetic advice** or community health services such as **physiotherapy, speech and language therapy** and **chiropody**. It should also include **specialist medical or nursing equipment** (for instance specialist **feeding equipment**) not on prescription and normally only available through hospitals. It would not cover basic equipment such as **incontinence** supplies, which should instead be included in the basic price charged by the home to the local authority or the person.'

The guidance also refers to **community health services** as a 'crucial part of the provision of continuing care for people or in residential care'.

(5) **Hospital discharge.** The guidance deals with hospital discharge as a separate issue: see **Hospital discharge**

■ **CONTINUING DUTY:** see **Duty: continuing**

Continuing inpatient care in hospital or nursing homes. Such care is an NHS **continuing care** service for which, **guidance** states, **criteria of eligibility** and **priorities** should be set within available **resources** (HSG(95)8). It is provided under the *NHS Act 1977*.

■ CONTORTIONS OF LOCAL AUTHORITIES

When faced with a severe shortage of **resources** and overwhelming demand for services, local authorities are likely to execute various contortions in interpreting (and reinterpreting) the meaning of **legislation**.

For instance, looking to minimise obligations towards **disabled people** under s.2 of the *CSDPA 1970*, they might explore the legal implications of each word or phrase in the **legislation** (e.g. **needs, satisfied, necessary, make arrangements,** facilitating, assistance). Thus, when the Court of Appeal judgment in the *Gloucestershire* case had temporarily (ie before the decision was reversed by the House of Lords) shut off an **escape route** via the words 'needs' and 'necessary', by holding that resources could not be taken into account, some authorities looked at how they could tighten their definition of **disability** under the *National Assistance Act 1948*, and thus prevent certain groups of people ever being **assessed** for *CSDPA* services (for which disability is a pre-condition).

■ **CONVENIENCE:** see **Safety, comfort or convenience**

■ **CONVEYANCE:** see **Travel**

■ CO-OPERATION BETWEEN STATUTORY SERVICES GENERALLY

Policy **guidance** states bluntly that effective 'local collaboration is the key to making a reality of community care' (DH 1990). More recently, recognising the importance of housing services to community care, even though they are not legally **community care services**, guidance from the Department of Health and Department of Environment has stressed the importance of partnership between housing authorities, social services departments and health authorities (DH 1997a).

However, co-operation is more easily talked about than achieved, owing to the essentially weak **duties** of co-operation imposed by **legislation**, the corrosive effects of a shortage of **resources**, and the disparate aims and funding underpinning different statutory services. Even where legislation imposes a **duty** of co-operation, the duty is typically **qualified** and difficult to enforce, as demonstrated by the *Harrow* and *Northavon* cases which involved questions of co-operation between authorities under, respectively, the Education Act 1996 and the *Children Act 1989*. Nevertheless, the importance of co-operation should not be underestimated; the alternative path of dispute and resort to law is generally a barren one not only for the service users who lose out, but ultimately for authorities also.

Co-operation: children. A local authority **may** request help from other authorities when exercising its functions under Part 3 of the *Children Act 1989*. The authorities listed include any other local authority, local education authority, local housing authority, or health authority. It should be noted that this is a **power**, not a **duty**. However, a **qualified duty** is placed on the authority receiving the request; it must comply, but only if it is 'compatible' with its own 'statutory or other duties and obligations and does not unduly prejudice the discharge' of any of its functions (*Children Act 1989*, s.27).

Co-operation: community care assessments. Local authorities have a **duty** to invite the relevant health and housing authorities to assist in a community care **assessment** if it **appears** to the local authority that the person being assessed has health or housing needs. There is no duty – not even a qualified one – imposed explicitly on the health or housing authority to accept the invitation (*NHS and Community Care Act 1990*, s.47). Unless the refusal of the invitation was blatantly **unreasonable**, the *Northavon* case suggests how difficult it might be to enforce a prompt and thorough response through the law courts.

Co-operation: community care plans. Local authorities have a **duty** to **consult** relevant health authorities, housing authorities and voluntary organisations about their **community care plans** (*NHS and Community Care Act 1990*, s.46).

Co-operation: disabled facilities grants. When a **disabled facilities grant** is being applied for, **a duty** is imposed on a housing authority to **consult** the social services authority (where the two are not one and the same) about whether the proposed works of **home adaptation** are **'necessary and appropriate'** to meet the **needs** of the disabled occupant. No explicit duty is placed on the authority being consulted to respond (*Housing Grants, Construction and Regeneration Act 1996*, s.24).

Where a unitary authority (i.e. the social services and housing authority is one and the same) is involved, **guidance** states that the housing department should still consult the social services department (DoE 17/96), although this is not an explicit statutory requirement.

Co-operation: health and welfare. A duty of co-operation is imposed by s.22 of the *NHS Act 1977*: local authorities and health authorities must co-operate to 'secure and advance the health and welfare' of the population. In addition, health authorities may make payments to local authorities towards expenditure incurred in carrying out their **social services functions** (*NHS Act 1977*, s.28A; and see guidance and Directions in LAC(92)17).

COST-EFFECTIVENESS

Community care **guidance** states that the aim of a care package should be 'to secure the most cost-effective package of services that meets the user's care **needs, taking account of** the user's and carers' own **preferences**'. It points out, in addition, that the costs of not acting in time might lead to greater costs in the future and the placing of 'even greater burdens on particular services' (DH 1990). No direct reference to cost-effectiveness is to be found in **legislation**. (Compare s.12 of the Social Work (Scotland) Act 1968, which says that assistance can only be given where it will avoid the local authority incurring greater expense: either by having to provide assistance in another form, or having to provide it at a later date).

In practice, this issue is highly relevant given shortages of **resources**, 'crisis intervention' and the tendency of local authorities to target those in most **need**. The question of weighing up both present and future costs, in **balancing** provision for the needs of a person with efficient use of resources, has been considered in the context of special education (*Staffordshire* case).

■ **COST-SHUNTING:** see **Buck-passing and cost-shunting**

■ **COUNCIL TENANTS:** see **Home adaptations: council tenants**

■ COUNCILLORS

Sometimes local councillors who pass restrictive **policies** in **social services committee** one week, protest the next when they discover that their own constituents have been adversely affected. For local authority staff attempting to rationalise their services when demand outstrips **resources**, this can be immensely frustrating. For service users, enlisting the support of local councillors might be one effective means of attempting to obtain services, since – questions of benevolence aside – adverse **publicity** and restrictive policies affecting significant numbers of people and their relatives do not win votes.

■ COUNSELLING: CHILDREN

In respect of **children in need** who are living with their **families**, local authorities have a **duty** to make 'such provision as they consider **appropriate**' for various services including counselling (*Children Act 1989*, schedule 2).

■ **CRAG:** see **Charging for Residential Accommodation Guide**

■ CRITERIA OF ELIGIBILITY

Criteria of eligibility are not referred to in **legislation**, but feature in various **guidance** and are widespread in practice. Used by local authorities to target and **ration** services, they might determine, for example, whether a person receives an **assessment** at all, how promptly, or in what depth; and then whether any services will be provided, how quickly and of what type. Criteria of eligibility are closely related to **priorities**, **policies** and resources; as these latter reduce over time, so criteria are tightened and provoke disputes in the law courts when, following **reassessment**, services are reduced or **withdrawn** (eg. *Gloucestershire, Bucke, Haringey* and *Farley* cases).

Local authorities should ensure that criteria are not: (a) applied over-rigidly – if they are, the authority might be **fettering its discretion**; or (b) simply **illegal** by contravening the wording of legislation (e.g. the *Ealing* case). It is difficult for authorities to strike the right balance between adopting criteria which enable them to deal efficiently and equitably with the large volume of requests received, and maintaining the individual approach to assessment demanded by legislation (*NHS* *and Community Care Act 1990*, s.47) and advocated by both policy and practice guidance (DH 1990, and SSI/SWSG 1991a).

Health authorities, too, should be aware of applying criteria of eligibility too strictly – since the principle of fettering of discretion applies to all public bodies. This consideration might be one of the reasons why, for instance, Department of Health guidance sets out a formal procedure for reviewing **hospital discharge** decisions (HSG(95)39.

■ **CSDPA 1970:** see **Chronically Sick and Disabled Persons Act 1970**

■ CULTURAL ACTIVITIES

Cultural activities: children. In respect of **children in need** who are living with their **families**, local authorities must make 'such provision as they consider **appropriate**' for various services including cultural activities (*Children Act 1989*, schedule 2).

Cultural activities: disabled people. Local authorities have a **duty** to **make arrangements** to provide cultural activities for **disabled people**. In respect of non-residents, the duty becomes only a **power** (Direction and Approval under *National Assistance Act 1948*, s.29).

***Cultural and religious needs*:** see **Needs: cultural and religious**

■ CUMBRIA CASE

The case concerned an association of proprietors of private sector **residential homes,** who made a wide-ranging attack on the decisions of the local authority in respect of the provision of **residential accommodation** – including the way in which the authority performed its **statutory duties**, and its failure to comply with **guidance, Directions** and a European Community directive on public contracts. The judge found in favour of the local authority, the Court of Appeal subsequently refusing the association leave to appeal.

Cumbria Case: High Court

(1) **Respite care contracts.** The court found that the authority's decision not to contract with the applicants for planned **respite care** was not **unlawful**. The argument that the local authority had erred, in relation to the 85% of the special transitional grant (STG) which should have been spent on private sector provision, failed. This was in part because it was:

> 'fallacious to pick out one particular of the budget with a view to showing that that particular area may have been treated unevenly, or even favourably towards the public sector, as the basis of an argument that the local authority is to that extent in breach of its public law duty'.

(2) **Public services contracts: European directive.** The judge rejected the claim in relation to the directive on public service contracts (EEC Directive 92/50), on the basis that an administrative decision by a public body, that a service be delivered by an inhouse service provider, could not amount to a contract: 'a body cannot make a contract with itself'. Therefore, the directive could not apply.

(3) **Allocation of resources to the local authority's homes.** The judge rejected the assertion that the authority had acted unfairly by allocating capital resources to its own residential homes.

(4) Waiting lists. Lastly, the judge dismissed the claim that the local authority had been operating unlawful waiting lists and denying potential residents a choice of home. He referred to the Rixon case in which the judge had stated that 'even an unequivocal set of statutory duties cannot produce money where there is none or by itself repair gaps in the availability of finance'. He went on to state that it was:

> 'manifest that the duty to assess and to provide accommodation is one that is owed by the respondents to the potential resident and not to any providers of private sector homes. There is no direct evidence that the respondents ever had, let alone operated, an unlawful policy in regard to waiting lists¡ It was never submitted¡ nor could it properly have been, that the [authority] operated a system which cynically disregarded its own declared policy'.

Cumbria Case: Court of Appeal: At a subsequent hearing, the Court of Appeal denied the Association leave to appeal from the High Court judgment, pointing out that for **judicial review** to have any prospect of case, **unreasonableness** would have to be demonstrated: yet there was no prospect of this. The court also agreed that there where the authority had made arrangements with one of its own Departments, there was no public service contract to which the European directive could apply.

■ **DAILY LIVING EQUIPMENT:** see **Disability equipment**

■ DAMAGES

Damages are not usually available in **judicial review** cases (with which this book is mostly concerned). This is one of the factors that distinguishes **judicial review** (public law) cases from those brought, for instance, in **private law** actions for **negligence** or **breach of statutory duty**.

■ DATA PROTECTION ACT 1984

Concerns data protection. Relevant **regulations** made under it include: the *Data Protection (Subject Access Modification) (Social Work) Order 1987*. See: **Information: personal**.

■ DAY CENTRES

Day centres and other types of centre (e.g. drop-in) are provided under various **powers** and **duties** in **legislation**. For instance, they might be provided for: (a) **disabled people** under s.2 of the *CSPDA 1970* or s.29 of the *National Assistance Act 1948*; (b) for **elderly people** under s.45 of the *Health Services and Public Health Act 1968*, (c) for preventing **illness** (including **mental disorder**) or for people who are, or who have been ill under schedule 8 of the *NHS Act 1977*; and (d) for certain mentally disordered people under s.117 of the *Mental Health Act 1983*.

■ DAYKIN CASE

This case illustrates: (a) the confusion which can arise in the absence of formal procedures for **assessment**, especially if recommendations are made by staff not authorised – according to an authority's policy of **delegation** – to take decisions about providing services; (b) the significance of differentiating clearly between **needs**, and the options to meet those needs; and (c) that, in the absence of statutory timescales, local authorities should perform their duties as soon as is **reasonably practicable.**

(1) **Staff with no authority to make decisions.** The case concerned a couple in their 60s, both **disabled**, she suffering from rheumatoid arthritis, he with chronic obstructive airways disease and a short time to live. A health authority **occupational therapist** recommended that they should have installed either a vertical lift or a stairlift to give them ingress and egress from their first floor council flat. The recommendation was also backed by an 'advocacy officer' of the council. The recommended **home adaptations** were eventually refused by the housing department of the council on grounds of cost. The applicant claimed that having assessed the need, the council was obliged to meet it.

(2) **Failure to assess.** The judge decided that, in fact, the council had failed to make an **assessment** and decision about services under s.47 of the *NHS and Community Care Act 1990* and s.2 of the *CSDPA 1970.* Confusingly for the service users, the statements of the advocacy officer, the care plan she had drawn up, and the recommendation of the occupational therapist, did not carry sufficient weight, since the provision of services was 'the concern of the council itself or of any committee or officer to whom a specific power is delegated'. Thus, under the policy of delegation, these staff were not authorised to carry out assessment and to decide about service provision.

(3) **Distinguishing need from means to meet the need – and getting on with meeting a need.** The judge stated that *need* should be differentiated from the *means to meet the need,* and that the requirement of the stairlift fell into the latter, but not the former, category; so it was 'impossible to regard the provision of stair lift at home as "the need"'. Instead the need was 'for the applicants to get in and out of the premises', for which the authority could review various options and take account of cost. Thus, the judge found not that the authority was in breach of its **statutory duty** to provide the stairlift, but that it had been profiting from its failure to carry out the assessment. This was because, if a decision about need is properly made, then:

> 'it is the duty of the authority to meet the needs and that means to meet them as soon as is reasonably practicable... Once they have identified after discussion the manner in which those needs are to be met, then the Act requires that they get on with it and meet those needs.'

DEAF

People who are deaf are eligible for **welfare** services under s.29 of the *National Assistance Act 1948*, s.2 of the *CSDPA 1970*, part 3 of the *Children Act 1989*, and also for **disabled facilities grants** under the *Housing Grants, Construction and Regeneration Act 1996*, s.100. See: **Disability**

DECLARATION

The courts can grant a declaration in **judicial review** cases. The purpose of a declaration is to let the parties know the legality of a particular situation. For example, at the High Court stage of the *Gloucestershire* case, a declaration was granted stating that the authority had **unlawfully** withdrawn services under s.2 of the *CSDPA 1970,* because: (a) lack of **resources** had been the sole factor involved in the decision; and (b) service users were not **reassessed** individually before the **withdrawal**.

DEFAULT POWERS

The Secretary of State has the **power** to make an order declaring a local authority to be in default of its **duty** in relation to any of its **social services functions**. The order **may** contain **Directions** as to what the local authority should do, which are enforceable by court order (*Local Authority Social Services Act 1970*, s.7).

These default powers are sometimes cited by the courts as an **alternative remedy** and a reason why resort to the courts is inappropriate (e.g. *Southwark, Wyatt* and *Good* cases), though in other cases, they might be deemed no obstacle (e.g. *Devon* case). It appears that the powers have never been formally exercised by the Secretary of State, although their use is sometimes threatened.

DELAY

The provision of some **community care services** is subject to considerable delay at both **assessment** and provision stages. For example, people might have to wait many months or even years for an assessment by an **occupational therapist**; and then have to wait a further period for the provision of services such as the installation of a stairlift or a level access **shower**. Unless timescales are imposed by legislation, duties should, legally, be carried out within a 'reasonable time'. Nevertheless, the courts are sometimes reluctant to interfere with the speed at which authorities perform their duties.

(1) **Intervention of the law courts.** The courts might state that cases involving delay only, without accompanying questions of law or fact, should be dealt with through local authority **complaints** procedures. This was held recently in the *Birmingham* case, involving delay in provision for a **child in need** under the *Children Act 1989*, s.17. **Home adaptations** for **disabled people** have featured regularly over the years in investigations of the **local ombudsman**: delay is a common ground for a finding of **maladministration**.

(2) **No timescales in legislation.** Neither community care **legislation** nor **guidance** specifies timescales within which assessment and provision should take place, although guidance issued about **community care charters** does state that such timescales should be drawn up and published (LAC(94)24). In addition, s.47 of the *NHS and Community Care Act 1990* clearly envisages that provision of services will in some circumstances be made very quickly, since it empowers authorities to make provision in **urgent** cases without carrying out an assessment first (although an assessment must then follow as soon as practicable).

(3) **Reasonable time.** Where no statutory timescales are specified, the courts might be reluctant to rule exactly how quickly authorities should carry out their duty, although it should still be performed in a **reasonable** time. Thus, in the *Macwan* case, a housing authority had a duty to provide permanent **accommodation** under the *Housing Act 1985*, but its provision of temporary accommodation for three years was seen by the court as an acceptable interim step – even though it meant that overall performance of the duty was delayed.

On the other hand, more recently, in the *Tucker* case, the judge ruled that by delaying its decision for some two years about what services were **called for**, the authority had actually failed to carry out its duty under s.47 of the *NHS and Community Care Act 1990*. And in the *Daykin* case the court stated that once the local authority had decided how to act under s.2 of the *CSDPA 1970*, it had a duty to 'meet the needs and that means to meet them as soon as is reasonably practicable'. Even so, the *Hendy* case demonstrates the reluctance with which the courts might intervene in situations of delay, even if there has been a breach of **statutory duty**; and the *Birmingham* case, their hesitation even in hearing cases about delay.

(4) Delay: statutory timescales. Sometimes **legislation** includes statutory timescales. For example, housing authorities have a duty to deal with an application for a **disabled facilities grant** within six months and, if the application is approved, make payment within 12 months of the original application date.

The inclusion in legislation of timescales clearly makes their enforceability potentially easier. However, what would seem to be a straightforward situation is sometimes obscured because of a shortage of **resources**. For example, some local authorities have developed 'preliminary enquiry' forms for housing grants, which they do not treat as formal applications; this means that the time laid down in legislation does not begin to run. This device has been used, therefore, to slow down the approval of grant applications. The local ombudsman, though sometimes censuring authorities for denying people grants in this fashion, has also recognised that the shortage of resources has left authorities with little choice. Guidance from the Department of Environment now encourages the use of preliminary (i.e. informal) enquiry schemes, but at the same time states that people must be told of their right to make a formal application at any time (DoE 17/96).

DELEGATION OF FUNCTIONS

Legislation gives local authorities duties and powers to do things. Authorities have the **power**, under the *Local Government Act 1972*, to delegate performance of their functions to committees and officers (e.g. care managers, social workers, or **occupational therapists**). But, unless expressly permitted by legislation, local authorities cannot simply delegate their functions to an independent body or person.

For instance, the **duty** of **assessment** and decision about provision of **community care services** is placed on local authorities (*NHS and Community Care Act 1990*, s.47), and no express provision is made for delegation. However, in contrast, authorities do have the express power – under both s.29 of the *National Assistance Act 1948*, and under s.45 of the *Health Services and Public Health Act 1968* – to employ as agents, independent organisations to deliver **services** (i.e. following an assessment and decision about provision). In any case, ubiquitous use of the term **'make arrangements'**, envisages indirect (i.e. through a third party) as well as direct provision.

(1) Delegating to staff within local authorities. If an authority delegates decision-making to particular officers, further unsanctioned delegation might be deemed **unlawful** by the law courts. This happened, for instance, in the *Aldabbagh* case involving **housing allocation**, whilst in the *Daykin* case the court ruled that the recommendations of both the local authority 'advocacy officer' (on behalf of the applican)t and of an occupational therapist, did not amount to a community care assessment and decision about services, because neither were authorised to perform these functions.

The question sometimes arising is whether an authority is bound by such an unauthorised assessment if it seems to the client that the assessing officer had 'ostensible authority' to take the decision. The answer seems to be that, depending on circumstances, the courts might rule either way; although they are more likely to say that the authority is not bound. However, the extent to which the client has acted in reliance on what was said might be a countervailing factor.

(2) Delegation of functions outside of local authorities. There are some functions which local authorities cannot legally delegate to external bodies.

For example, as already explained, the overall duty of community care assessment of **needs** and decision about services is quite clearly placed on the local authority (*NHS and Community Care Act 1990*, s.47). It is difficult to see how, legally, this decision-making can be wholly contracted out. If it cannot, then while independent agencies might be heavily involved – for example, carrying out fast-track assessments for older people (in low **priority** groups) requiring daily living **equipment**, or for misusers of drugs and alcohol – they should not, in principle, be taking the final, overall decision about individual people's needs and services. Department of Health **guidance** on alcohol and drug misuse, commenting on fast-track assessment by independent agencies, states that authorities retain 'ultimate responsibility' (LAC(93)2).

How an authority might demonstrate that it has retained final, overall control over assessment will no doubt vary. In the *Woolgar* case, involving the investigation of people's **homelessness** by a housing association, the judge ruled that the housing association could play a dominant role in the assessment, so long as the authority remained the ultimate decision-maker. The law in respect of such delegation of functions relating to housing allocation and homelessness has in fact now been altered by **regulations** (SI 1996/3205). However, no such contracting out legislation has been passed in relation to community care assessment.

■ DEVON CASE (AND DURHAM CASE)

These two cases, heard together in the Court of Appeal, highlighted the **duty** which local authorities have in certain circumstances to **consult** service users before **withdrawing** or changing services.

(1) Scrupulous fairness. The cases concerned the closure of local authority residential homes. The appeal of the residents was dismissed in the *Devon* case, the court finding that the residents knew about the proposed closure of the homes long before the final decision was made; that they had had ample time to make representations; and that council's officers were 'scrupulously fair' in putting before councillors representations and objections. In addition, it was held that residents did not have an individual right to be consulted face to face, but that consultation could be achieved by meetings held with residents generally.

(2) Informing people at the last minute. In the *Durham* case, however, the court found that the residents had been informed only at the eleventh hour about the closure of the home. The **duty** of the authority to act fairly to the residents would have been satisfied if the residents (a) had known well in advance of the final decision about closure, (b) had been given a **reasonable** amount of time to object to the council, and (c) had had their objections considered by the council. This did not happen.

(3) Appropriateness of judicial review. The court went on to consider the nature of **legitimate expectation**. It also pointed out that it was appropriate that the dispute had come before the law courts, rather than being channelled toward the Secretary of State's power to declare an authority in **default** of its duty. This was because: (a) it was not clear that the duty to consult residents was a statutory **social services function** (if it was not, the Secretary of State had no **power** to intervene); and (b) the matter was one of law in a developing field and thus for the courts and not the Secretary of State to deal with.

■ DIABETIC ADVICE

Diabetic advice is an NHS **continuing care** service which, **guidance** explains, people – in **nursing** or **residential homes**, or in their own homes – might require and for which **criteria of eligibility** and **priorities** should be set within available **resources** (HSG(95)8). Such advice is provided under the *NHS Act 1977*.

DIAGNOSIS

Diagnosis: illness. Diagnosis of **illness** is one of the purposes for which the Secretary of State has a **duty to provide a comprehensive** health service (*NHS Act 1977*, s.1). The duty is difficult to enforce in the law courts because of the wide **discretion** it confers, as confirmed in cases such as *Hincks*.

Diagnosis: mental disorder. Local authorities have a duty to **make arrangements** for the provision of **social work** and related services to help in the diagnosis of **mental disorder** (Direction under *NHS Act 1977*, schedule 8).

DICTIONARIES

Sometimes in **judicial review** cases, the judges resort to dictionaries to support their decisions; either in contrast to, or in tandem with, consideration of other factors such as the will of **Parliament**. For instance, the Shorter Oxford English Dictionary (3rd edition, 1944) has been used to shed light on certain words in s.2 of the CSDPA 1970: **'need'** and **'necessary'** in the *Gloucestershire* case (Court of Appeal stage), and 'facilitate' in the *Hargreaves (no.2)* case. Conversely, one of the judges at the House of Lords stage of the *Gloucestershire* case stated dismissively: 'reference to dictionary definitions does not seem to me to advance the construction' of the words in issue.

DIRECT PAYMENTS

Local authorities have the **power** to make payments to certain groups of people, in order to enable the latter to buy their own **community care services** (*Community Care (Direct Payments) Act 1996*). This Act stands in stark contrast to the *National Assistance Act 1948* passed nearly 50 years before: s.29 of the Act forbids cash payments in respect of welfare services, while the courts have stated that they are not permissible under s.21 in connection with residential accommodation (*Hammersmith and Fulham (no.2)* case). This illustrates how disparate community care **legislation** is, and points perhaps to the need for consolidation and **law reform**. (The *Children Act 1989*, s.17, allows assistance for **children in need** to be given in cash, rather than kind, in 'exceptional circumstances').

Accompanying **regulations** restrict payments to people under the age of 65 such as those with **physical disabilities, sensory disabilities, learning disabilities,** various other illnesses (such as **HIV** and **AIDS**), and people with a **mental illness** (SI 1997/734). (A number of categories of people, to whom mental health or criminal justice legislation applies, are excluded from eligibility; such as patients detained under mental health legislation and patients subject to Home Office restrictions, guardianship, supervised discharge, compulsory court order, or probation/combination order involving requirement of treatment for mental health condition or drugs/alcohol dependency). Payments can only be made to a person 'who **appears** to the authority to be capable of managing a direct payment by himself or with assistance'.

Some of the details of direct payments are as follows.

(1) **Residential accommodation.** Payments cannot be used for **residential accommodation**, except for short periods of up to four weeks at any one time. Within a 12-month period, more than one four-week period would qualify for payments, so long as the gap between any two periods is greater than four weeks (SI 1997/734).

(2) **Repayment of money.** The Act itself makes provision for repayment of the money if the authority is not **satisfied** that it has been used to secure the intended services or has been used to pay certain people barred by the regulations (e.g. spouse, partner, parent). However, policy **guidance** points out that the power to recover money is not intended to enable authorities to penalise honest mistakes. Importantly, it also states that authorities should inform people of the various legal responsibilities which they might incur if they contract directly, as employer, with care staff (DH 1997).

(3) **Payments for equipment.** Payments are available for **community care services**, including, therefore, for **disability equipment** and **home adaptations** provided by local authority social services departments (but not by housing authorities or the NHS). However, guidance states that direct payments 'are unlikely to be appropriate for purchasing complex and expensive pieces of equipment' because of issues of safety, appropriateness, and responsibility for ongoing care and maintenance (DH 1997).

■ DIRECTIONS AND APPROVALS

Community care **legislation** gives the Secretary of State the **power** to make Directions and Approvals, which form yet another part of the community care legal and administrative framework, lying somewhere between legislation and **guidance**. They are not the same as legislation (Acts of Parliament and **statutory instruments**) which passes through **Parliament**, but Directions are regarded nevertheless as placing **duties** on authorities. In contrast, Approvals give authorities the power to do things. The Secretary of State has issued Directions or Approvals about, for example, **complaints procedures, residential accommodation, choice of residential accommodation, welfare services** for **elderly people**.

Although Directions and Approvals are usually identifiable because they are clearly labelled 'Directions' and 'Approvals', this is not always so. The courts have held that strong language used in what otherwise might appear to be guidance, is capable of being a Direction – even if it is not called by that name (*Manchester* case; but see also the *Fisher* case on the same issue).

■ **DIRECTORS OF SOCIAL SERVICES:** see **Social services: directors**

■ DISABILITY

Disability is a concept central to community care (and related) legislation.

Disability: access to goods and services. The Disability Discrimination Act 1995 (DDA), which is not community care **legislation**, makes it unlawful to discriminate against disabled people, on account of their disability, in the provision of goods and services. Public authorities, including both local authorities and the NHS, are covered by the Act.

However, the detailed implications in relation to the delivery of **community care services** are unclear at present, since: (a) various parts of the Act are not yet in force; (b) it is not yet known how terms such as **'reasonable'**, which govern some duties in the Act, will be interpreted by the law courts in particular situations; and (c) there is an uncertain 'interface' between the DDA and community care legislation, in that nothing in the DDA can make **unlawful** any act done 'in pursuance of' other legislation (DDA 1995, s.59).

Disability: adjustment to: see **Adjustment to disability**

Disability: children: see **Children: disabled**

Disability: chronically sick and disabled people. It is sometimes assumed by practitioners that a person qualifies for services under the *CSDPA 1970* if he or she is 'chronically sick or disabled' in the normal sense (whatever that might be) of the phrase. In fact, **eligibility** depends, legally, on the person being **blind, deaf, dumb, substantially and permanently handicapped** or **mentally disordered** under s.29 of the *National Assistance Act 1948* (or the *Children Act* 1989, schedule 2).

Disability: disabled facilities grants and home repair assistance. For the purposes of awarding **disabled facilities grants** or giving **home repair assistance** for a disabled person under housing **legislation**, disability is defined twofold. First, a person is disabled if (a) his or her **sight, hearing** or **speech** is substantially **impaired**; (b) he or she has a **mental disorder** or impairment of any kind; or (c) he or she is substantially physically disabled by **illness, injury, impairment** present since birth, or otherwise. Second, a person is taken to be disabled if he or she is **registered**, or registerable, under the definition of disability given in s.29 of the *National Assistance Act 1948* (or the *Children Act* 1989, schedule 2) (see **Disability: welfare services**) (*Housing Grants, Construction and Regeneration Act 1996*, s.100).

Disability: equipment. Regarded as the 'Cinderella' even of cinderella services, policy **guidance** nevertheless refers to equipment as part of the preferred aim of community care: to enable people to remain in their own homes (DH 1990).

Equipment is provided by local authorities mainly as **additional facilities** for greater **safety, comfort or convenience,** either for disabled people under the *CSDPA 1970* or for **elderly people** under the *Health Services and Public Health Act 1968*. Items covered include hoists, high-seat chairs, riser chairs, special cutlery, electric bath-seats, bath-boards, reaching-sticks and so on.

Guidance suggests that housing authorities **may**, unusually, provide some types of equipment (the installation of which requires little or no structural modification to a dwelling) as part of **home repair assistance** or even of a **disabled facilities grant** (DoE 17/96). The NHS also provides many types of equipment, including wheelchairs, walking aids, **communication aids,** hearing aids, nebulisers, **incontinence** pads and so on, under the *NHS Act 1977*.

Disability: home help and laundry facilities. Local authorities have a **duty** to provide, or **arrange** for the provision of, **home help** 'on such a scale as is adequate for the **needs** of their area' which is **required** because of the presence of a person who, amongst other things, is 'handicapped' by '**illness** or by congenital deformity'. There is a **power** to provide **laundry facilities** in the same circumstances (*NHS Act 1977*, schedule 8). The term 'handicap' in this Act is not qualified by the words 'substantial' or 'permanent': compare the *National Assistance Act 1948*, s.29.

Disability: housing needs. Housing authorities have a **duty**, when considering their own housing stock under s.8 of the *Housing Act 1985*, to consider the special **needs** of 'chronically sick and disabled persons' (*CSDPA 1970*, s.3). The phrase 'chronically sick and disabled persons', in relation to this particular duty, is not subject to the definition of disability supplied in the *National Assistance Act 1948*, s.29, and remains undefined.

Disability: health services. The *NHS Act 1977* defines **illness** to include 'any injury or disability requiring **medical** or dental **treatment** or **nursing**' (s.128).

Disability: learning disabilities. People with learning disabilities come within the **legislation** both as disabled people or – in some cases – as people with a **mental disorder** (which takes on the meaning given in the *Mental Health Act 1983*, including 'arrested or incomplete development of mind').

In 1992, the Department of Health issued **guidance** specifically about services for adults with learning disabilities. Included is the statement that services should be arranged on an individual basis, 'taking account of **age, need,** degree of disability, the personal **preference** of the individual' etc. (LAC(92)15). This guidance was referred to by the judge in the *Avon* case, when he confirmed that a person's preference could in some circumstances amount to a **psychological need** and thus trigger a **duty**.

Disability: residential accommodation. Local authorities have **duties** and **powers** to **make arrangements** for the provision of **residential accommodation** for people who, because of disability, are in need of **care and attention** not **otherwise available** to them (**Directions and Approvals** under *National Assistance Act 1948*, s.21). It should be noted that disability is defined to include mental as well as physical disability, but is not governed by the 'substantially and permanently handicapped' condition which controls provision of **welfare services** under s.29 of the *National Assistance Act 1948*.

Disability: welfare services. For adults, eligibility for services under s.29 of *National Assistance Act 1948* and s.2 of the *CSDPA 1970* is restricted to people 'aged 18 or over who are **blind, deaf** or **dumb**, or who suffer from **mental disorder** of any description and other persons aged 18 or over who are substantially and permanently handicapped by **illness, injury,** or **congenital deformity** or such other disabilities as may be prescribed'. The same conditions (save the age condition) cover childrens' eligibility for services under s.2 of the *CSDPA*. **Hearing impairment, sight impairment** and **speech impairment** are taken to come under substantial and permanent handicap (see: LAC(93)10).

Some authorities, faced with a shortage of **resources**, might attempt to limit the number of people qualifying for *CSDPA* services by narrowing their definition of disability. While authorities might believe that they have considerable **discretion** to do this, they should be aware that Department of Health guidance has urged a generous and inclusive approach to disability (LAC(93)10).

***Disability Discrimination Act 1995*: see Disability: access to goods and services**

- **DISABLED CHILDREN:** see **Children: disabled**

- **DISABLED FACILITIES GRANTS:** see **Home adaptations**

DISABLED OCCUPANT

'Disabled occupant' is the term used in the *Housing Grants, Construction and Regeneration Act 1996* in relation to **disabled facilities grants** (see **Disability: housing grants**).

- **DISABLED PEOPLE:** see **Disability**

DISABLED PERSONS (SERVICES, CONSULTATION AND REPRESENTATION) ACT 1986

(1) **Assessment of disabled people.** Section 4 of the Act imposes a **duty** on local authorities to **assess** a **disabled person** on request (by the disabled person or a **carer** providing care on a regular and substantial basis) for services under s.2 of the *CSDPA 1970*: see **Assessment**.

(2) **Disabled school-leavers.** Sections 5 and 6 place duties on local authority social services departments and local education authorities to **co-operate**, carry out assessments, exchange **information** etc., in relation to **disabled children** with a statement of special educational needs when they approach school-leaving age. See: **School leavers**.

(3) **Carers.** Section 8 stipulates that when assessing the needs of a disabled person for services under Part 3 of the *National Assistance Act 1948*, s.2 of the *CSDPA 1970*, schedule 8 of the *NHS Act 1977* or under Part 3 of the *Children Act 1989*, the local authority must have regard to the ability of a carer, who is providing a 'substantial amount of care on a regular basis' 'to continue to provide such care on a regular basis'.

(4) **Guidance.** Associated **guidance** is to be found in LAC(87)6, LAC(88)2, LAC(93)12.

- **DISCHARGE FROM HOSPITAL:** see **Hospital discharge**

DISCRETION

Public authorities use discretion when they take decisions in the performance of their statutory functions. For instance, when performing its duty to assess people's needs and deciding what **community care services** are **called for** (*NHS and Community Care Act 1990*, s.47), a local authority is exercising its discretion. The law courts, through **judicial review**, attempt to prevent authorities from abusing their discretion: for example, either from **fettering** it through excessively **rigid policies**, or, at the other extreme, from exercising unfettered discretion (i.e. an authority cannot do whatever it wants, but should act within the general purpose of the **legislation**).

DISCRETIONARY SERVICES

A discretionary service refers to a service provided under a **power** rather than a **duty**. For instance, housing authorities have the power to award discretionary **disabled facilities grants** for the **welfare, accommodation** or **employment** of **disabled people**. The term 'discretionary' should be differentiated from the **discretion** which authorities exercise in respect of both duties and powers.

DOMICILIARY SERVICES

Domiciliary services: community care generally. Policy **guidance** refers to 'domiciliary care' as a means of achieving the preferred aim of community care namely, to enable people to remain in their own homes (DH 1990). Domiciliary services might take the form of, for instance, **practical assistance in the home, home help, meals on wheels** etc.

Domiciliary services: mental disorder. For the prevention of **mental disorder**, or for people who are, or have been, suffering from mental disorder, local authorities have a **duty** to **make arrangements** for the provision of **social work** and related services to provide domiciliary and **care services** for people in their own homes or elsewhere (Direction under the *NHS Act 1977*, schedule 8).

DUMB

People who are 'dumb' are eligible for **welfare** services under s.29 of the *National Assistance Act 1948*, s.2 of the *CSDPA 1970*, part 3 of the *Children Act 1989*, and also for **disabled facilities grants** under the *Housing Grants, Construction and Regeneration Act 1996*, s.100. See: **Disability**

DUPLICATION

Within **legislation**, measures to avoid overlap in the provision of services are sometimes found. However, even where they do exist they sometimes fail to shed light on **grey areas** of responsibility lying between statutory services.

For instance, s.29 of the *National Assistance Act 1948* states that nothing in it authorises or requires the provision of services **required** to be provided under the *NHS Act 1977*. This is capable of two interpretations: narrow and broad. The narrow interpretation would mean that *local authorities* cannot provide under s.29 of the 1948 Act anything which they must provide under the 1977 Act; the broad interpretation would be stating that local authorities should not be providing anything at all which either they or the NHS are required to provide under the 1977 Act.

(1) **Broad interpretation.** Given the vagueness of the *NHS Act 1977*, referring to the provision of **medical services, nursing services** etc., are **incontinence** pads, wheelchairs, pressure mattresses, bed-raising blocks, bathing services or **communication aids**, for example, 'required' to be provided under the Act? Indeed, in the *Fox* case, the court

conceded that a health authority might have no **duty** to 'provide any particular type of health care to any particular person at any particular time'.

The question is further complicated because it can be asked on four different levels: (a) is the service or item something which the NHS as a whole has a duty to provide *generally* and *in principle*; (b) does the NHS as a whole provide it *generally* and *in practice*; (c) does the *particular* health authority involved provide it *generally* and *in practice* and (d) will the *particular* health authority provide it for this *particular* person *in practice*? For example, in the *Connick* case, a woman was being denied incontinence pads by the Social Fund on the basis that the rules precluded assistance being given with provision of medical items (which were for the NHS to supply). If one applies this four-fold test to the case, the answer to the first three questions is in effect affirmative, but to the fourth negative: the health authority did provide pads, but only according to strict **criteria of eligibility** which the woman did not meet.

(2) Narrow interpretation. Even the narrow approach (i.e. relating only to local authority functions under the 1948 and 1977 Acts, rather than to the NHS as well) is not totally straightforward to understand. First, the anti-duplication measure applies only to what is 'required' to be provided, i.e. presumably involving a duty; yet a number of the services in schedule 8 of the *NHS Act 1977* are provided under powers: **laundry facilities** for example.

Second, s.2 of the *CSDPA 1970* is often assumed to be an extension of s.29 of the *National Assistance Act 1948* and on this basis, it might be thought, services provided under a duty in the *NHS Act 1977* could be provided neither under the 1948 Act nor under s.2 of the *CSDPA*; for instance, **home help** for disabled people. Nevertheless, this very contention was dismissed by the High Court in the *Gloucestershire* case as 'unattractive', since by failing to **make arrangements** for home help for a **disabled person** under the **general duty** contained in the 1977 Act, the authority would also be relieving itself of the more **specific duty** to provide it under s.2 of the *CSDPA*. The judge pointed out that this argument was erroneous because: 'What is authorising the local authority to make arrangements under section 2 is section 2': i.e. home help could be provided under the *CSDPA 1970*.

■ **DURHAM CASE:** see **Devon case**

■ DUTY

A duty is what authorities must do under **legislation**, while a **power** *permits* – but does not oblige – them to act. A duty is usually identified in legislation by the word 'shall'. The courts sometimes distinguish between two types of duty: (a) a strong, **specific duty** towards individual people, and (b) a less strong **general duty** or **target duty** toward the local population. However, as a general rule, the actual words 'specific', 'individual', 'absolute', 'general' (but see s.17 of the *Children Act 1989*), 'target' do not appear in legislation.

Duty: absolute. A duty is sometimes described as absolute, which once certain conditions are met, has to be performed irrespective of **resources** – such as the duty under s.2 of the *CSDPA 1970*, once an authority has accepted that it is **necessary** for it to meet a person's **needs**. Such a duty is amenable to enforcement through **judicial review**. See below: **Duty: general or specific.**

Duty: continuing. A continuing duty is sometimes referred to in the context of s.2 of the *CSDPA 1970*, when a local authority has **assessed** a **need**, and assumed or hoped that somebody else will meet the need (e.g. that a housing authority will fund a **home adaptation**), but this does not happen. In this situation, the local authority, having in the first place assessed the need and a necessity to meet it, might remain under a duty to **make arrangements** to meet it (see e.g. **guidance** in DoE 17/96).

Duty: general and target, or specific. The courts sometimes distinguish between what they call general or target duties on the one hand, and specific or individual duties on the other. The latter are sometimes seen to be stronger and easier to enforce than the former.

(1) **Specific, individual duties.** A specific, individual duty can be identified by a combination of the words 'shall' (indicating a duty) and 'any person' (indicating that is a duty towards individuals). These words are found, for instance, in s.2 of the *CSDPA 1970* (**welfare services** for disabled people), s.47 of the *NHS and Community Care Act 1990* (community care **assessment**), and s.117 of the *Mental Health Act 1983* (**after-care** for people with a **mental disorder**).

The existence of an individual duty under s.2 of the *CSDPA 1970* was recognised in the *Gloucestershire* case to mean that once an authority had accepted that it was necessary for it to meet a person's **needs**, it had an **absolute duty** to do so, irrespective of whether it had adequate **resources** (and subject only to **reassessment**). The terms 'individual' and 'specific' are used variously and interchangeably in, for instance, the *Bexley, Gloucestershire* and *Rixon* cases. In the *Gloucestershire* case, the House of Lords referred to the duty under s.2 of the *CSDPA 1970* towards **disabled people** as 'not a general but a particular duty and it gave a correlative right to the individual which he could enforce in the event of a failure in its performance'.

(2) **General, target duties.** In contrast, general duties omit mention of 'any person' and are regarded as being towards the local population rather than individuals. The courts generally seem to accept that target duties are not so easily amenable to judicial enforcement. This is, first, because it might be possible for an authority in some circumstances to take into account **resources** when deciding whether to perform such duties. Second, it is also because unless there is a drastic, general dereliction of the target duty – such as a decision to 'stop production' altogether, rather than simply fail in a single instance – the court might state that any solution should be through the Secretary of State's **default powers**, rather than the law courts (see *Rixon* case). (The term, 'stop production', was originally used in an education case when an authority's schools were closed down because of a strike).

In the *Rixon, Goldsack* and *Gloucestershire* cases, too, the duty under s.29 of the *National Assistance Act 1948* was identified as less easy to enforce – because resources can be taken into account – than specific, individual duties. Also in the *Gloucestershire* case (High Court), the judge referred to the 'general arrangements' for **home help** under schedule 8 of the *NHS Act 1977*, implying too a target duty here, in contrast to the specific duty to provide **practical assistance** under s.2 of the *CSDPA 1970*. In the *Fox* case, the judge distinguished between the general duty to provide after-care under s.3 of the *NHS Act 1977* and the specific duty owed under s.117 of the *Mental Health Act 1983*; whilst the Court of Appeal in the *Hincks* case agreed that s.3 does not impose an **absolute duty** (see above). Last, the *Children Act 1989*, s.17, actually contains the term 'general duty' to describe the obligations of local authorities to safeguard and promote the welfare of **children in need**, as if emphasising that the duty is not towards individual children (in the light of the *Tilley* case).

(3) **Blurring the distinction between different types of duty?** However, the distinction between the two types of duty, general and specific, is not totally clear. First, in community care legislation, the various duties to provide **community care services** are overlaid by

the individual duty to assess people (*NHS and Community Care Act 1990*, s.47). Inevitably, the question arises as to whether, for the purpose of enforcement by a service user, this means that a target duty underpinning provision of a community care service (e.g. as contained in s.29 of the *National Assistance Act 1948*) becomes 'personalised' and thus an individual duty after all. The answer in, for instance, the *Rixon* case, was no.

Second, in the *Sefton* case (High Court), analysing the duty to provide **residential accommodation** 'for persons' in need of **care and attention** under s.21 of the *National Assistance Act 1948*, the judge stated that once an authority had identified 'in a particular case' the need which triggers its duty, then it cannot 'pray in aid its own lack of resources as an excuse for failing to make the necessary provision'. The Court of Appeal in the same case agreed with this aspect of the High Court judgment. This would appear to place s.21 of the 1948 Act on a par with s.2 of the *CSDPA 1970* as an individual and specific, rather than a target, duty.

Third, although a general duty might ultimately be more difficult to enforce than a specific duty, this does not necessarily mean that an authority can simply ignore it. For instance, in the *Tower Hamlets* case, the authority mistakenly took too narrow a view of what it could provide under s.17 of the *Children Act 1989*, and thus failed to carry out a proper assessment under that section.

Duty: of care: see **Negligence**

Duty: qualified. Duties to provide services are often hedged around with qualifying wording. For example, the duty to provide NHS **medical services** is to the extent 'necessary to meet all **reasonable requirements**' (NHS Act 1977, s.3). Or, the duty on local authorities is not simply to provide **home adaptations** for **disabled people**: it is to **make arrangements** for the provision of assistance for the carrying out of works of home adaptation, and only if the authority is **satisfied** that it is **necessary** for it to meet that person's **needs** (*CSDPA 1970*, s.2). First, need and necessity have to be established; second, the arrangements made by the authority do not necessarily have to be in the form of direct provision; and third, the provision, whoever makes it, is not straightforwardly provision of, but only assistance in carrying out, home adaptations.

EAST SUSSEX COUNTY COUNCIL CASE

This education case concerned the reduction in the amount of home tuition received by a girl suffering from myalgic encephalomyelitis. The High Court and Court of Appeal judgments made ample reference to the *Gloucestershire* case, since the question was at heart the same in both cases: could local authorities take account of **resources** when deciding what services to provide.

In this case, the issue was whether they could be taken into account when deciding on 'suitable education' (under s.298 of the Education Act 1993) for a child who could not attend school as a result of ill health. The High Court ruled that resources could not be a **relevant factor** in deciding this question; the Court of Appeal, in a split 2-1 decision, overturned the lower court's decision. However, the case might be taken on further appeal to the House of Lords in early 1998.

East Sussex County Council case: High Court. In distinguishing the *Gloucestershire* case from the present one, The judge pointed out that whilst the words **'necessary'** and **'needs'** are not defined in the *CSDPA 1970*, **Parliament** had by contrast ensured that the term 'suitable education' was explained in s.298 of the 1993 Act. Suitable education for a child or young person was defined as 'efficient education suitable to his age, ability and apptitude and to any special educational needs he may have'. Nowhere was there mention of resources. Not only had the authority taken account of an **irrelevant** consideration, but had also made its decision in an **irrational** way.

However - and in this respect he followed the *Gloucestershire* judgment - the judge pointed out that this did not mean that resources were altogether **irrelevant:** having decided on what suitable education is, there might be different options - some cheaper than others - for **making arrangements** for its provision. At this stage, the authority could take into account its resources in deciding how to provide the suitable education.

East Sussex County Council case: Court of Appeal. In overturning the High Court decision, a number of points were made, including the following.

(1) **Making arrangements and considering costs.** Whilst the **legislation** defined 'suitable education' in relation to each individual child, the duty to make arrangements for suitable education was for sick children (in the plural). The court contrasted provision for 'children' in s.298, as opposed to 'each child' elsewhere in education legislation. This meant that such arrangements 'have to be made with an eye to meeting the needs of all the sick children to whom the LEA are beholden' – and that inevitably the cost of making such arrangements had to be taken into account.

(2) **Budgetary issues: political not legal.** Furthermore, it was pointed out that even the 'lode-star' of five hours of tuition, the original provision, involved questions of cost, since the child's:

> 'true need, considered from her best interest alone, would be for a home-tutor to be available to her during those days when she is fit and well enough to concentrate and make best use of the service. It may be more than five hours on a good week, less on a bad. But that degree of personal service cannot be provided. It is simply too expensive. The decision to afford hours [sic] home tuition is itself a decision taken with an eye to the management of the available budget. In reduced times, all have to suffer. That may not be a satisfactory position from [the child's] point of view but the remedy is a political one, not a legal one. Consequently it is not for us'.

(The dissenting judge, like Lord Lloyd (dissenting) in the *Gloucestershire* case, pointed the finger at central government, by saying that once a local authority had made what savings on non-mandatory items it could – by, for example, cancelling a proposed leisure centre or a football ground – then its inability to carry out its **statutory duty** could only be remedied by Parliament.)

(3) **Predominance of resources.** It was suggested that the education authority had treated budgetary considerations as paramount and that the decision was tainted by an improper purpose or that only lip service had been paid to the needs of the particular child. The court rejected this contention, stating that it was quite clear that the individual child had been considered, and that, so long as the authority had had regard to all material considerations, it was not for the court to say what weight should have been given to each consideration.

(4) **Irrationality of the decision.** The authority's decision was attacked as **irrational** on a number of counts, and both majority judges pointed to the shortcomings of the decision. One suggested that it 'may seem hard to justify when there was so little evidence to show any diminution in ... need for five hours home-tuition a week'. The other conceded that his concerns were stirred about the detail of the decision-making. But neither were

prepared to strike the decision down as irrational, since if they were to examine decision-making over-critically, they would be dealing with the **merits of the decision,** something which had to be avoided: 'there is a danger that a legitimate exercise in review of legality becomes an impermissible appeal on the merits and that imperfections in the process are equated with irrationality in the result'.

■ EDUCATIONAL FACILITIES: DISABLED PEOPLE

If a person is **disabled** and **ordinarily resident** within the area of a local authority, then the authority has a **duty** to **make arrangements** for the provision of assistance to the person in taking advantage of educational facilities available to him or her, if the authority is **satisfied** that it is **necessary** for it to make those arrangements in order to meet the person's **needs** (*CSDPA 1970*, s.2).

■ ELDERLY PEOPLE

See also: **Age**

Elderly people: home repair assistance. Some of the statutory conditions for the provision by housing authorities of **home repair assistance** are relaxed in the case of 'elderly' people, who are defined as being 60 years old or over (*Housing Grants, Construction and Regeneration Act 1996*, s.77–78,101).

Elderly people: welfare. Local authorities have the **power** to 'meet the **needs** of the elderly' by **making arrangements** to provide various **welfare services** (Approval under *Health Services and Public Health Act 1968*, s.45). Elderly people are not defined in terms of age.

■ ELIGIBILITY CRITERIA: see **Criteria of eligibility**

■ EMPLOYMENT: DISABLED FACILITIES GRANTS

Making a dwelling or building suitable for the employment of a **disabled occupant** is one of the statutory purposes for which a housing authority **may**, but is not obliged to, approve an application for a **disabled facilities grant** (*Housing Grants, Construction and Regeneration Act 1996*, s.23). See: **Work**

■ ENFIELD CASE

A case concerning the extent to which, if any, local authorities can be found liable in **negligence** in respect of their **social services functions.**

(1) **Background.** Concerning child care, the case involved a claim that a local authority acted negligently towards a child who was in its care from the age of ten months until he was eighteen years old. Amongst the complaints were failure to arrange for adoption, inappropriate foster placements, lack of proper monitoring and supervision whilst at different placements.

(2) **Distinction between exercise of discretion, and implementing a decision.** The Court of Appeal ruled that the plaintiff had no prospect of succeeding, and that the local authority and its staff would not be liable for negligent exercise of **discretion** in caring for the plaintiff. This was in accord with the House of Lords decision in the *Bedfordshire* case. However, the court stated generally that if a social worker was careless in implementing a decision, either of his own or of the authority, then the authority could in principle be vicariously liable in negligence if it were proved according to the ordinary rules of negligence.

- **EQUIPMENT:** see **Additional facilities; Disability equipment; Medical and nursing equipment: specialist; and Safety, comfort or convenience**

EQUITY

A criticism of community care is that provision varies considerably in quality and quantity between local authorities, resulting in a lack of equity. In other words, area postcode rather than individual **need** might determine provision. **Priorities, policies, criteria of eligibility** and the amount of money spent on community care per head of the population might all vary from place to place.

The counter-argument, often advanced by central government, is that local authorities should be free to act flexibly, and to make different policies and priorities according to local circumstances. The flaw in this counter-argument is that when it wants to, central government attempts to keep tight control on what is happening locally; not only by means of the plentiful **guidance** sent to local authorities, but also through the **rate-capping** system.

Within a local authority, inequitable treatment might appear to flourish when one person receives a service which a second person in similar circumstances is denied, either for no apparent reason or because of a change of policy. As to why the courts might be reluctant to intervene, see: **Inconsistency, Fettering of discretion, Policies**

ESCAPE ROUTES

Local authorities sometimes attempt to avoid obligations by actively seeking escape routes through the maze of **legislation**. For instance, in the *Sefton* case – at the High Court stage, but not subsequently, in the Court of Appeal – the authority successfully identified circumstances in which the charging **regulations** for **residential accommodation** did not apply. Similarly, the *Gloucestershire* case was about detecting the points in s.2 of the *CSDPA 1970* at which local authorities could take account of **resources** and thus reduce, or at least set realistic limits to, their obligations.

ESSEX CASE

A negligence case involving child care, in which the court ruled that the authority could potentially be liable in **negligence**, notwithstanding the House of Lords decision in the Bedfordshire case which had demonstrated the courts' reluctance to impose negligence liability on local authority social services departments.

(1) Background. It was alleged that the local authority and/or its social worker knew at the time that a child, who went to live with a foster family, was a sexual abuser. He subsequently sexually abused the family's two children. The local authority attempted to have the case struck out and prevent it proceeding to trial; it claimed that it owed no **duty of care** to the family, and would not have owed it even if the child had 'previously been convicted of rape, indecent assault, robbery or an offence of violence' – and even if the social worker had deliberately deceived the family.

(2) Potential duty of care. Having dealt with the various obstacles to imposing a duty of care listed in the *Bedfordshire* case, the judge did not strike out the parts of the claim relating to a duty of care – finding essentially that the relationship between social worker and foster carer could, in principle, give rise to vicarious liability in negligence on the part of the local authority. (This meant the case could go to trial, where the ordinary principles of negligence would be applied to attempt to establish actual liability.)

■ ETHICAL CONFLICTS

Local authority staff might sometimes find themselves confronted by conflicting loyalties and possible ethical dilemmas. For instance, a professional code of conduct might state that they should advocate for the client, yet they are under an obligation, as employees, to their employer. The two obligations might not always sit easily together.

For example, how should staff act if they are asked to carry out fast-track **assessment** of people's **bathing** needs, but to ignore any other needs which **appear** to them to exist – especially as this could, arguably, be in breach of s.47 of the *NHS and Community Care Act 1990*? Or, what if they see how the authority's stringent **criteria of eligibility** can be circumvented: should they tell clients?

■ EXCEPTIONS

The **policies, criteria of eligibility** and **priorities** of local authorities should somehow allow for exceptions, if authorities are not to be found **fettering their discretion** by the law courts in **judicial review**, or by the **local ombudsman**.

■ EXPECTANT AND NURSING MOTHERS

Expectant and nursing mothers: care. Local authorities have the **power** to **make arrangements** for the care (other than **residential accommodation**) of expectant and nursing mothers of any age (Approval under *NHS Act 1977*, schedule 8).

Expectant and nursing mothers: residential accommodation. Local authorities have the **power** to **make arrangements** for the provision of **residential accommodation**, in particular, mother and baby homes, for expectant and nursing mothers of any age who are in **need** of **care and attention** not **otherwise available** to them (Approval under *National Assistance Act 1948*, s.21).

Expectant mothers or women lying-in: home help. Local authorities have a **duty** to provide, or **arrange** for the provision of, **home help** for households 'on such a scale as is adequate for the **needs** of their area', which is **required** because of the presence of a person who is lying-in, or of an expectant mother (*NHS Act 1977*, schedule 8).

Expectant and nursing mothers: NHS. To 'such extent as he **considers necessary** to meet all **reasonable requirements**', the Secretary of State has a **duty**, **delegated** to health authorities, to provide 'such other' facilities for the care of expectant and nursing mothers 'as he **considers** are **appropriate** as part of the health service' (*NHS Act 1977*, s.3). This represents a vague duty, difficult to enforce in the law courts because of the wide discretion it confers on authorities, as illustrated in the *Hincks* case.

Expectant mothers or women lying-in: laundry facilities. Local authorities have the **power** to provide, or **arrange** for the provision of, **laundry facilities** for households for which **home help** is being, or could be, provided; i.e. because of the presence of a person who is lying-in or an expectant mother (*NHS Act 1977*, schedule 8).

■ EXPECTATIONS

People's expectations are distinguished, both legally and practically, from their **needs,** for the purpose of **assessment** and provision of various **community care services**. See: **Choice** and **Preferences**

■ **FACILITIES FOR SAFETY, COMFORT OR CONVENIENCE:** see **Additional facilities;** also **Safety, comfort or convenience**

■ FAMILIES

The **legislation** does not always refer to provision specifically for the individual in **need** or **disabled person**. For example, when providing services appropriate for **children in need** under the **duty** contained in s.17 of the *Children Act 1989*, local authorities **may** also provide services for the family as a whole, or for particular members of the family. Local authorities also have a duty to provide **home help**, and a **power** to provide **laundry facilities**, for 'households' (*NHS Act 1977*, schedule 8). See: **Carers**

■ **FAMILY ROOM, PRINCIPAL:** see **Principal family room**

■ FARLEY CASE

This concerned an 86-year old woman who, following a **reassessment** which resulted in an altered **care plan** and the loss of the **night-sitter service** which had previously been provided. Pending the full hearing of the case, an interim **injunction** was sought restoring the original care package. The local authority argued also that if such an order were made it would submit to it on condition that the applicant should reimburse the costs of such interim provision if she were eventually to lose the case.

(1) **Background.** The woman suffered from severe arthritis and had poor mobility and a very weak bladder, which meant that she needed assistance, from chair or bed to commode or toilet, throughout the day and night. The night-sitter service under the original care plan involved a person in attendance between10pm and 7am to help with undressing, ensure that she was properly provided for and able to visit the toilet frequently during the night. The revised care plan involved only a person in attendance between 10pm and 10.30 pm, to undress the woman, make her a drink and see that she was comfortable for the night.

(2) **Potential unreasonableness.** The judge noted that nothing in the new care plan suggested a change either in the woman's needs or in any other relevant circumstances. Thus:

> 'there is a very strong case here in support of the applicant's submission that the respondent's apparent decision, that she no longer has an identified need for night care services appears to have been based on no evidence whatsoever and is, therefore, irrational or unreasonable... In those circumstances, I have no hesitation in coming to the

conclusion that an interim injunction would…be appropriate in these proceedings for judicial review.'

(3) **Undertaking to pay the cost of the care should the case be lost.** Exceptionally, the judge decided that the woman should not have to give an undertaking to pay the cost of the interim care should she eventually lose the case at the full hearing. This was for the following reasons.

First the woman was 'indisputably very infirm' and attempts by her to go to the toilet would result in physical problems, danger and possible extreme physical discomfort: to 'expose her to that sort of indignity and risk would be, in my judgment, inhumane to say the very least'. Second, she had no means to pay. Third, her family had done all it could but could no longer meet further costs. Fourth, if the injunction were not granted, the woman would undoubtedly lose her night sitter service. Finally, the amount of money involved, over the four weeks before the full hearing, would amount to about £800 – a 'trivial' amount of money, compared to the degree of risk the woman would be exposed to.

FEEDING EQUIPMENT

Feeding equipment is an example of specialist equipment which, as **guidance** on NHS **continuing care** explains, people – in **residential** or **nursing homes**, or in their own homes – might **require**, and for which **criteria of eligibility** and **priorities** should be set within available **resources** (HSG(95)8). Such equipment is provided under the *NHS Act 1977*.

FETTERING OF DISCRETION

This is a concept used both by the law courts in **judicial review** and by the **local ombudsmen** when investigating **maladministration**.

Essentially, when local authorities perform **duties** and use their **powers**, they are exercising their **discretion**. They must not fetter (i.e. not restrict) this discretion by adopting **rigid policies, priorities** or **criteria of eligibility** which prevent them applying that discretion to individual cases. In other words, they must not make up their minds in advance.

It should be noted that the principle applies not only to policies adopted in relation to a duty, but also to a power; as illustrated by the *Bristol* case involving **renovation grants**, the *British Oxygen* case involving a policy not to give grants for items costing under £25, and the *Collymore* case involving education grants. In the *Hargreaves (no.2)* case, the local authority was held to have fettered its discretion under s.2 of the *CSDPA 1970*, by operating a policy which ruled out paying the basic or **ordinary** costs (as opposed to the extra costs stemming from **disability**) of a disabled person's **holiday**.

The individual nature of community care **assessment**, and the diversity of people's **individual needs**, make it all the more important that authorities do not make up their minds in advance. Indeed, the High Court stage of the *Gloucestershire* case confirmed that assessment or **reassessment** must be individually orientated and cannot be made on a **blanket** basis.

FIDUCIARY DUTY

Applied by the House of Lords in the *GLC* case, the term 'fiduciary duty' (e.g. the duty a trustee has to a beneficiary, a duty of trust) described a local authority's duty to act for the benefit of local rate (now council tax) payers, by not placing an inordinate burden on them through thriftlessness. This duty was hinted at in Department of Health **guidance** about charging for non-residential **community care services**, which suggested that failure of a local authority to make use of its **power** to make **charges** might place an additional burden on the local population (LAC(94)1).

FINE WORDS

At the House of Lords stage of the *Gloucestershire* case, Lord Lloyd referred to **central government's** departure from the 'fine words' of the White Paper on community care (DH 1989) as the reason why the local authority had been placed in an **'impossible position'**.

FISHER CASE

A notable case, insofar as the court curtailed a health authority's **discretion** to **ration** services – on the basis that it had blatantly disregarded Circular **guidance** from the Department of Health. The court also dismissed, on the facts of the particular case, the health authority's arguments in relation to **resources**.

(1) Directions or guidance? The case concerned a person with multiple sclerosis who was being denied treatment with a new drug, Beta Interferon, by the health authority. The NHS Executive, part of the Department of Health, had issued a Circular (EL(95)97) in connection with the prescription of such drugs for multiple sclerosis. The judge considered the effect of the Circular and the obligations it placed on the authority.

First, he decided that the Circular did not amount to **Directions** which would have created an 'absolute duty' of compliance, since although it carried words such as 'asks', 'suggested' and 'taking into account', it did not include the word 'shall', or any of the other 'badges of mandatory requirement'. Nevertheless, he found that the Circular constituted 'strong guidance' and that the health authority, contrary to it, had in effect operated a **blanket** ban on treating patients in Derbyshire.

(2) Having regard to guidance. Was the policy **unlawful**? The judge stated that the health authority:

> 'had to have regard to that national policy [in the Circular]. They were not obliged to follow the policy, but if they decided to depart from it, they had to give clear reasons for so doing, and those reasons would have been susceptible to a Wednesbury [i.e. on grounds of unreasonableness] challenge... Moreover, if the [health authority] failed properly to understand the Circular, then their policy would be as defective as if no regard had to [sic] been paid to the policy at all... [The health authority] did not take the Circular into account and decide[d] exceptionally not to follow it. They decided to disregard it altogether throughout 1996, because they were opposed to it ... and did not properly take it into consideration'.

(3) Resources and clinical decisions. The health authority argued that under s.97 of the *NHS Act 1977*, it had a duty not overspend; and that **clinical** decisions had to be taken with due regard to available resources. The judge 'unreservedly accept[ed] both propositions as correct. But on the facts of this case, they do not assist the [health authority, which] had funds available, but chose not allocate them. As for clinical decisions, they were not for the [health authority] to take'.

The applicant also maintained that the health authority had **fettered its discretion** by operating a blanket ban, and also given rise – through a letter written to the applicant about the possibility of treatment – to either a substantive or procedural

legitimate expectation. The judge did not go on to rule on these issues, having already found the authority's policy unlawful on the grounds explained above.

■ FLOODGATES

In times of short **resources**, local authorities sometimes attempt to minimise provision of certain services or equipment, so as to keep the floodgates of demand, if not closed, at least manageably ajar. For instance, faced with overwhelming demand and long **waiting lists**, an authority might be tempted to state that, under the CSDPA 1970, it will never provide: (a) bathing equipment where this is the only need; (b) equipment under £20; (c) access to the service user's garden; or (d) the ordinary or basic costs of a **holiday**. Both the authority and services users then know where they stand.

However, the potential problem with such policies is that, unless they are thought through and applied carefully, they risk **fettering an authority's discretion** (e.g. *Hargreaves (no.2)* case) or even **illegality** (e.g. *Leaman* case). This illustrates the tension between setting general **criteria of eligibility** and carrying out an **assessment** which takes account genuinely of **individual needs**.

■ **FOOD:** see **Preparation and cooking of food; Meals;** and *Gorenkin* case

■ FOX CASE

Amongst other things, this case contrasted **specific** and **general duties**.

It concerned a **hospital discharge** decision and **after-care** arrangements to be made under s.117 of the *Mental Health Act 1983*. The judge found that the **duty** to provide after-care services under that section is 'not only a general duty but also a specific duty owed to the applicant to provide him with aftercare services'. This was contrasted with the more general duty under s.3 of the *NHS Act 1977* to provide after-care. However, the judge did seem to state that his judgment did not extend to the situation where an authority refuses to perform the duty under s.117 because of lack of **resources**.

■ FRUSTRATING THE PURPOSE OF LEGISLATION

Frustrating the purpose of **legislation** is sometimes part of the reasoning of the law courts when they rule against local authorities in **judicial review** proceedings. For example, in the *Cleveland* case, the authority's behaviour was **unreasonable** because its new contract terms might have caused the closure of local residential **accommodation**, which would in turn have been to 'defeat the purpose' of the *NHS and Community Care Act 1990* of providing people with a **choice** of home.

■ GAMES: DISABLED PEOPLE

If a person is **disabled** and **ordinarily resident** within the area of a local authority, then the authority has a **duty** to **make arrangements** for the provision of games outside the person's home if it is **satisfied** that it is **necessary** for it to make those arrangements in order to meet the person's **needs** (*CSDPA 1970*, s.2).

■ **GENERAL DUTY:** see **Duty: general**

GENERAL PRACTITIONERS

General practitioners: community care assessment: see **Needs: medical**

General practitioners: functions. General practitioners (GPs) have various functions, including advice-giving, diagnosis, referral to hospital, prescription of drugs, dressings and appliances listed on the Drug Tariff (published monthly by the Stationery Office), etc. In particular, they also have a duty to give patients advice about local authority services and to offer annual consultations and home visits to each patient aged 75 years or over. In respect of the latter, the GP has to assess and **record** his or her observations about a number of matters including sensory functions, **mobility**, physical condition including **incontinence**, social environment, and use of medicines (SI 1992/635).

General practitioners: fundholding. In addition to providing general medical services (under Part 2 of the *NHS Act 1977*) like non-fundholding general practitioners, fundholders have the **power** to purchase on behalf of their patients various services normally associated with Part 1 of the 1977 Act (SI 1996/706).

These services include, for instance, **nursing** and **therapy** services and an extended range of equipment such as **communication aids, incontinence** aids, hoists, nebulisers, orthotic equipment, special beds and mattresses, suction equipment, syringe drivers and walking aids. Excluded are items prescribable on the Drug Tariff (wigs, fabric supports, elastic hosiery), prostheses (other than breast), wheelchairs, environmental control equipment, and equipment costing over £6000 (Approval in HSG(96)46: made under SI 1996/706).

GENEROSITY

Local authorities should beware of being over-generous for two reasons. First, they might step outside the **legislation** if they provide what they are not empowered to. For instance, in the *Jennifer Lewis* case the housing authority was using its housing revenue account **illegally** to fund the provision of certain **welfare services** in sheltered housing. Second, the courts have held that local authorities have a **fiduciary duty** to be thrifty and not to place an inordinate burden on local tax payers (*GLC* case).

GIVING REASONS FOR DECISIONS: see **Reasons**

GLC CASE

This case illustrated how the courts might interfere with policy-making in local government. It involved a scheme of the Greater London Council to cut substantially London Transport fares in 1983. The scheme had been a plank of the GLC's election manifesto, although its implementation necessitated the raising of an unforeseen extra precept from rate-payers; the House of Lords ruled that this would place the GLC in breach of its **fiduciary duty** to be thrifty and to avoid placing an inordinate burden on rate-payers.

GLOUCESTERSHIRE CASE

A major community care case which culminated in a House of Lords decision on 20 March 1997 to allow local authorities to take account of **resources**, under s.2 of the *CSDPA 1970*, both when assessing people's **'needs'** and when deciding whether it is **necessary** to meet them.

The case arose when the council informed about 1,500 people that their **home help** services would be reduced or **withdrawn** – owing to an unexpected shortfall of about £3 million in grant money from central government. The original four users making the challenge were as follows:

Applicants. The first applicant was 71 years old, lived alone, suffered from decreased **mobility**, pain and stiffness, had suffered a stroke, and received income support and attendance allowance. He was receiving assistance with bed-making, ironing and **cleaning**: the council now informed him that he would no longer be provided with housework assistance.

The second was 79 years old, had suffered several heart attacks, had previously fractured his femur, had a hip replacement, could only walk short distances aided by a stick, and was partially-sighted and receiving income support. He had been provided with cleaning, **laundry, shopping** and community **meals**; now the cleaning services were withdrawn and the laundry provision reduced.

The third was 76 years old, and his wife 71. He was a double amputee, wheelchair-bound and suffering from prostate cancer. His wife had arthritis, high blood pressure and a heart condition. He had been assessed as needing **respite care** for a period of two weeks in every six, to give his wife short-term breaks. Both had been assessed as requiring assistance in the home; now the respite care was cancelled and the assistance drastically reduced.

Last, the fourth was 79 years old, and suffering from severe rheumatoid arthritis, unable to walk. She had been assessed as needing a hoist: now the council 'rescinded' the decision to provide it. As a consequence, she had been unable to leave hospital and return to her own home.

All the decisions – High Court, Court of Appeal and House of Lords – are summarised below.

Gloucestershire case: High Court. The decision of the High Court was overturned by the Court of Appeal before being reinstated by the House of Lords (see below). The judge acknowledged, but did not succumb, to the force of the argument that **resources** were totally **irrelevant** to the **assessment** of disabled people's community care **needs**.

(1) **Balancing exercise.** The assessment (or **reassessment**) of a person's needs should involve a **balancing exercise**, involving the needs of the individual, the needs of others, and the resources available.

(2) **Individual focus of assessment and role of resources.** The balancing exercise must be conducted in respect of each individual: the council could not simply make **blanket** decisions as it had **unlawfully** done in this case. So, in order even to contemplate reducing or **withdrawing services**, the council would have to reassess each individual, and even then resources could not be the sole factor taken into account (because of the nature of a balancing exercise).

(3) **Triggering an absolute duty.** Once the authority was **satisfied** that it was **necessary** to **make arrangements** to meet the needs, then – subject only to a reassessment – there was an **absolute duty** to make them, since at that stage 'resources do not come into it'.

The judge also acknowledged the 'impossible task faced by councils, unless they could 'have regard to the size of the cake so that in turn they know how fairest and best to cut it'.

(4) Taking account of resources for both need and necessity to meet the need. The local authority 'was right to take account of resources both when assessing needs and when deciding whether it is necessary to make arrangements to meet those needs'.

Gloucestershire case: High Court (no.2). In the first High Court case (see above), the court had ordered that, although the authority could take **resources** into account when **reassessing** people's **needs** and reducing or **withdrawing** services, it must nevertheless reassess people individually before doing so. The council began the process of reassessment gradually, since the cost was estimated at £200,000. The Royal Association for Disability and Rehabilitation (RADAR) claimed that the Council had not complied with the original High Court judgement.

Extensive duty of reassessment. The judge found that the practicalities of the situation meant that it was **reasonable** for the council not to restore services (which had been **withdrawn** or reduced) pending reassessment. However, he also ruled that the duty of reassessing people individually was not satisfied by the authority's writing to them, and offering a reassessment only if they replied in the affirmative to the offer. This was because in:

> 'some areas of the law that might be an adequate response, where those affected can be assumed to be capable of looking after their own interests, and where silence in response to an offer can be treated as acceptance or acquiescence. However, that approach is not valid in the present context. The obligation to make an assessment for community care services does not depend on a request but on an 'appearance' of need. Indeed, under Section 47(2) of the 1990 Act, where it appears that a person is disabled, the authority is specifically required to make a decision as to the service he requires without waiting for a request. Of course, the authority cannot carry out an effective reassessment without some degree of co-operation from the service user or his helpers. However, that is a very different thing from saying that they can simply rest on having sent a letter of the type to which I have referred.'

The judge also concluded that RADAR did have the **standing** to bring the case, and that the local authority's **complaints** procedure would not have been a 'suitable or **alternative remedy**' because the case was about 'a general issue of principle as to the authority's obligations in law'.

Gloucestershire case: Court of Appeal. The Court of Appeal, by a majority of two to one, overruled the High Court (see above); but was, in turn, overruled by the House of Lords (see below). The reasoning of the majority was attractively, though deceptively, simple.

(1) Judgement about need. Ascertaining a person's **needs** involved **assessment** and **judgement**, not an exercise of public law **discretion** by the authority which might allow **resources** to be taken into account.

(2) Absurdity of measuring need in terms of resources. It was 'difficult to see how a third party's resources or the needs of others can be relevant' to assessment of a person's **needs**. Indeed, were such factors to be taken into account, 'the logical consequence would be that if the local authority had no resources, then no disabled person in its area could have any needs'.

(3) **Necessity of meeting needs.** Resources could not be **relevant** to a judgement about whether it was necessary to meet the assessed needs. Otherwise it would be:

> 'inescapable that if a local authority has no money in the relevant budget, then it would be open to the local authority to make an assessment or judgement that a disabled person has a need which it is necessary to meet applying objective criteria, but they are not required to meet it because of shortage of funds, resulting in an unmet need.'

But this would seem to 'fly in the face of the plain language' of the 1970 Act.

(4) **Taking account of resources when deciding how to meet needs.** However, resources could be taken into account when deciding how to meet needs, since 'the manner in which the need was met, for example, by someone doing his laundry at home in a washing-machine or by it being taken away, was within the discretion of the authority and costs would be a relevant consideration'.

Gloucestershire case: House of Lords (majority decision). In a split decision (three to two), the House of Lords finally ruled in this crucial and long-drawn out case, that local authorities could take account of **resources** when determining, under s.2 of the *CSDPA 1970*, both the **needs** of **disabled people** and then whether it is **necessary** to meet them. The original High Court decision of 1995 was restored (see above).

(1) **Resources and needs.** It was stated that 'needs for services cannot sensibly be assessed without having some regard to the cost of providing them', and that 'when assessing needs under section 2(1) a local authority may take its resources into account'.

(2) **Resources and necessity.** The court held as well, that resources could be taken into account when determining whether it is necessary to meet needs. In:

> 'deciding whether there is a necessity to meet the needs of the individual some criteria have to be provided... The determination of eligibility...requires guidance not only on the assessment of the severity of the condition or the seriousness of the need but also on the level at which there is to be satisfaction of the necessity to make arrangements. In the framing of the criteria to be applied...the severity of a condition may have to be matched against the availability of resources.'

(3) **Standards.** The court felt that general standards of living alone were too imprecise to measure a person's need, not least because they vary, and different people's expectations about them vary also. In addition, the words 'necessary' and 'needs' are relative terms; and in the context of the Act, their role is not explained by reference either to a dictionary or to the 'values of a civilised society'.

(4) **Balancing exercise.** Like the High Court, the House of Lords referred also to a **balancing exercise**: 'the relative cost will be balanced against the relative benefit and the relative need for the benefit'.

(5) **Stringency of eligibility criteria.** Depending on the financial position of the authority, its **criteria of eligibility** 'may properly be more or less stringent'.

(6) **Collapse of duty?** A safeguard against the 'collapse' of the duty contained in s.2 of the 1970 Act was that authorities must carry out their **duty** reasonably, i.e. not lapsing into legal **unreasonableness**. The duty anyway still retained its force because once it arose (i.e. the authority has had accepted it was necessary for it to meet a person's needs), it had to be performed and lack of resources was no defence for non-performance.

(7) **Parliament's intentions.** There was no basis for supposing that **Parliament** had intended that resources be ignored when assessing disabled people's needs.

Gloucestershire case: House of Lords (minority decision). In a powerful dissenting judgement, Lord Lloyd made various points, including the following:

(1) **Civilised standards.** The yardstick for measuring a person's **needs**, be they simple or complex, were 'the standards of civilised society as we know them in the United Kingdom, or, in the more homely phraseology of the law, the man on the Clapham omnibus'.

(2) **Professional judgement.** The measurement of needs was for the 'professional judgement of the **social worker** concerned, just as the need for a by-pass operation is left to the professional judgement of the heart specialist'.

(3) **Setting of standards.** The standards were to be decided upon by the local authority.

(4) **Irrelevance of resources.** Any imprecision associated with the attempt of an authority to identify such standards could not be alleviated by taking account of **resources**, which might be able to impose cash limits on what is provided but could not 'help to measure need'. **Criteria of eligibility** clearly could be set without reference to resources, and there was 'no necessity on grounds of logic, and no advantage on grounds of practical convenience, in bringing resources into account as a **relevant** factor when assessing needs'. Thus, if a child needed a new pair of shoes, its need was 'not the less because his parents cannot afford them'.

(5) **Collapse of duty.** The arbitrary reduction in assessed need by raising the threshold of need artificially, because of lack of resources, would collapse the duty under s.2 of the *CSDPA* into a **power**.

(6) **Central government.** It was pointed out that the local authority was in an 'impossible position; truly impossible, because even if the council wished to raise the money themselves to meet the need by increasing council tax, they would be unable to do so by reason of the government-imposed rate capping'. Furthermore, it was the government's departure from its 'fine words' in the community care White Paper that had brought about the situation.

(7) **Parliament's intention.** It could not have been **Parliament's** intention in 1970 (a) that the **threshold of need** should be artificially manipulated because of lack of resources, and (b) that 'the standards and expectations for measuring the needs of the disabled in Bermondsey should differ from those in Belgrave Square'.

GOING WRONG

Sometimes the law courts in **judicial review** cases simply find that an authority has gone 'wrong', as happened in the *Leaman* case involving assistance with holidays under the *CSDPA 1970*, s.2.

GOLDSACK CASE

A case which looked, amongst other things, at (a) the provision of walking assistance under the *National Assistance Act 1948*; (b) the strength of the **duty** under the 1948 Act compared with that under s.2 of the *CSDPA 1970*; (c) distinguishing **needs** from **arrangements** to meet those needs; and (d) the **relevance** of **health and safety** matters.

(1) **Walking assistance at day centre.** The case concerned a 21-year-old woman who had suffered brain damage at the age of two, and later (at the age of 15) developed a viral illness which caused serious **disability** and loss of walking ability. By 1992 she could walk again, although only with assistance. She had cerebral palsy, a right hemiplegia,

and was partially-sighted and epileptic. She had been attending a day centre until her parents removed her, feeling that her needs were being grossly neglected. They were particularly disturbed that she was being pushed around the centre in a wheelchair, rather than walking. Their formal **complaints** had been rejected by the council.

When she first attended the centre, the woman had received assistance with walking; but latterly a wheelchair and a rollator (a walking frame with wheels) was being used because, the council claimed, staff had complained of back pain when they walked with her. At one stage, the council offered to allow the woman to walk alone with protective headgear so long as the parents would absolve the council of liability in case of accident and injury. However, no agreement about this was reached.

(2) Distinguishing the need from the means to meet it. The judge had to consider the following: within the 15 hours of one-to-one assistance with mobility which the council had decided that the woman needed each week, how much – if any – of the assistance was to involve walking? Was the term 'mobility' to be taken in a narrow sense of walking, or in a wider sense which might or might not include walking? And was assistance with walking a need, or simply an arrangement to meet the need?

The judge had some difficulty in ascertaining exactly what the **assessment** of need had been, as opposed to the decision about what services were to be provided to meet the need. The decisions had not been formally **recorded**, and it was not clear even when the assessment had been completed. Nevertheless, he decided that the assessment of need was at the general level: i.e. 15 hours of one-to-one mobility assistance. The particular content of this assistance, assistance with walking, was not part of the assessment of need. If it had been, it would have represented a level of excessive detail. The judge pointed out that, in general, if assessments of need are too detailed, then this would in turn mean that whenever provision needed to be varied – even slightly – to take account of changing circumstances, a formal reassessment would be required. This would be cumbersome and would also mean that until **reassessment** was complete the authority would be in breach of its **statutory duty**; something **Parliament** could not have intended.

(3) General duty under the 1948 Act. Therefore, withdrawal of the walking element of the assistance did not involve a breach of statutory duty in failing to meet agreed needs. Furthermore, given that the assistance was being provided under the **general duty** contained in s.29 of the *National Assistance 1948*, it was also quite clear that **resources** could be a relevant factor in deciding both whether or how to meet needs.

(4) Health and safety. The judge also stated that health and safety (i.e. potential back injury to staff) was also a material consideration in deciding what should be provided.

GOOD CASE

The case was about an application for **home adaptations** and the **relevance** of the *Carers (Recognition and Services) Act 1995* and the *CSDPA 1970*.

(1) Adaptations for carers in the dwelling upstairs. The case concerned an elderly, **disabled** couple (Mr and Mrs Good senior) living on the ground floor, and Mr and Mrs Good junior with a **family** of four children who lived on the floor above. The dispute was about whether in addition to providing housing improvement work downstairs, the Goods junior upstairs should also receive a grant so as to alleviate their situation and enable them to provide improved care for Mr and Mrs Good senior downstairs. The *Carers (Recognition and Services) Act 1995* was argued in support of this.

(2) Relevance of legislation. The judge pointed out, however, that simply making an **assessment** under the 1995 Act 'does not get anyone anywhere'. It was actual provision of assistance that was in question, and the Act did not require the authority to provide a grant for the **carers** in respect of the upstairs premises. Indeed, the 1995 Act was simply not relevant to an application for a grant under housing **legislation** (then, the *Local Government and Housing Act 1989*). The judge also went on to consider whether the authority came under a **duty** towards the family upstairs under s.2 of the *CSDPA 1970*, which refers to adaptations to the home – and found that no duty arose (though it did for the elderly couple downstairs).

GOOD PRACTICE

Good practice is generally taken to go beyond just basic compliance with **legislation**. However, some of the principles applied by the courts in **judicial review**, and by **the local ombudsman** when investigating **maladministration**, coincide with professional good practice: for example, being **fair** to people in terms of listening to and informing them, taking account of their **legitimate expectations**, and not adopting **blanket** or excessively **rigid policies**. Even the **legislation** – which demands that **assessment** be of an individual person's **needs**, and that the assessment be separate from a decision about service provision – equates with good practice if it means that staff explore more fully both needs, and the range of options for meeting them. See also **Standards**

GORENKIN CASE

This was a case, following on from the **Hammersmith and Fulham** case, concerning **residential accommodation, resources, asylum-seekers** and continued logic-chopping over the meaning of particular words in s.21 of the *National Assistance Act 1948*.

Need for food without accommodation. The court held, somewhat reluctantly, that s.21 of the 1948 Act meant that local authorities could provide food (or food vouchers) with accommodation, but not food vouchers alone; because the **'care and attention'**, which was a condition for provision, had to be seen in the context of residential accommodation. The authority therefore simply had no **power** to provide the food without the accommodation. It was on this basis that the authority had, for the most part lawfully, **reassessed** individual applicants, offering assistance only to those who were 'either without accommodation or are likely to become so imminently'. However, the judge stated that in the following respect, the authority's policy went too far:

> 'where someone has accommodation of some sort, but is otherwise wholly destitute, it is certainly possible that he may reach a stage where he is in need of care and attention as defined in the section. A person who is starving in a garret may certainly need such attention, and it would be very odd if the authority could not review his position while he remains there. What the authority have to consider is whether, looking at the person's position overall, it has arrived at a position where they ought to take responsibility for him by securing residential accommodation and the food that goes with it, and that position may, as I say, be arrived at while he still has a roof over his head.'

GREY AREAS

A number of services occupy grey areas lying between statutory authorities, in that they might be provided by either one authority or another. For instance, a particular service might be capable of being regarded either as **health care**, and therefore the responsibility of the NHS, or **social care**, and therefore falling to local authority social services departments.

Thus, **bathing services** formerly provided by NHS district nurses are now, in many areas, increasingly supplied by personal care assistants on behalf of social services departments. **Continuing** care, too, has been shifting markedly away from the NHS. And some **disability equipment** (for example, **mobility** equipment, beds, children's equipment and **communication aids**) falls into these grey areas between local authority social services departments, local authority education departments and the NHS.

Sometimes, responsibilities are claimed or denied not just in terms of the type of equipment, but of its purpose in respect of a particular person. For instance, two bed-raising blocks needed for medical purposes (e.g. breathing or fluid drainage) might be an NHS responsibility, but four blocks (for easier transfer to and from the bed) that of social services. And **speech and language therapy** has been the subject of regular dispute between education authorities and health authorities (e.g. *Harrow, Oxfordshire* and *M* cases).

See: **Buck-passing and cost-shunting;** also **Duplication**

GUIDANCE

Apart from **legislation** (Acts of Parliament, statutory instruments) and **Directions** and **Approvals** (both of which have the effect of legislation), the community care framework includes guidance issued by the Department of Health.

On the one hand guidance is welcome because it assists authorities in carrying out their functions: for example, suggesting what they should be doing and how they might go about it, and putting forward interpretations of the relevant legislation. On the other hand, guidance sometimes causes confusion and uncertainty and might be, as stated in the *Patchett* case, 'four-times cursed' being: (a) unseen by Parliament, (b) inaccessible, (c) a jumble of legislative, administrative and directive provisions, and (d) imprecisely expressed.

Indeed, the profusion of guidance, some of it distinctly unclear in meaning and in its implications, allows both sides in a dispute to muster plentiful material in their cause, sometimes from the same part of the same document. One of the judges at the Court of Appeal stage of the *Gloucestershire* case noted that 'unsurprisingly, both sides found passages which assisted their respective cases'. And, in the second High Court hearing of the *Gloucestershire* case, the judge politely expressed his puzzlement about the coherence of Department of Health practice guidance.

(1) Statutory, policy and practice guidance. Authorities are sometimes unsure about the extent to which they must follow guidance, since some types are more legally binding than others.

The stronger form of guidance is sometimes referred to as 'statutory guidance', so called because it is made explicitly by the Secretary of State under s.7(1) of the *Local Authority Social Services Act 1970*, which places a **duty** on authorities to act under general guidance. Some of the guidance issued under this Act is labelled 'policy guidance', in contrast to 'practice guidance' not issued under the Act. Various policy guidance has been issued including on community care generally (DH 1990), **carers** (DH 1996) and community care **direct payments** (DH 1997). Practice guidance has been issued on the same subjects (SSI/SWSG 1991a, SSI 1996, DH 1997).

The courts have indicated that in some circumstances authorities must follow policy guidance, and that failure to do so amounts to a **breach of statutory duty** (e.g. *Hargreaves* case); while authorities should at least **'have regard to'** practice guidance

– and a series of omissions, rather than the occasional omission, might suggest that it had been **unlawfully** disregarded (*Rixon* case).

At the same time, the courts are disinclined to rely on guidance for interpreting the meaning of **legislation**. In the *Beckwith* case about the closure of the local authority's **residential homes**, the outcome hinged on the meaning of a particular phrase in legislation; the House of Lords ruled that the Department of Health's interpretation, contained in a Circular, of the phrase was simply wrong. And in the *Gloucestershire* case in the House of Lords, one of the judges stated that he did not regard guidance as 'proper material for the construction of the critical provision' in the legislation.

(2) **Guidance: status and currency.** It is not always apparent whether guidance for local authorities has been issued as statutory guidance (see above) or not; for instance, when it does not declare itself clearly one way or the other. This is apt to cause confusion. In addition, the courts have even held that a document which at face value appears to contain only guidance, could – if the language used is sufficiently peremptory – in fact amount to a **Direction** (see the *Manchester* case – and also the *Fisher* case, in which the same question arose, but resulted in a different outcome). This illustrates that the legal effect of a document is not necessarily determined by what it is called on its face – for instance, 'guidance', **'standards'**, 'advice note', 'Directions' and so on.

It has been extremely difficult in the past for authorities, lawyers, voluntary organisations – in fact everybody in the field – to know which guidance is current and which obsolete. This is because of an absence, in the past, of accurate, up-to-date **information** about the existence, currency or obsolescence of guidance. Indeed, when in 1995 the Department of Health was asked in **Parliament** for a list of its community care **legislation** and guidance, it was unable to produce it. However, in 1996, the Department produced a list of current social services Circulars (LASSL(96)10).

Guidance (counselling): children. In respect of **children in need** who are living with their **families**, local authorities have a **duty** to make 'such provision as they consider **appropriate**' for various services including guidance and **counselling** (*Children Act 1989*, schedule 2).

GUARDIANSHIP

For the prevention of **mental disorder** or for people who are, or have been, suffering from mental disorder, local authorities have a **duty** to **make arrangements** for the exercise of their functions towards people received into guardianship under Parts 2 or 3 of the *Mental Health Act 1983* (Direction under *NHS Act 1977*, schedule 8).

HAMMERSMITH AND FULHAM CASE

A case involving asylum-seekers and illustrating the **safety net** function which community care **legislation** sometimes performs.

(1) **Horrendous plight.** The case focused on whether asylum-seekers, while they were waiting for their applications to be dealt with by the Home Office, were entitled to assistance under s.21 of the *National Assistance Act 1948*. The question had arisen because under the Asylum and Immigration Act 1996, asylum-seekers who had not immediately claimed asylum at the port of entry, were not entitled (as from August 1996) either to public housing assistance or social security benefits. The Court of Appeal upheld the decision of the High Court that the applicants were potentially entitled to assistance. It noted that their:

'plight is indeed horrendous... The 1948 Act brought to an end 350 years of the Poor Law... We emphasise the significance of the Act because it is a prime example of an Act which is 'always speaking', and so should be construed on a construction which continuously updates its wording to allow for changes since the Act was initially framed (for this last point, the court here drew on Bennion's *Statutory Interpretation*).'

The court went on to find that, under s.21 of the 1948 Act, the applicants might be in **need of care and attention**, not through **age, illness** or **disability**, but owing to **other circumstances**. The meaning of this later term, 'other circumstances', was not necessarily limited by the words (age, illness, disability) preceding it. However, even if it did have such a limited meaning, it was clear that the circumstances of the asylum-seekers could result in illness or disability, and thus trigger eligibility for assistance. The circumstances were a combination of:

'lack of food and accommodation...their inability to speak the language, their ignorance of Britain and the fact that they had been subject to the stress of coming to this country in circumstances which at least involved their contending to be refugees.'

The court stressed the *combination* of these circumstances, because the Act was not a 'safety net provision on which anyone who is short of money and/or short of accommodation can rely'.

(At the High Court stage, the judge had stated that the applicants were entitled to relief, since he felt that it was impossible to believe that **Parliament** intended that an asylum seeker, who was lawfully here and who could not be lawfully removed from the country, should be left destitute, starving and at risk of grave illness and even death because he could find no one to provide him with the bare necessities of life.)

Hammersmith and Fulham (no.2) case. Following the Court of Appeal judgment (see immediately above) in relation to the eligibility of asylum-seekers for **residential accommodation** under s.21 of the *National Assistance Act 1948*, a further case was brought. The council had been providing bed and breakfast accommodation for the asylum-seekers, but had otherwise been making **cash payments** to them for meals other than breakfast, and for other other everyday necessities such as toiletries. The making of such payments was inconsistent with **guidance** issued by the Department of Health (LAC(97)6); the council now challenged the correctness of the guidance. The court found that under s.21 of the 1948 Act, the term **'make arrangements'** envisaged provision 'in kind' but not in cash; the payments were therefore illegal and the Department of Health's guidance correct.

■ **HANDICAP: see Disability**

■ HARCOMBE CASE

This case was about the application of the **charging** rules for **residential accommodation**, and in particular about the **power** of the local authority to disregard the value of the home of a woman who had been admitted to residential care – and whether it had exercised it **reasonably**.

(1) Looking after a parent. The case concerned a man who gave up his job in Australia to return to England to look after his mother who was suffering from Parkinson's disease and had been forced to go into residential care. On his arrival, she returned home, but suffered a series of strokes and had to return to residential care.

Under the **regulations** governing the **assessment** of people's means in relation to payment for **residential accommodation**, the local authority had a power to disregard the value of the woman's home (see: **Charges: residential accommodation**). The authority did not do this and, although it did not force the son to sell the house, it created a charge of £500 a month on it. In April 1997, the mother died with a bill of £25,000 outstanding and interest beginning to accrue on death.

(2) **Reasonable decision in all the circumstances.** The judge decided that 'in all the circumstances of the case it was not reasonable to disregard the value of the house'. One factor, but not the only one, in the overall decision was that the son had returned to Australia after his mother had gone into residential care for the second time, in order to attempt to resume his career. This meant that on his second return to England, occupation of the house had become attributable not to the need to look after his mother, but to the decision to give up the job and accommodation in Australia. Overall, the judge was satisfied that the decision had been taken by the local authority's officer within the ambit of the regulations, was 'properly based on conclusions of fact to which he was entitled to come on the material which he had to consider', and 'was based on full and proper assessment of all the facts and circumstances of the case'.

HARGREAVES CASE

The case illustrates how the law courts might find fault with local authorities which follow neither statutory **guidance** nor the recommendations of a **complaints** review panel.

(1) **Respite care.** The case concerned a 55-year-old woman with serious intellectual impairment who was heavily dependent on daily support from her brother. The dispute centred on the amount and type of **respite care** which the council would provide each year, in particular, whether it should be at an establishment such as the Winged Fellowship or simply provided through domiciliary support at home. The council accepted that both brother and sister needed respite care.

(2) **Preferences of the user.** The judge granted an order against the council on the grounds that when it had carried out its **assessment**, it had failed to discover the **preferences** of the woman herself and could not assume that they were necessarily the same as her brother's. The judge accepted that it was not necessarily easy to ascertain the woman's preferences since the brother was protective of his sister, and the social worker might well have thought that he was being obstructive. Nevertheless, such difficulties did not absolve the council of its **duty**. It is notable that the judge based this breach of **statutory duty** on the failure of the authority to follow policy guidance, since the **legislation** does not itself explicitly refer to ascertaining people's preferences.

(3) **Review panel recommendations.** The judge also found that it was not **unlawful** for the council to have failed to follow the recommendations of the complaints review panel, about the transitional arrangements to be made during the course of the dispute. He made it plain that, despite the *Avon* case, there was no general rule that review panel recommendations must be followed, although in particular circumstances the failure to do so without a rational reason might be unlawful.

Hargreaves (no.2) case. The case illustrates the pitfalls for authorities when they attempt to limit provision of services for **disabled people** under s.2 of the *CSDPA 1970*.

(1) **Not relieving poverty by paying for basic costs.** Under s.2 of the *CSDPA*, the authority had a **duty**, if it was **satisfied** that it was **necessary** for it to meet the **needs** of a disabled person, to **make arrangements** for facilitating the taking of a **holiday**. The authority

was prepared to pay the holiday costs of the woman's brother (as carer), but not her own costs. First, it argued that the section did not envisage direct provision of a holiday since the word 'facilitate' was used. Second, the holiday was an **ordinary** cost incurred by everybody – not just by disabled people – and that the authority's obligations under the Act did not amount to the **relief of poverty**, but only to relieving the extra expense of **disability**. Therefore it would meet additional costs such as special transport or accommodation expenses, but not basic costs unrelated to disability.

(2) Facilitating holidays. The judge ruled that the authority's reasoning was awry. The authority did have a **discretion**, under the word 'facilitate', to provide holidays directly, because the section envisaged that one means of facilitating was in fact to provide council-arranged holidays. Therefore, depending on the applicant's ability to contribute to the costs (under the *HASSASSA 1983*, s.17), the authority might in some circumstances end up having to pay all the costs.

(3) Fettering of discretion. The authority had **fettered its discretion** by adopting a policy which denied the possibility of making such provision: it had misunderstood the scope of the **legislation**. The question the authority should have been asking was whether the need for the holiday arose from the disability. If it did, 'then the cost of the holiday to the disabled person must be capable of being an additional cost which is the result of the disability, although the question may well arise as to whether in the particular case it is necessary, in order to facilitate the holiday, to assist with that cost'. However, the judge also indicated that the **escape route** of **reassessment** might remain open to local authorities even when they are apparently committed to provision under s.2 of the *CSDPA 1970*:

> 'It follows that the policy adopted by the Council unlawfully fetters its discretion, and the decision based upon that policy is flawed and must be quashed. However, this will not inevitably result in any different decision in relation [to the applicant]. The Council may well wish to reassess her needs, both because of the passage of time, and the decision of the House of Lords [in the *Gloucestershire* case].'

HARINGEY CASE

A case illustrating that when assessing people's **needs** and formulating **care plans**, local authorities should beware of limiting their conception of needs to **personal care**; social, **recreational** and leisure needs should also be at least considered and subject to proper **assessment**.

(1) Background. Since being assessed in 1994, a man suffering from multiple sclerosis had received a 24-hour-a-day package of care from the local authority, via a voluntary organisation. In early 1997, a **reassessment** of his needs led to a reduction of care to about three hours a day. This was subsequently increased to five hours a day to cover assistance with **personal care** (getting in and out of bed, washing, dressing, cleaning teeth, washing hair and using a toilet), meal preparation etc, shopping, laundry, cleaning, laundry, ironing.

Details of this assistance was set out in a **letter** outlining the care plan which could only cater for the man's personal needs; the letter explained that in relation to the man's social, recreational and leisure needs, he could approach a local resource centre himself. The authority was unable to meet these needs because it was not in a position 'to meet or address all the demands made [and so was] forced to make decisions upon prioritising need and working within existing resources'.

The local authority argued that the 1994 assessment and care plan had been generous, did not reflect the person's real needs (which would have been less than 24-hour care each day) and so should not be taken at face value.

(2) **Irrational or unreasonable decision?** The judge, avoiding a ruling on the merits of the local authority's decision, decided that the reassessment and revised care plan did not constitute **unreasonableness** or **irrationality**, since on the evidence available, the authority had not 'taken leave of its senses'. Nevertheless, he did say that he had 'grave misgivings as to whether five hours per day of care plus meals on wheels and domiciliary nursing can meet the applicant's needs consistent with the [authority's] resources'.

He did however give an example of an authority taking leave of its senses. Under its housing allocation system, it had awarded 0 points, on a scale from 0 to 250, to a woman:

> 'with possibly recurrent cancer and gross breathing difficulty, of whom two consultants at London teaching hospitals said in categorical terms that were she to have climb stairs this would endanger her life. In such circumstances a Court can properly but most exceptionally conclude that the authority must have taken leave of its senses.'

The judge also sharply criticised the attempt to use the report of an expert, an **occupational therapist**, to 'adduce evidence' that the authority had behaved unreasonably. Such questions were:

> 'for the Court, and the Court alone...it can never be permissible for an expert either to express an opinion that a local authority's decision was or was not reasonable... The opinion is all the more objectionable in this case because an occupational therapist cannot claim to know as much as the [authority] about its available resources and competing needs, nor perhaps about Haringey's local standards'.

(3) **Unlawful decision: misdirection in law.** However, the judge did find the decision **unlawful** on the basis that the authority had misdirected itself in law, because it was:

> 'impermissible to carry out the reassessment by putting social, recreation and leisure needs on one side and saying that "I would be happy to provide you with details of the Winkfield Road Resource Centre". The care package which should have been assessed ... had to be a multi-faceted package. This Applicant has been able to overcome or at least live with some of the most awful characteristics of his illness by the social intercourse achieved in recreational facilities such as the playing of bridge, swimming etc. A reassessed care package should have comprehended such matters and should not have discriminated in the manner that it did'.

He went on to quote the Department of Health guidance (SSI/SWSG 1991a) which refers to need as a 'multi-facted concept'.

HARROW CASES

Two linked cases involved a dispute about whether a health authority or an education authority should provide **speech and language therapy** (one hour a week), **occupational therapy** (one hour a week) and **physiotherapy** (at least 45 minutes a week) for a six-year-old child with cerebral palsy. The cases provide an example of a dispute over a **grey area** of provision and a failure of **co-operation** between statutory services.

(1) **Education authority against the NHS.** Under s.166 of the *Education Act 1993*, a health authority was obliged to assist with provision for **children** with special educational needs, unless, in the light of **resources**, it was not **reasonable** for it to comply with the obligation. On this basis, the court decided that the health authority was entitled to refuse the education authority's request that the health authority provide the **therapy** for a child.

(2) **Child against the education authority.** The court accepted that underlying the dispute and an 'unhappy state of affairs' was 'the problem of chronic under-funding of public bodies who have a statutory duty to fulfil but only a limited budget out of which to meet their statutory obligations'.

Under s.168 of the *Education Act 1993*, the court held that the education authority had a non-delegable duty to **arrange** the special educational provision set out in a statement of special educational **needs**. This meant that it was no defence for the education authority to argue that it was not required to make the provision on the grounds that it was the health authority which had failed to provide the necessary resources. In other words, though assistance was indeed not forthcoming from the health authority, s.168 of the 1993 Act did not release the education authority from its obligations; otherwise the Act would 'manifestly fail to serve the child for whose benefit' it exists.

- **HASSASSA 1983:** see **Health and Social Services and Social Security Adjudications Act 1983**

HAVING REGARD TO

When authorities must 'have regard' to something, it seems that they must take account of it but not necessarily be totally ruled by it.

For example, 'having regard' to its **assessment** of a person's **needs** for **community care services**, a local authority has a **duty** to decide whether those needs **call for** the provision of services by it (*NHS and Community Care Act 1990*). This means that the authority can decide what to provide or not to provide, in the light of various duties and powers, and the varying degrees of obligation entailed by them, in the community care legislation. And, in the *Rixon* case, the judge ruled that local authorities must at least 'have regard' to practice **guidance**. This meant that although the occasional omission to follow the guidance would not be evidence that the authority had disregarded the guidance, a series of omissions would. Similarly, the judge stated in effect that authorities must have regard to the recommendations of a local authority **complaints** review panel; since if they depart from those recommendations without good reasons, then a court might infer that the recommendations had been 'overlooked'. As the *Fisher* case shows, health authorities also must have regard to guidance when they formulate policies.

HEALTH: PHYSICAL AND MENTAL

Health: physical and mental (community care). For the prevention of **illness**, the care of people who are ill, and the **after-care** of people who have been ill, local authorities have the **power** to **make arrangements** to provide social services – including **support** and **advice** – to prevent the **impairment** of physical or mental health of adults in **families** where such **impairment** is likely (Approval under the *NHS Act 1977*, schedule 8).

Health: physical and mental (NHS). The Secretary of State has a **duty** to **promote a comprehensive health service** designed to improve the physical and mental health of the population (*NHS Act 1977*, s.1). The difficulty of enforcing the duty, because of the wide **discretion** it confers, has been confirmed in cases such as *Hincks*.

HEALTH AND SAFETY

This book does not deal with health and safety as a subject in its own right: but see: **Lifting and handling**

HEALTH AND SOCIAL SERVICES AND SOCIAL SECURITY ADJUDICATIONS ACT 1983 (SHORTENED TO: *HASSASSA* 1983)

This Act gives local authorities the **power** to make **charges** for most non-residential **community care services** (s.17). **Guidance** has been issued in Circular LAC(94)1 and in an advice note (SSI 1994). See **Charges: non-residential services**

HEALTH CARE

Health care is a term used sometimes to indicate what the NHS, rather than social services departments, will provide; and as a contrast to **social care**. However, the existence of **grey areas** sometimes renders the distinction imprecise.

Health care: support. Special health care support for people in **residential** or **nursing homes**, or in their own homes, is an NHS **continuing care** service, listed in **guidance** as a service for which **criteria of eligibility** and **priorities** should be set within available **resources** (HSG(95)8). Such support is provided under the *NHS Act 1977.*

HEALTH SERVICE OMBUDSMAN

The health service ombudsman has the power to investigate any **maladministration**, failure in service, or failure to provide a service which there is a **duty** to provide, which has allegedly caused **injustice** or hardship. In addition, from April 1996, he has been able to investigate **clinical judgement** (Health Service Commissioners Act 1993).

HEALTH SERVICES AND PUBLIC HEALTH ACT 1968: WELFARE OF ELDERLY PEOPLE

Under s.45 of the this Act, local authorities '**may** with the **approval** of the Secretary of State, and to such extent as he may direct **shall, make arrangements** for promoting the welfare of **old people**'. Approvals and **guidance** were issued in Circular DHSS 19/71. It should be noted that the services listed in the Approvals are similar to those contained in the *CSDPA 1970.* However, guidance explains that these approved services are intended for those older people who are not **disabled (substantially and permanently handicapped)**, and so not covered by the 1970 Act. The Approvals mean that local authorities have the **power**, but not the **duty**, to make arrangements:

> 'for any of the following purposes to meet the needs of the **elderly**: for the provision of **meals and recreation** in the home and elsewhere; for **informing** the elderly of services available to them and to **identify** elderly people in need of services; for providing facilities or assistance in **travelling** to and from the home for the purpose of participating in services provided by the authority or similar services; for assistance in finding suitable households for **boarding** elderly people; for providing **visiting** and **advisory** services and **social work support**; for providing **practical assistance in the home**, including assistance in the carrying out of works of **adaptation** or the provision of any **additional facilities** designed to secure greater **safety, comfort or conven-**

ience; for contributing to the cost of employing a warden on welfare functions in warden assisted housing schemes; for provision of **warden services** for occupiers of private housing.'

HEARING IMPAIRMENT

People with a hearing impairment are eligible for **welfare services** under s.29 of the *National Assistance Act 1948*, s.2 of the *CSDPA 1970*, and Part 3 of the *Children Act 1989*; and also for **disabled facilities grants** under the *Housing Grants, Construction and Regeneration Act 1996*, s.100. See: **Disability**

HEAT

Facilitating the use of a source of heat by a **disabled occupant** is one of the statutory purposes for which a housing authority has a **duty** to approve an application for a **disabled facilities grant**, assuming various other conditions are also met (*Housing Grants, Construction and Regeneration Act 1996*, s.23).

HEATING

Improving or providing a heating system for a **disabled occupant** is one of the statutory purposes for which a housing authority has a **duty** to approve an application for a **disabled facilities grant**, assuming various other conditions are also met (*Housing Grants, Construction and Regeneration Act 1996*, s.23).

HENDRY CASE

A case in which a local authority officer acted outside his authority by departing informally from the authority's **policy** on taxi licences: this was **unlawful**.

HENDY CASE

A case illustrating circumstances in which the courts (a) will tolerate delay; and (b) will in some cases not intervene even if an authority is breaching its **statutory duty**.

Reasonable delay, and the authority doing it all it can. It concerned the provision of accommodation for a person under the Land Compensation Act 1973. In fulfilling its duty to provide longer-term accommodation, the housing authority was first of all offering **temporary accommodation**. The applicant claimed that there was a breach of duty and asked for an order from the court forcing the authority to remedy this. On the issue of delay in providing the longer-term accommodation, the court stated that in carrying out its duty, the authority was acting **reasonably**, since it was not required 'to give the applicant as a displaced person any priority other than, on his displacement, immediate accommodation, albeit temporary'. Furthermore, even if there were to be a clear breach of duty, but:

> 'in a situation such as this, there is evidence that a local authority is doing all that it honestly and honourably can to meet the statutory obligation, and that its failure, if there be failure, to meet that obligation arises really out of circumstances over which it has no control, then...it would be improper for the court to make an order...compelling it to do that which either it cannot do or which it can only do at the expense of other persons not before the court who may have equal rights with the applicant and some of whom would certainly have equal moral claims.'

HILLINGDON CASE

A case which illustrates how swiftly the courts seize on a **precedent** established in one field (community care) and apply it to another (education). The case was decided with reference to the Court of Appeal judgment in the *Gloucestershire* case (before the latter was overturned by the House of Lords in March 1997).

Resources and children's special educational needs. The case concerned a funding formula used by the education authority, which effectively reduced the amount it was making available to the school for meeting the requirements of pupils with special educational **needs**. The judge ruled that a lack of **resources** could play no part in the **assessment** of a child's special educational needs, and that financial constraints could be considered only in deciding how to meet those needs (so long as the needs were still actually met). This followed from the *Gloucestershire* judgement. The duty of the education authority to provide for **children's** needs specified in statements of special educational needs was non-delegable, and thus it could not force the school to make up the shortfall with the school's own funds.

HINCKS CASE

This case illustrates the difficulty in enforcing the **duty** imposed on health authorities to provide health services.

Health services within the resources available. The case concerned people in Staffordshire who had been on a **waiting** list for NHS orthopaedic treatment for some years and who sought a **declaration** that the Secretary of State was not providing a **comprehensive health service**. The judge (Lord Denning) agreed that s.3 of the *NHS Act 1977* did not impose an **absolute duty**, since it was inevitably governed by **resources**. Indeed, the only way it could be read was to supply extra words which did not actually appear in the Act at all.

These were as follows (the added words are italicised): 'duty to provide throughout England and Wales, to such extent as he considers necessary to meet all reasonable requirements *such as can be provided within the resources available*'. He went on to point out that it 'cannot be supposed that the Secretary of State has to provide all the latest equipment [or] to provide everything that is asked for... That includes the numerous pills that people take nowadays: it cannot be said that he has to provide all these free for everybody'.

HOLIDAYS

Holidays: children. In respect of **children in need** who are living with their **families**, local authorities have a **duty** to make 'such provision as they consider **appropriate**' for 'assistance to enable the child concerned and his family to have a holiday' (*Children Act 1989*, schedule 2).

Holidays: disabled people. Local authorities have a **power** to **make arrangements** to provide holiday homes for **disabled people** (Approval under *National Assistance Act 1948*, s.29).

In addition, if a person is **disabled** and **ordinarily resident** within the area of the authority, then the authority has a **duty** to make arrangements for facilitating the taking of a holiday, whether at holiday homes or elsewhere, and whether or not arranged by the authority. However, the authority must be **satisfied** that it is **necessary** for it to make those arrangements in order to meet the person's **needs** (*CSDPA 1970*, s.2).

The *Leaman* case concerned an authority which acted **unlawfully** by operating a **blanket policy** under the *CSDPA* of assisting people only with holidays that it (the authority) arranged, and not with holidays otherwise arranged, despite the clear wording of the Act. The *Hargreaves (no.2)* case involved a local authority which was **fettering its discretion** by applying a policy which precluded assisting disabled people with the **ordinary** costs of a holiday (i.e. costs which anybody, disabled or non-disabled, would be expected to pay).

Holidays: illness. For the prevention of **illness**, the care of people who are ill, and the **after-care** of people who have been ill, local authorities have the **power** to **make arrangements** for the provision of recuperative holidays (Approval under *NHS Act 1977*, schedule 8).

HOME ADAPTATIONS

If community care aims to enable people to remain in their own homes, then home adaptations are of prime importance, as community care policy **guidance** points out (DH 1990).

However, although some home adaptations are available in the guise of **community care services**, they are also provided through housing (or environmental health) departments and thus under housing **legislation**, which is not legally within the community care framework. That said, community care legislation does make provision for **co-operation** between local authorities and housing authorities; for example, in drawing up **community care plans** and carrying out community care **assessments**. In addition, community care guidance not only urges full co-operation between different authorities but suggests that the success of community care depends on it (DH 1990). The paragraphs below provide an overview.

(1) **Housing authorities/departments.** *Housing departments* have the **power** to adapt their own council stock. They also have the power, and in some circumstances, **duty**, to award **disabled facilities grants** to both council tenants and private sector landlords and tenants. In addition, they have the power to provide **home repair assistance** for some types of adaptation (though not for council tenants).

(2) **Social services departments.** In some circumstances, social services departments have a duty to **make arrangements** in relation to home adaptations. Usually they provide only minor adaptations, defined either in terms of removability (i.e. non-permanence) or of cost (e.g. up to a certain limit such as £500). However, they might 'top up' grants given by housing departments towards major adaptations and even, sometimes, meet the whole cost, for example, through outright provision, or an interest-free loan.

(3) **Housing associations.** Tenants of **housing associations** have a right to apply for adaptations through any of the above routes as well as through their own housing association (now called, under the *Housing Act 1996*, **registered social landlord**) either from the association's revenue, or through a grant from the Housing Corporation.

Home adaptations: complexity. The system of provision of home adaptations is complex, and obtaining suitable assistance might not be straightforward. The appropriate source of funding has to be identified, and various people might need to be involved – for example, **occupational therapists,** housing technical officers, planning officers, housing finance officers, architects, builders. Even when major adaptations are under way, the process can be lengthy and disruptive – and be further complicated if the person's **needs** change during the process – which, from initial application, might take years. Indeed, the **local ombudsman** has investigated cases of delay in the provision of grants for **disabled people**, and found **maladministration** on a number of occasions.

Home adaptations: council tenants. Council tenants are entitled to apply for **disabled facilities grants** and to apply to social services departments for adaptations, but not for **home repair assistance**. The ombudsman has on occasion found **maladministration** when housing authorities have refused to consider applications for DFGs from council tenants, or have simply omitted to publicise the availability of DFGs: so denying tenants their statutory right to apply. A difficulty for housing authorities is that disabled facilities grants awarded to council tenants do not attract the 60 per cent contribution from **central government** which is available to authorities for grants awarded to private sector tenants (DoE 17/96).

Home adaptations: disabled facilities grants (DFGs). Housing departments (or environmental health departments) of local authorities have a **duty** to award disabled facilities grants if they are for particular purposes and if various other conditions are met. These purposes basically concern access by a **disabled occupant** to various parts of his or her dwelling. Grants **may** also – but do not have to – be awarded for other purposes, namely for making the dwelling suitable for a disabled occupant's **welfare**, **accommodation** or **employment**. The following is an outline of the legal requirements: for further detail see *Housing Grants, Construction and Regeneration Act 1996.*

(1) **Necessary and appropriate, reasonable and practicable.** The housing department must be **satisfied** that the works are **necessary and appropriate**, as well as **reasonable and practicable** in relation to the age and condition of the building. However, fitness for habitation is not an absolute requirement, although it must be taken into account. The **legislation** stipulates that the housing authority **consult** the social services authority (if they are not one and the same authority) about necessity and appropriateness.

(2) **Statutory means-test.** Even if the above conditions are met, the housing department then has a duty to conduct a means-test, the result of which might mean that the cost of the works (up to a maximum of £20,000 in England, and £24,000 in Wales) is met fully, partially or not at all. Thus, the formal approval of a grant application does not necessarily mean that a full – or indeed any – grant will be forthcoming. Conversely, authorities do have the **power** – where the cost of the adaptation exceeds the maximum amount (£20,000) – to pay a further amount of money to increase the value of the grant beyond the maximum (SI 1996/2888).

(3) **Reasons and time limits.** If the authority rejects an application, it has a duty to give **reasons** for doing so. And if a grant is approved, payment must be made no longer than 12 months from the date of application (*Housing Grants, Construction and Regeneration Act 1996*, Part 1).

(4) **Preliminary or ancillary services and charges.** The costs of various services may be included within **disabled facilities grants**, including surveys, **advice,** assistance in

completing forms, considerations of tenders etc., as well as those of **occupational therapists** (but not assessment) (SI 1996/2889).

Home adaptations: home repair assistance. For more minor works, home repair assistance is available in the form of grant or materials for works of **repair, improvement** or **adaptation**. However, authorities are not under a **duty** to provide it – they **may** if they wish (but even in respect of such a **power**, they should beware of **fettering their discretion**).

Various conditions have to be met, although if the works are to enable an **elderly, infirm** or **disabled** person to be cared for, then some are relaxed – for example, the condition that the applicant be receiving State benefits, or that he or she live in the dwelling as his only or main residence. Although the applicant must be over 18 years old, the works need not be for his or her benefit, and so could be applied for in respect of **children**. The maximum amount of assistance available in respect of one dwelling is £2,000 per application and a total of £4,000 over a period of three years (*Housing Grants, Reconstruction and Regeneration Act 1996*, s.76–80, and SI 1996/2888).

Home adaptations: housing authorities' own stock. Housing authorities have a **duty** to consider housing **needs** in the district, and a **power** to alter, enlarge, repair or improve their own stock. Thus, they **may** carry out adaptations to their own stock (e.g. for disabled council tenants) without making use of **disabled facilities grants** (*Housing Act 1985*, s.8–9). In discharging their duty under s.8 (considering housing needs) of the *Housing Act 1985*, housing authorities have a **duty** to 'have regard to the special needs of chronically sick or disabled persons' (*CSDPA 1970*, s.3).

Home adaptations: social services (disabled people). If a person is **disabled** and **ordinarily resident** within the area of a local authority, then the authority has a **duty** to **make arrangements** for the provision of assistance for that person in arranging for the carrying out of works of adaptation to his or her home for greater **safety, comfort or convenience**, if the authority is **satisfied** that it is **necessary** for it to make those arrangements in order to meet the person's **needs** (*CSDPA 1970*, s.2).

In practice, social services departments provide 'minor' adaptations defined either by a financial limit (e.g. up to £500 or £1,000) or by their non-structural nature. In addition, assistance is sometimes given with more major adaptations – for example, by meeting part of the cost with a social services 'top-up' to a housing grant, or the whole cost in the form of a loan.

Home adaptations: social services (elderly people). In order to meet the **needs** of **elderly people**, local authorities have the **power** to **make arrangements** to provide **practical assistance in the home**, including assistance in the carrying out of works of adaptation for greater **safety, comfort or convenience** (Approval under *Health Services and Public Health Act 1968*, s.45).

HOME CARE

Nothing in community care **legislation** states that it is preferable for people to remain in their own homes, rather than in **residential accommodation**. However, policy **guidance** states that the preferred aim of community care should be 'support for the user in his or her own home including day and **domiciliary care, respite care,** the provision of **disability equipment** and **adaptations** to **accommodation** as **necessary**' (DH 1990).

Nevertheless, achieving this preferred aim is partially dependent on the weight given by authorities to people's **choice**, and on the **resources** available. The *Lancashire* case demonstrated that so long as a person's **needs** can be met either in **residential accommodation** or by care in the person's home, then a local authority can opt to provide residential accommodation if it is cheaper, irrespective of the person's **preference**.

HOME HELP

Home help is provided under various legislation, although the precise term appears only in the *NHS Act 1977* and the *Children Act 1989*. However, it is also covered by **practical assistance in the home**, a phrase occurring in both the *CSDPA 1970* and the *Health Services and Public Health Act 1968*.

Local authorities have a **duty** to provide – or to **arrange** for the provision of – home help on a scale adequate for the **needs** of their area, for households where such help is **required** because of a person who is **ill**, lying-in, an **expectant mother, aged**, – or **handicapped** by **illness** or **congenital deformity** (*NHS Act 1977*, schedule 8). This duty applies in respect of both adults and children.

In addition, in respect of **children in need** who are living with their **families**, local authorities have a **duty** to make 'such provision as they consider **appropriate**' for various services to be available including home help (*Children Act 1989*, schedule 2). See also **Domiciliary services**

HOME SUPPORT SERVICES: see **Domiciliary services; Home help; Practical assistance in the home; Respite care**

HOMELESSNESS

This book does not cover the **law** of **homelessness** as set out in the *Housing Act 1996*. However, a number of decisions of the law courts in the homelessness field are referred to in order to illustrate relevant aspects of **judicial review**.

HOOPER CASE

A case, essentially a dispute between a local authority and a health authority, in which the court considered whether the local authority was exercising its **power** reasonably under s.17 of the *HASSASSA 1983*, when **charging** for services provided under s.29 of the *National Assistance Act 1948*, and schedule 8 of the *NHS Act 1977*.

(1) **Background.** The local authority had been providing services for a person who had been seriously brain-damaged at his birth in 1978 due to foetal anoxia; he was consequently severely disabled, both physically and mentally, and died in 1991. The

services provided were **residential accommodation** under schedule 8 of the *NHS Act 1977* (no longer possible from April 1993, when the Act was amended), and welfare services under s.29 of the *National Assistance Act 1948.*

In 1989, a **negligence** award was made, under which the health authority paid £289,000 to the person. In 1991, the local authority brought a case to recover the cost (£232,000) of some of the care which it had been providing. The case was brought against both the disabled person's estate and the health authority, which – when the negligence claim was settled – had originally agreed to indemnify the disabled person against any liability for care provided prior to the date of the settlement. Thus, the local authority was now in effect attempting to recover the cost of the care not from the person's estate, but from the health authority.

The local authority was attempting to make charges retrospectively; the question was whether this was a lawful exercise of its power to make **reasonable** charges, which it is **reasonably practicable** for the person to pay, under s.17 of the *HASSASSA 1983*.

(2) **Reasonableness of charging.** The judge found in favour of the local authority, emphasising the all-embracing effect of the term 'reasonable'. First, he observed that s.17 of the *HASSASSA 1983* was the starting point, under which the local authority had a power, but not a **duty**, to charge; it

> 'was implicit both in the language of the section and in the general law governing the activities of local authorities that the power must be exercised reasonably, that is to say, that the local authority must have relevant and reasonable grounds for choosing to exercise the power... Thus, there is an overriding criterion of reasonableness'.

Second, in assessing whether an authority is acting reasonably by imposing charges the following should be considered:

> 'If the right to charge has been waived, clearly no charge can be recovered. If the service was provided in circumstances under which it would be unreasonable for the authority subsequently to charge for it, then the authority is not entitled later to seek to recover a charge. Similarly, if having provided a service, the local authority seeks to recover a charge, it must be prepared to justify the reasonableness of doing so. The reasonableness of any conduct falls to be assessed at the time of the relevant conduct and having regard to all the relevant circumstances then existing. If the claim is first made some time after the provision of the services, the local authority must be prepared to justify the reasonableness of making the claim notwithstanding the delay'.

(3) **Making charges after services have been provided?** The judge considered separately the argument that charges had to be made at the time of providing services, not afterwards. The argument, which he proceeded to reject, was that the power to charge under s.17 of the *HASSASSA 1983* was phrased in the present tense and should be exercised only when the services were provided, not later: 'like a shopkeeper asks a purchaser for the price at the time of sale or a hotel-keeper tells the visitor the room charge on arrival'. However, he stated that:

> 'This is not a reasonable interpretation of the section. The primary duty of the local authority is to provide the services to those in need of them. The power to charge is consequential upon the provision of the service. Whether it is reasonable to charge has to be considered at an appropriate time which will not necessarily be before the time the services are rendered and will most probably be later when the local authority has put itself in possession of the relevant information. Similarly, the question of means and the practicability of paying will very often have to be the subject of later enquiry and consideration'.

(4) **Imposing a reasonable charge which it is reasonably practicable to pay.** The judge stated that first an authority has to decide to make a charge and has to be 'acting

reasonably in doing so' - but then the person has to persuade the authority about whether it is reasonably practicable for him or her to pay the charges. Then:

> 'the person availing himself of the service has, in those circumstances, to satisfy the authority under [s.17 of the 1983 Act] that his means are insufficient for it to be reasonably practicable for him to pay the amount which he would otherwise be obliged to pay. It is for the recipient of the service to discharge his burden of persuasion. He must show that he has insufficient means. The time at which he has to do this is the time when the local authority is seeking to charge him for the service. If his means have been reduced, as might be the case with a business man whose business had run into difficulties after his being injured, the reduction in his means is something upon which he would be entitled to rely as making it impracticable for him to pay, even though at an earlier date he might have been better off'.

(5) **Assessing the 'means' of a person.** The judge stated that the word 'means' in s.17 of the 1983 Act referred to more than just cash, since as a 'matter of the ordinary use of English, the word 'means' refers to the financial resources of a person:

> 'his assets, his sources of income, his liabilities and expenses. If he has a realisable asset, that is part of his means; he has the means to pay... If he has an asset which can reasonably be expected to realise and which will (after taking into account any other relevant factor) enable him to pay, his means make it practicable for him to pay'.

■ HOSPITAL DISCHARGE

The co-ordination of effective hospital discharge for patients has always been difficult for the NHS and social services departments: as, for example, when attempting to ensure that adequate support services are in place before discharge. The **health service ombudsman** has regularly investigated this issue. More recently, the attempt by the NHS to reduce its responsibilities has led (a) to increased likelihood of premature discharge and inadequate **rehabilitation** for patients in hospital; and (b) to significant reductions in the number of long-stay beds available.

Hospital discharge: criteria. Precipitated by the **health service ombudsman's** well-publicised **Leeds investigation** about the discharge of a severely disabled man, **guidance** was issued in 1995 by the Department of Health in order to staunch the flow of responsibilities away from the NHS. It states that health authorities should draw up and operate **criteria of eligibility** in order to decide three main questions about the **requirements** of patients.

(1) **Special or complex needs**. Whether inpatient care is required (a) because the patient needs 'ongoing and regular specialist clinical supervision' (e.g. weekly or more frequent); (b) because of the 'complexity, nature or intensity of his or her **medical, nursing** or other needs'; (c) due to 'the need for frequent not easily predictable interventions'; or (d) 'because after acute treatment or inpatient **palliative care** in hospital or hospice his or her prognosis is such that he or she is likely to die in the very near future and discharge from NHS care would be inappropriate'.

(2) **Rehabilitation.** Whether a period or **rehabilitation** or **recovery** funded by the NHS is required.

(3) **Discharge location.** Whether the person can be discharged from NHS inpatient care either into a **residential** or **nursing home**, or back to his or her own home with a package of **health care** and **social care support** (HSG(95)39).

Hospital discharge: information and review. Guidance states that patients and their families 'should be kept fully informed' about hospital discharge procedures and be given **information** relevant to the decisions they have to make about **continuing care**. They should be given the right to challenge a discharge decision through an independent **review panel**. The guidance also points out that people do not have a right to occupy an NHS bed indefinitely, although they can refuse to be discharged into **residential** or **nursing homes** (HSG(95)8).

Further guidance was issued about the procedure for reviewing decisions to discharge patients from NHS inpatient care. It states that the review panel should have an independent chairman on it, and – restrictively – that the review procedure is not appropriate for challenging the content of an authority's **criteria of eligibility**, only their application. The **NHS complaints** procedure is suggested as the appropriate route for such a challenge (HSG(95)39).

- **HOSTELS:** see **Workshops**

HOUSE BOATS

House boats are eligible for **home repair assistance** (*Housing Grants, Construction and Regeneration Act 1996*, s.78).

HOUSING ACT 1985

Housing authorities have a **duty** to consider housing needs in the district, and a **power** to alter, enlarge, repair or improve their own stock (s.8 and 9).

HOUSING GRANTS, CONSTRUCTION AND REGENERATION ACT 1996

This Act now underpins the provision of **disabled facilities grants** and **home repair assistance** (formerly minor works assistance), having superseded the relevant parts of the *Local Government and Housing Act 1989*. **Regulations** governing various aspects of grants and assistance include: SI 1996/2887, SI 1996/2888, SI 1996/2889, SI 1996/2990, SI 1996/2891, SI 1996/3119. A substantial guidance document was issued in the form of Circular DoE 17/96 *Private Sector Rnewal: A Strategic Approach*.

Housing Grants, Construction and Regeneration Act 1996: disabled facilities grants (DFGs). Housing authorities have a **duty** in some circumstances, and a **power** in others, to approve applications for **disabled facilities grants,** subject to various other qualifying conditions. The duty is towards each individual applicant.

(1) Mandatory access purposes etc. These are (in paraphrase) to **facilitate access** by the **disabled occupant** (a) to and from the dwelling; (b) to a room used as the **principal family room;** (c) to, or providing for the disabled occupant, a room used or usable for **sleeping;** (d) to, or provide for the disabled occupant, a room in which there is a **lavatory** – or facilitating its use by the disabled occupant; (e) to, or providing for the disabled occupant, a room in which there is a **bath or a shower** (or both) – or facilitating its use by the disabled occupant; (f) to, or providing for the disabled occupant, a room in which there is a **washhand basin** – or facilitating its use by the disabled occupant (s.23).

Other purposes are: (g) making the dwelling or building **safe** for the disabled occupant and other persons residing with him/her; (h) facilitating the **preparation**

and cooking of food by the disabled occupant; (j) improving any **heating system** in the dwelling to meet the needs of the disabled occupant or – if there is no existing heating system or an existing system is unsuitable for use by the disabled occupant – providing a heating system suitable to meet his/her needs; (k) facilitating the use by the disabled occupant of a source of **power, light or heat** by altering the position of one or more means of access to, or control of, that source – or by providing additional means of control; and (l) facilitating access and movement by the disabled occupant around the dwelling in order to enable him/her to **care for a person** who normally resides in the dwelling and needs such care (s.23).

(2) **Other discretionary purposes.** Disabled facilities grants which do not come under the above purposes **may** – but do not have to – be awarded for making the dwelling suitable for the **accommodation, welfare** or **employment** of the disabled occupant (s.23).

(3) **Owner and tenant certificates.** Applications by tenants for **disabled facilities grants** must be accompanied by a tenant's certificate, making clear that the **disabled occupant** will live in the dwelling as his/her only or main residence. An owner's certificate from the current landlord to the same effect will normally be required as well as the tenant's certificate (i.e. to confirm both the occupancy position and the landlord's permission). When it is an owner who is making the application, then an owner's certificate is required. Certificates must declare that the disabled occupant will live in the dwelling as his/her only or main residence throughout the grant condition period, or for as long as his/her health or other relevant circumstances permit (*Housing Grants, Construction and Regeneration Act 1996*, s.21–22).

(4) **Works must be necessary and appropriate, and reasonable and practicable.** A grant cannot be awarded unless the housing authority is **satisfied** that the 'relevant works are **necessary and appropriate** to meet the needs of the disabled occupant'. If the housing authority is not itself also a social services authority, then it is under an obligation to consult the latter (s.24).

In addition, the housing authority must be satisfied that 'it is **reasonable and practicable** to carry out the relevant works having regard to the age and condition of the dwelling or building'. In deciding this, the authority must at least take into account whether the dwelling is **fit for human habitation** (i.e. this is a **relevant**, but not necessarily decisive, factor).

(5) **Disabled occupant (s.100).** Disabled facilities grants are available only in respect of disabled occupants, and the Act provides a definition of **disability** which both overlaps with, but also departs from, that provided in s.29 of the *National Assistance Act 1948* (see **Disability**).

(6) **Giving reasons and time limits (s.34–35). Reasons** must be given if applications for grants are refused, and applications must be approved or refused within six months of the date of application. If approved, payment must be made no longer than 12 months after the original date of application.

Housing Grants, Construction and Regeneration Act 1996: home repair assistance (HRA). Housing authorities have the **power** to provide assistance 'in the form of a grant or the provision of materials for the carrying out of works of **repair, improvement** or **adaptation** to a dwelling'. The assistance is **discretionary:** i.e. it may, but does not have to be, given. Parents can apply on behalf of their children.

(1) **Conditions.** The applicant must (a) be aged 18 or over; (b) live in the dwelling as his/her or only main residence (this condition is treated as met if the works are for an **elderly, disabled** or **infirm** person to be cared for – whether or not he/she is the applicant –

who lives or proposes to live in the dwelling as his/her only or main residence); (c) have an owner's interest in the dwelling or be a tenant (but not a **council tenant**), alone or jointly with others; (d) have a **duty** or power to carry out the works in question; (e) be (or his/her partner be) in receipt of income support, family credit, housing benefit, council tax benefit or disability working allowance. This last condition (e) does not apply if the applicant is elderly or disabled or infirm, or if the application is for works to adapt a dwelling to enable an elderly, disabled or infirm person, who lives or proposes to live in the dwelling, to be cared for.

(2) **Mobile homes and house boats.** Mobile homes and house boats are eligible for home repair assistance – subject to special residence requirements, which do not, however, apply in relation to applications in respect of elderly, disabled or infirm persons.

■ HOUSING ALLOCATION

Housing authorities are under various obligations when they allocate public housing **accommodation** to people. One of these requires them to operate an 'allocation scheme' for determining priorities, within which preference must be given to various groups of people, including **families** with dependent **children**, and households containing a person who needs settled **accommodation** on **medical** or **welfare grounds** (*Housing Act 1996*, s.167).

■ HOUSING ASSOCIATIONS

Now known as registered social landlords, housing associations play an increasingly important role in the provision of housing for **elderly** and **disabled people** – not only because of the specialist housing they provide, but also because of the large scale voluntary transfer (LSVT) of council housing to housing associations.

Housing associations can apply to the Housing Corporation for **social housing grants,** including grants to adapt the dwellings of tenants with physical **disabilities**. The Housing Corporation has a **power**, but not a **duty**, to award such grants to associations (*Housing Act 1996*, s.18). Indeed, its policy – contained in a procedural manual – is not to assist with **home adaptations** for disabled tenants costing less than £500. Housing associations can use their own revenue to fund adaptations costing under £500; although, again, there is no statutory obligation to do so. In addition to these two routes, housing association tenants could apply to housing authorities for **disabled facilities grants** or for **home repair assistance,** or to social services departments under s.2 of the *CSDPA 1970* or under s.45 of the *Health Services and Public Health Act 1968*.

■ HOUSING CORPORATION: see **Housing associations**

■ HOUSING NEEDS

Housing authorities have a **duty** to consider housing conditions in their area (*Housing Act 1985*, s.8), and when doing so, '**shall** have regard to the needs of chronically sick or **disabled** persons' (*CSDPA 1970*, s.3).

■ HYGIENE

Local authorities have a **duty** to **make arrangements** for the supervision of hygiene in **residential accommodation** they provide (Direction under *National Assistance Act 1948*, s.21).

IDENTIFICATION OF MENTAL DISORDER

Local authorities have a **duty** to **make arrangements** for the provision of **social work** and related services to help in the identification of **mental disorder** (Direction under *NHS Act 1977*, schedule 8).

IDENTIFICATION OF NEED

The **duties** placed on local authorities (and listed immediately below) to identify the extent of **need** in the area do not necessarily involve identifying individuals. However, the **power**, under the *Health and Public Services Act 1968*, does appear to involve such identification, as is made clear by accompanying **guidance** (DHSS 19/71). See also: **Registration**

Identification of need: children. Authorities have a **duty** to 'take **reasonable** steps' to identify the extent to which there are **children in need** in their area (*Children Act 1989*, schedule 2).

Identification of need: disabled adults. A local authority has a **duty** to find out the number of people in their area who are **disabled** (under s.29 of the *National Assistance Act 1948*), and the extent to which it needs to **make arrangements** for such people (*CSDPA 1970*, s.1).

Identification of need: elderly people. In order to meet their **needs**, local authorities have the **power** to identify **elderly people** in need of services (Approval under *Health Services and Public Health Act 1968*, s.45).

ILLEGALITY

Illegality is one of the grounds on which the law courts sometimes rule against a local authority in **judicial review** proceedings. It might consist simply of not adhering to **legislation**.

For example, in the *Leaman* case, the local authority had adopted a policy on assistance with **holidays** which was 'wrong' because it excised wording from the *CSDPA 1970*, s.2. And, in the *Redezeus* case, a housing authority added, to the conditions already laid down in legislation, its own restrictive condition governing the payment of **renovation grants**. This policy lay outside its statutory powers and so was **unlawful**. Authorities might behave illegally by being too generous, as well as too mean. In the *Jennifer Lewis* case, the Court of Appeal found that the legislation at that time (it was subsequently changed) did not allow the housing authority to use its housing revenue account to fund certain welfare activities of wardens in sheltered housing.

ILLNESS

Illness is mentioned in both the *National Assistance Act 1948* and the *NHS Act 1977*. However, it is defined only in the latter Act, and so as to include **mental disorder** and any **injury** or **disability** requiring **medical** or dental treatment or **nursing** (*NHS Act 1977*, s.128). See also: **Infirmity**

Illness: home help. Local authorities have a **duty** to provide, or **arrange** for the provision of, **home help** for households – 'on such a scale as is **adequate** for the **needs** of their area' – which is **required** because of the presence of a person who is ill (*NHS Act 1977*, schedule 8).

Illness: laundry facilities. Local authorities have the **power** to provide, or **arrange** for the provision of, **laundry facilities** for households for which **home help** is being, or could be, provided because of a person who is ill (*NHS Act 1977*, schedule 8).

Illness: mental disorder: see **Mental disorder**

Illness: prevention of (NHS). The prevention of illness is one of the purposes for which the Secretary of State has a **duty** to provide a **comprehensive health service** (*NHS Act 1977*, s.1).

In addition, in relation to the prevention of **illness**, the care of people who are ill and their **after-care**, and to 'such extent as he **considers necessary** to meet all **reasonable requirements**', the Secretary of State has a **duty,** exercised by health authorities, to provide such facilities 'as he **considers** are **appropriate** as part of the health service' (*NHS Act 1977*, s.3). These represent vague duties, difficult to enforce in the law courts because of the wide discretion they confer (e.g. *Hincks* case).

Illness: prevention of illness, care, after-care (residential accommodation). Local authorities have the **power** to **make arrangements** to provide **residential accommodation** for these purposes (Approval under *National Assistance Act 1948*, s.21).

Illness: prevention of illness, care, after-care (non-residential services). Local authorities have various **powers** and **duties** to **make arrangements** for these purposes (Approval and Direction under *NHS Act 1977*, schedule 8). The **legislation** makes it clear that these arrangements should not overlap with provision of health services for the same purposes, under s.3 of the *NHS Act 1977*: see immediately above (*NHS Act 1977*, s.21).

Illness: residential accommodation. Local authorities have both a **duty** and **power** to **make arrangements** for the provision of **residential accommodation** for people who, because of illness, are in **need** of **care and attention** not **otherwise available** to them (Direction and Approval under *National Assistance Act 1948*, s.21).

Illness: welfare services. People who are **substantially and permanently handicapped** by illness are eligible for **welfare services** under s.29 of the *National Assistance Act 1948* and s.2 of the *CSDPA 1970* (*National Assistance Act 1948*, s.29), and also for **disabled facilities grants** (*Housing Grants, Construction and Regeneration Act 1996*, s.100). See: **Disability**

IMPAIRMENT

For the prevention of **illness**, the care of people who are ill, and the **after-care** of people who have been ill, local authorities have the **power** to **make arrangements** to provide social services – including **advice** and **support** – to prevent the impairment of physical or mental **health** of adults in **families** where such impairment is likely (Approval under *NHS Act 1977*, schedule 8). See: **Disability**

IMPOSSIBLE POSITION

An 'impossible task' and a 'truly impossible position' were phrases used by, respectively, the High Court and the House of Lords in the *Gloucestershire* case in relation to the local authority and its attempts to meet the **needs** of **disabled people** within available **resources**.

IMPROVEMENT (OF A DWELLING)

Improving a dwelling is one of the purposes for which housing authorities have the **power** to provide **home repair assistance** (*Housing Grants, Construction and Regeneration Act 1996*, s.76).

INCONSISTENCY OF DECISIONS

Sometimes, of two people with apparently similar **needs**, the first person receives a service but the second does not. The courts might regard the decisions underlying such apparent inconsistency as **unfair** in some circumstances (see points 5–6 below). However, there are also reasons why they (or the **local ombudsman**) might not fault the decisions (1–4 below).

(1) **No two cases exactly alike.** It can be argued that no two cases are exactly alike and that therefore there is no inconsistency anyway.

(2) **Fettering of discretion.** The obligation on local authorities to avoid **fettering their discretion** and to take account of exceptional cases cuts both ways, sometimes in favour of an applicant, sometimes not: i.e. it might lead to apparent inconsistencies.

(3) **Change of policy.** The courts will generally accept that local authorities have to change their **policies** from time to time, and apparent inconsistency might in fact be due to just such a change. If authorities could not change policies in this way, their discretion would be fettered.

(4) **Same decision-maker: different outcomes.** Inconsistent decision-making is not necessarily **unlawful**, even where the same decision-maker reaches different conclusions about the very same person (e.g. *C* case). And even three different decisions, recommending different types of home lift for a woman with multiple sclerosis, might not be deemed **maladministration** by the local ombudsman. For instance, he might accept the authority's explanation that all the decisions were professionally and technically correct, and that the difference in outcome was attributable to a shift in the weight given to different factors in the **assessment** process.

(5) **Legitimate expectation.** If an authority has departed from its own policy for no good reason, arbitrarily and informally, the courts might in some circumstances rule that the non-adherence is unlawful, for instance, because the policy gave rise to a **legitimate expectation**.

(6) **Maladministration.** The local ombudsman, too, might find **maladministration**; for instance, if inconsistent decision-making has allowed unjustifiable **queue-jumping**, or represents an absence of, or chaotic application of, a policy.

INCONTINENCE

Incontinence remains a taboo subject for many sufferers and professionals. It is a symptom which has various causes, from the psychological to the physical, and which affects millions of people in the United Kingdom. The last 20 years have seen huge developments in its recognition and **treatment** by the NHS, but, still, management of the condition might typically be poor, expertise remains thin on the ground, and services, e.g. incontinence pads, seem to be a favourite target for **rationing**.

Advice about incontinence is listed in guidance as an **NHS continuing care** service which people – in **nursing** or **residential homes**, or in their own homes – might **require**, and for which **criteria of eligibility** and **priorities** should be set within available **resources** (HSG(95)8). The guidance also states, however, that incontinence supplies should be included in the basic price charged by nursing homes to local authorities or directly to residents (i.e. those who are funding themselves).

Incontinence services are provided under the *NHS Act 1977*.

■ INDEPENDENT ASSESSMENT

Local authorities sometimes employ independent bodies to carry out some aspects of **assessment** of people's **needs**, although they should not lose control of the final decision-making function (see **Delegation**). In addition, authorities sometimes seek expert, professional opinions. Although it is still the local authority which ultimately takes the decision, such opinions might carry considerable weight. For instance, in the *Avon* case, where the expert evidence had been 'largely one way' and been accepted by the **complaints** procedure review panel, the judge found the authority's rejection of the panel's recommendations to be **unlawful**. On the other hand, the court in the *Haringey* case emphatically made clear that it is not for an expert to give an opinion about the legal **reasonableness** or general lawfulness of an authority's decision.

■ **INDIVIDUAL DUTY:** see **Duty: general or specific**

■ INDIVIDUAL NEEDS

Community care **legislation** places a **duty** on local authorities to assess 'any person' – i.e. any individual – who appears to be need of **community care services** (*NHS and Community Care Act 1990*, s.47).

Practice **guidance** reinforces the notion of individual needs, stating that no two individuals will perceive or define their needs in the same way, and that local authority staff should attempt to 'identify the unique characteristics of each individual's needs and to develop individualised, rather than stereotyped responses to those needs', although still within the limits of **policies** and **resources**. And elsewhere, it states that in setting **priorities**, authorities should take account of people's attitudes and aspirations (SSI/SWSG 1991a).

Therefore, given both the dictates of the legislation and the content of the guidance, local authorities should beware of adopting **rigid policies** or **blanket policies** which **fetter their discretion** to the extent that they fail to make a genuine decision about each person. In other words, there is a fine line to be drawn between the use of priorities and **criteria of eligibility** as tools for handling a large volume of applications, and the retention of an individual approach.

INFIRMITY: HOME REPAIR ASSISTANCE

Some of the statutory conditions for **home repair assistance** are relaxed in the case of infirm people (*Housing Grants, Construction and Regeneration Act 1996*, s.77–78). See also **Illness**

INFORMATION

The need for good quality information about **community care services** is frequently stressed. Indeed, local authorities have a **duty** to provide information for **disabled people**, both individually and generally, under s.2 of the *CSDPA 1970* (see below). In addition, **guidance** puts a premium on information – whether it be, for instance, publishing general information about services, or providing people with written copies of their individual **care plans** (SSI/SWSG 1991a). Nevertheless, providing information remains an inexact art and might be difficult to enforce, especially in the case of a **general duty** to publish information (e.g. *Bradford* case).

Information: access to personal information. In order to understand what is happening to them, service users sometimes require two types of information, general and personal. General information might tell them about, for example, an authority's **policies** and **criteria of eligibility**. Personal information might indicate how those policies and criteria have been applied in their particular case. There are specific rights of access to personal information under **legislation**.

(1) Computer-held records. In the case of computer-held information, the Data Protection Act 1984 allows people access to personal information held about them. However, **regulations** specifically applying to social work, state that access can be restricted if it would result in physical or mental harm befalling either the person or anybody else (SI 1987/1904).

(2) Manually-held records. Access to manually-held records is governed by the *Access to Personal Files Act 1987*, and, more particularly, by the Access to Personal Files (Social Services) Regulations 1989 (SI 1989/206). One restriction on access is that consent must be sought of any third party (other than a social services employee, or a health professional involved) who could be identified from the information. A second restriction is, in the case of health information, if physical or mental harm to the person or to anybody else is likely. A third, in the case of other (i.e. non-health) information, is if disclosure is likely to cause serious harm to the person's physical or mental health or emotional condition.

It should be emphasised that access by an individual under this legislation is limited to his/her own personal information; access to information about other individuals (which perhaps might assist the person's arguments) is not permitted. However, personal information is not limited necessarily to a case record, since it is defined as any 'information which relates to a living individual who can be identified from that information'. Hence, for example, **guidance** was issued which urged local authorities to be cautious when **recording unmet need** if they did not want individual service users to identify possible breaches of **statutory duty** (CI(92)34).

Information: care plans. Practice **guidance**, but not **legislation,** states that people should be given written copies of their individual **assessment** and **care plan** (SSI/SWSG 1991a). In practice, it is far from clear that this happens with any regularity, despite the rulings of the law courts that authorities should **have regard** to this guidance (e.g. *Rixon* case).

Information: carers. The right of a **carer** to an **assessment** under the *Carers (Recognition and Services) Act 1995* depends on the carer making a request. However, so that carers are not deprived of the opportunity of asking, policy **guidance** states that they should be informed about their **rights** *generally* through published information, and *individually* as part of standard assessment **procedures** (DH 1996).

Information: children. Authorities have a **duty** to publish **information** about services they provide for **children in need** and, where they consider it **appropriate,** about services which they have the **power** to provide themselves but which are in fact provided by other bodies (in particular voluntary organisations). Authorities must take **reasonably practicable** steps to ensure that those who might benefit from services receive relevant information (*Children Act 1989*, schedule 2).

Information: disabled people. Authorities have a **power** to **make arrangements** for informing **disabled people** about available **welfare services** (Approval under *National Assistance Act 1948*, s.29). In addition, a local authority has a **duty** to inform individual disabled people who are using the authority's services about other relevant services, either provided by the authority or other organisations. Local authorities also have a duty to publish, from time to time, general information about their welfare services provided under the 1948 Act (*CSDPA 1970*, s.1).

Information: elderly people. In order to meet the **needs** of **elderly people**, local authorities have the **power** to **make arrangements** for informing them of available services (Approval under *Health Services and Public Health Act 1968*, s.45).

Information: hospital discharge. Guidance emphasises that patients and relatives should be kept fully informed about **hospital discharge** procedures and given information relevant to the decisions they have to make about **continuing care** (HSG(95)8).

INJUNCTION

An injunction is a seldom-used remedy in **judicial review** proceedings – ordering an authority either to do, or not to do, something. For example, the court in the *Farley* case granted an interim injunction to force the local authority to restore **night-sitter services** for a vulnerable **elderly** woman.

INJURY

People who are **'substantially and permanently handicapped'** by injury are eligible for **welfare** services under s.29 of the *National Assistance Act 1948* and s.2 of the *CSDPA 1970*, and also for **disabled facilities grants** (*Housing Grants, Construction and Regeneration Act 1996*, s.100). Under the *NHS Act 1977*, and for the purpose of provision of health services by the NHS, injury which requires **medical** or dental treatment or **nursing** is included within the definition of **illness** (*NHS Act 1977*, s.128). See: **Disability**

INJUSTICE

For the **local ombudsman** to make recommendations against a local authority and in favour of the complainant, not only **maladministration** but also injustice must be caused as a result. The **health service ombudsman,** too, must find injustice or hardship in order to make recommendations.

INSPECTION UNITS

Each local authority has a **duty** to establish an inspection unit to inspect: (a) **residential accommodation** provided by the local authority; (b) other residential accommodation in its area which has to be registered under Part 1 of the *Registered Homes Act 1984*; and (c) community homes and registered children's homes (Direction under *Local Authority Social Services Act 1970*, s.7A, in LAC(94)16).

INSTRUCTION TO OVERCOME THE EFFECTS OF DISABILITY

Authorities have the **power** to **make arrangements** for the giving of instruction to people to overcome their **disabilities**, either in their own homes or elsewhere (Approval under *National Assistance Act 1948*, s.29).

■ INTER-AGENCY WORKING: see **Co-operation**

IRC CASE

A case in which the House of Lords stated that **maladministration** is not necessarily **unlawful**.

IRONING

Help with ironing might be part of **home help** or **practical assistance in the home.**

IRRATIONALITY

This is one of the grounds on which the law courts sometimes rule against local authorities in **judicial review** proceedings. Irrationality has been defined as characterising 'a decision which is so outrageous in its defiance of logic or of accepted moral standards that no sensible person who had applied his mind to the question to be decided could have arrived at it' (*CCSU* case). The courts are capable of raising or lowering the threshold test for irrationality from case to case, and even within the same case: compare the High Court and Court of Appeal judgments in the *East Sussex* case. For further explanation, see **Unreasonableness**

IRRELEVANT FACTORS

Irrelevancy is one of the grounds on which the law courts sometimes rule against local authorities in *judicial review* proceedings: for example, when an authority introduces factors beyond those stated in **legislation** into its decision-making (e.g. *Redezeus* case), or takes into account an immaterial consideration (*East Sussex* case:

High Court stage). Conversely, authorities must ensure that they consider all the **relevant factors** when taking decisions.

JENNIFER LEWIS CASE

This case shows what can happen if an authority, in over-generous mood, acts beyond the **legislation**. A council tenant, unhappy about recent rent increases, complained that the council was paying out of the housing revenue account for certain welfare services provided by wardens in its sheltered housing. The court held that the legislation (which was later changed) was not capable of supporting this arrangement which was therefore unlawful.

JUDICIAL REVIEW

The law courts supervise the decisions and actions of public bodies by means of judicial review. In the community care field, judicial review cases have proliferated in the last two or three years; this means that in order to understand community care **law**, a knowledge of both **legislation** and judicial decisions is required. The law courts employ an array of conceptual tools, which can be categorised under the following three umbrella terms: **unreasonableness, unfairness** and **illegality**.

Judicial review: aim of the courts. It is important to note that in judicial review the law courts are, in principle at least, ensuring that local authorities have acted within the **law**, rather than judging the **merits of decisions**. For example, they are not so much interested in whether a particular person has or has not received **community care services**, as in whether the local authority has arrived at its decision lawfully. If an authority has made an **unlawful** decision, the court orders it to go away and retake it – this time in a lawful manner.

Therefore, in the *Gloucestershire* case, the High Court ruled that the local authority's decision to withdraw services under s.2 of the *CSDPA 1970* was unlawful, because the **reassessment** process was flawed. The High Court did not step into the shoes of the authority and decide who should or who should not have services, it ruled instead that this was still for the authority to decide – but this time by means of lawful reassessment.

Judicial review: effectiveness. There are several general points to make about judicial review.

(1) **Precedents.** When a case goes to a full hearing (see below), the decision of the court sets a **precedent** for the future and has ramifications far beyond the particular applicant or applicants in the case.

(2) **Threats.** The threat alone of judicial review might be effective. For instance, if leave (permission) to bring a case is given by a judge, then the authority against whom the case is being brought will be aware that the case is an arguable one, and might be tempted to settle the dispute before it comes to a full hearing. Authorities might wish to avoid (a) adverse publicity, (b) high legal costs and (c) the danger of losing the case and the setting of an expensive precedent, which will apply to many other service users in a similar position to the applicant.

(3) **Public interest.** Judicial review might be used by voluntary organisations and others to highlight matters of public interest. For instance, in the *Lancashire* case the woman who did not wish to go into a **nursing home** had died by the time of the Court of Appeal hearing; but the court still allowed her daughter and the *Royal Association for Disability and Rehabilitation* to bring the case. The same voluntary organisation brought a second High Court case against *Gloucestershire* when it challenged the adequacy of the **reassessment** being offered by the local authority and its failure to restore services, following the first High Court ruling. In another example, *Help the Aged* joined with two service users to bring the *Sefton* case.

(4) **Legal compliance of local authorities.** A local authority does not necessarily learn from judicial review cases which have been brought generally, and might react only when it is itself threatened. In addition, the incidence of judicial review cases against particular authorities might not necessarily reflect the existence of good or bad local practices, but might simply depend, at least to some extent, on the activities and interests of local voluntary organisations or solicitors.

Judicial review: procedure. Various rules affect judicial review.

(1) **Permission.** First, 'leave' (permission) has to be sought in order to bring a judicial review case. Leave will be granted for a full hearing (at a later date) if a judge thinks there is an arguable case. This means that 'hopeless' cases will be weeded out.

(2) **Time limits.** Judicial review cases must be brought promptly and, in any event, within three months from the date when the grounds for the action arose. The court has the power to extend the time limit if it thinks there is a good reason for doing so.

(3) **Remedies.** The courts are not obliged (i.e. they have a **power**, but not a **duty**) to grant people remedies, even if an authority has behaved **unlawfully** (e.g. *Hendy* case). In addition, the courts sometimes state (either at a full hearing or at the leave stage) that an **alternative remedy** – such as the local authority's own **complaints** procedure (e.g. *Birmingham* case) or the Secretary of State's **default powers** (e.g. *Wyatt*) – should be used (or at least exhausted first) to obtain a remedy.

Conversely, the courts might rule that some matters are simply unsuitable for local authority complaints procedures or the default powers of the Secretary of State – if they involve, for instance, a question of law – and so should be subject to judicial review (e.g. *Durham*). In one case the judge stated that there was no point in the applicant going back to the local authority to ask for reconsideration of his case, since the authority would simply reapply a policy which was **illegal** (*Redezeus*). And in another, it would not have been 'convenient, expeditious or effective' for the applicant to argue points of law before a non-qualified body – i.e. the complaints procedure review panel (*Tucker*).

The courts make various orders including **certiorari** (quashing a decision), **declaration** (stating whether a particular decision or action is lawful), **injunction** (ordering an authority either to do, or not do, something) **mandamus** (ordering an authority to do something), and **prohibition** (ordering an authority not to do something). **Damages** are generally not available.

(4) **Complex problems.** Some of the community care disputes which have reached the law courts have involved complex problems, when, for instance, a local authority is attempting to identify affordable and appropriate services for severely **disabled people**. Indeed, some elements of a dispute might simply not be amenable to judicial resolution, since they are 'beyond the competence of courts of law' (*Rixon*).

JUDGEMENT

The question of judgement by local authorities about the **needs** of **disabled people** arose in the *Gloucestershire* case. The Court of Appeal stated that the needs of a disabled person were to be ascertained by **assessment** and judgement, and that this did not include consideration of the authority's **resources** – a factor which a local authority might otherwise take into account when exercising its **discretion** in making decisions.

When the Court of Appeal's decision was overturned by the House of Lords, both majority and minority views seemed to agree that professional judgements (e.g. of social workers) ultimately determine individual people's needs; but that such judgements are made against a **yardstick** provided by the **social services committee** of each local authority. Where the judges disagreed, was that the majority maintained that this yardstick could be defined by resources, the minority that it should be defined by the committee's notion of **civilised standards** of society.

It seems clear that the more restrictive is the yardstick (e.g. in the form of **criteria of eligibility**), the more curtailed professional judgement will become. At an extreme, some local authority staff question whether they are exercising their professional skills to assist people, or becoming mere administrative **rationers** of services.

JUMPING THE QUEUE

The **local ombudsman** is unlikely to look favourably on local authorities which allow queue-jumping, even if it is for the best of motives – for example, the soft-heartedness of individual staff in taking pity on the plight of individual people. This is because of the **injustice** to other people who are still waiting in line, and because queue-jumping represents a breakdown of an authority's **policies** and **priorities**; this might be deemed **maladministration**. Of course queue-jumping should not be confused with making an **exception** in special circumstances.

KINGSTON UPON HULL CASE

A case from a rather different field to that of community care – sewage treatment – but dwelling on the pervasive theme of this book: the **relevance** of **resources** to decision-making. The court held that cost could not play a part in defining the limits to an estuary: compare the House of Lords judgment in the *Gloucestershire* case which declared that cost was a relevant factor in determining people's **needs**.

(1) **Sewage treatment.** Under a European Community directive, countries are obliged to give two types of sewage treatment to waste water: primary or secondary. The latter is more stringent and expensive and applies to sewage discharged into estuaries; the former, cheaper and less thorough, applies to discharge into coastal waters. In order to save money, the Secretary of State for the Environment decided to limit the purported reach of certain estuaries, and thereby to extend coastal waters, with a wave of the financial hand, so to speak.

(2) **Irrelevance of resources to establishing geographical features.** The court pointed out that there were various relevant considerations in relation to establishing estuarine

limits. For example, the directive did not state that salinity or topography were the criteria which had to be used; thus there was a **discretion**. However, that discretion could not extend so far as to include the cost of sewage treatment as a factor, since such a consideration was **irrelevant** to a genuine and rational **assessment** of what an estuary is. The Secretary of State's decision was therefore quashed.

KHAN CASE

This immigration case illustrates how the courts might *at least in some contexts* state that people have a **legitimate expectation** not only to **consultation**, but also to the substantive benefit or service they had expected. The Court of Appeal ruled that the Secretary of State could only depart from **criteria of eligibility** set out in **guidance** if (a) the affected person was given a hearing, and (b) in any event only if overriding public interest demanded the departure.

LANCASHIRE CASE

This case confirms limits to the notion of **choice** within community care, and the importance of distinguishing between a **need** and the means to meet it.

It concerned a local authority's decision, taking **resources** into account, to cease to support an elderly woman in her own home, and instead to meet her needs in a **nursing home.** The High Court found in favour of the council. The Court of Appeal upheld the High Court's decision stating that an **assessed** need for '24-hour care' gave the authority the option of providing **home support services** or a residential placement, and in making that choice of how to meet the need, the authority could take account of **resources.**

LAUNDRY FACILITIES

Local authorities have the **power** to provide or **arrange** for the provision of laundry facilities for households for which **home help** is being, or could be, provided – i.e. because of a person who is ill, lying-in, an **expectant mother, aged,** or **handicapped** by **illness** or **congenital deformity** (Approval under *NHS Act 1977*, schedule 8). This power applies in respect of both adults and children. In addition, for **children in need** who are living with their **families**, local authorities have a **duty** to make 'such provision as they consider **appropriate**' for various services including **home help**, which may include laundry facilities (*Children Act 1989*, schedule 2).

Although not mentioned explicitly, laundry facilities might also be available for disabled people (adults or children) under s.2 of the *CSDPA 1970*, or for elderly people under s.45 of the *Health Services and Public Health Act 1968* (e.g. as **additional facilities** for **safety, comfort** or **convenience**, or **practical assistance in the home**).

LAVATORY

Facilitating access to the lavatory by, provision of it for, or facilitating its use by, a **disabled occupant** is one of the statutory purposes for which a housing authority has a **duty** to approve a **disabled facilities grant,** assuming various other conditions are also met (*Housing Grants, Construction and Regeneration Act 1996*, s.23).

LAW

The law of community care is to be found essentially in **legislation** and in **judicial review** decisions of the law courts. However, **Directions** and **Approvals** have the effect of legislation, whilst **guidance** is sometimes referred to as 'quasi-legislation'.

(1) **Knowledge of law.** The first two axioms listed in *Good Administrative Practice* (CLAE 1993), published by the **local ombudsman's** office, are that a local authority should (a) understand the requirements of the law, and (b) ensure that its staff understand and fulfil the relevant legal requirements. However, even if these axioms are followed, the complexity and uncertainty of community care law is such that **balancing the equation** and finding the **right answers** might still prove difficult in practice.

(2) **Gulf between law and everyday practice.** There is a considerable gulf between the letter of the law and everyday practice for a number of reasons. These include the complexity of community care **legislation** and accompanying **guidance**, a lack of knowledge of the law on the part of local authority staff, pressures exerted by scarce **resources,** and the fact that local authority **procedures** do not always reflect the legislation on which they are meant to be based. It is arguable that if the practices of all local authorities were scrutinised as closely as they have been in some community care cases (e.g. *Daykin, Rixon, Tucker*), then many authorities would be found to be acting **unlawfully** in one way or another.

(3) **Law and practice: Gloucestershire case.** Take, for instance, the House of Lords *Gloucestershire* judgment, which states that resources are a relevant factor both in **assessing** disabled people's needs and in deciding about the **necessity** of meeting them under s.2 of the *CSDPA 1970.* This case has been characterised as a serious blow to **disabled people**. However, it is arguable that such comments exaggerate the practical impact of the judgment (though not perhaps the overall plight of at least some disabled and elderly people).

First, local authorities have always tailored provision under the *CSDPA 1970* to available resources, and to this extent the judgment might not be quite as significant as has been suggested. Indeed, the elasticity of the concept of need in the 1970 Act has been referred to in Parliament by politicians of very different hue: Barbara Castle in the 1970s and Margaret Thatcher in the 1980s. Second, had the judgment gone the other way in the House of Lords, local authorities would now simply be looking to minimise provision by seeking alternative **escape routes** from their obligations. Alternatively, they might simply breach the law. Either way, it would seem clear that they cannot provide what they do not have the money for.

Third, although the judgment provides, at least in principle, more than one escape route from obligations under the *CSDPA 1970*, some local authorities will in practice still fail to formulate legally sound **policies**, which will therefore attract successful challenges. Last, even if the policies are sound, in the hurly-burly of everyday practice they are likely to be misapplied in a proportion of cases and so, again, will invite challenges.

(3) **Law reform.** Increasingly there are calls for fundamental reform of the morass of community care **legislation** in order to simplify the picture, much as the *Children Act 1989* did for **children's** legislation. Nevertheless, while consolidated and better drafted legislation might be a *necessary* condition for resolving problems in community care, it is unlikely to be a *sufficient* one. For instance, the problem of **resources** should not be underestimated: after all, it was this, rather than unclear drafting, which precipitated the *Gloucestershire* case.

(4) Resorting to law to solve disputes. Resort to law to decide major questions of community care seems (a) to indicate breakdown in the system for a number of reasons and on various levels, and (b) to provide only stop-gap solutions.

First, as one of the judges at the House of Lords in the *Gloucestershire* case pointed out, the national **policy** of **central government** lay at the heart of the dispute. Arguably, such comments suggest fundamental problems better resolved by public policy and politics, than by logic-chopping in the law courts. Second, when statutory services, arguing with each other over divisions of responsibility, retreat into their respective corners and reach for **legislation** as a weapon, **co-operation** has clearly failed. Third, when, for example, central government is asked in **Parliament** about its policy on **incontinence** pads but gives a carefully-worded answer about the legal position, it simply betrays an absence of policy. Last, although **judicial review** might benefit individual users and be a forum for airing issues of public interest, going to law cannot ultimately be the way to run a welfare system. This is especially so since a number of community care cases have not just concerned – as one might have expected – fringe questions and uncertainties, but have gone to the heart of community care law, policy and practice. This suggests a flawed or ill thought-out system.

■ LEAMAN CASE

This case illustrates how, by snatching at a **policy** in order to save money, an authority can find itself acting **illegally**.

(1) Restriction of holidays for disabled people. The case concerned an application by a **disabled person** under s.2 of the *CSDPA 1970* for assistance with a privately-arranged **holiday**. The authority responded to the request with the following statement: 'Due to financial cut-backs, Ealing [does] not currently provide grants, but will sponsor applicants for council-organised holidays for handicapped persons'. Yet s.2 of the 1970 Act clearly refers both to holidays arranged by the authority or 'otherwise' arranged.

(2) Unlawful policy. The applicant's lawyers claimed that this response amounted to **breach of statutory duty, fettering of discretion,** taking into account an **irrelevant** consideration and making a decision so **unreasonable** that no local authority could have taken it. The judge put it more simply: the authority was 'quite wrong': not because it ultimately failed to provide the assistance, but because it did not even consider the application in the first place. The authority had deprived itself of the 'opportunity of asking' the question of whether the person's **needs** were such that it was **necessary** for the authority to meet them by means of assistance with a privately-arranged holiday.

■ LEARNING DISABILITIES: see **Disability: learning disabilities**

■ LECTURES: DISABLED PEOPLE

If a person is **disabled** and **ordinarily resident** within the area of a local authority, then the authority must **make arrangements** for the provision of lectures, if the authority is **satisfied** that it is **necessary** for it to make the arrangements in order to meet the person's **needs** (*CSDPA 1970*, s.2).

■ LEEDS INVESTIGATION

In early 1994, the **health service ombudsman** published his report of an investigation into a health authority's refusal, as a matter of **policy**, to provide **continuing care** for a severely disabled man. He had suffered a brain haemorrhage, was doubly incontinent, could not eat or drink unassisted, could not communicate, and had a kidney tumour, cataracts in both eyes and occasional epileptic fits.

Notwithstanding the general disinclination of the law courts to intervene in such circumstances (e.g. the *Hincks* and *Cambridge* cases), the ombudsman concluded that the health authority's decision amounted to a failure in service. As a consequence of this investigation and the adverse publicity generated, the Department of Health published **guidance** on **continuing care** (HSG(95)8).

■ LEGISLATION

Legislation includes Acts of Parliament, **regulations** (statutory instruments), while **Directions** and **Approvals** have the effect of legislation. Legislation should be contrasted with **guidance**, although the boundary between the two blurs in some respects (see, for example, *Hargreaves* case) and guidance is sometimes referred to as quasi-legislation.

Community care legislation is composed of different statutory provisions passed at different times (from 1948 onwards) and with different aims in mind. Not only are the individual statutory provisions sometimes difficult to understand, but also their inter-relationship: witness the saga of the *Gloucestershire* case. This concerned both the meaning of s.2 of the *CSDPA 1970*, as well as its connection with other community care legislation. The case took up considerable amounts of time, and elicited significant judicial disagreement right up to the House of Lords.

■ LEGITIMATE EXPECTATION

Legitimate expectation is one of the grounds on which the law courts sometimes rule against a local authority in **judicial review** proceedings. A person's legitimate expectation might be disappointed if, for example, a local authority **withdraws** or reduces services without **consultation** – as occurred in the *Durham* case about closure of a residential home – or refuses to provide services which its **policy** had indicated would be provided.

Occasionally, in contexts other than community care, the courts have held that a person's legitimate expectation extends not only to consultation, but also to actual receipt of the service which had been expected. Thus, in an immigration case, the court ruled that a minister could not withdraw from an undertaking made to an individual by circular letter unless there was an overriding public interest (*Khan*). In another case, about taxi licences, it was ruled to be unlawful for the local authority to depart informally from its policy (*Hendry*). However, the courts are unlikely to advance too far down this avenue, because otherwise authorities would be excessively bound by their own policies, be unable easily to change them, and so **unlawfully** be **fettering their discretion**. Therefore, for instance, a **reassessment** of a person's community care **needs** in the light of a change of policy, followed by a reduction or **withdrawal** of services, might satisfy the test of legitimate expectation in the community care context.

■ **LEISURE:** see **Recreation**

LETTERS

Letters sent to service users containing decisions about provision can constitute evidence, both for the law courts and the **local ombudsman**, of **unlawful** formulation, or application (or both) of a **policy**. Thus, local authorities should ensure the content of such letters properly reflects underlying policies. For example, in the *Bristol* case, a particular letter written by the housing authority indicated a policy which **fettered its discretion**; but on closer scrutiny the judge decided that in practice, the authority had not in fact done so. In contrast, it is possible that despite a local authority's claim that its policy meant that it would consider **exceptions** to its strict **eligibility criteria** of 'high risk', a letter sent to a user, giving an unequivocal impression that the authority would not listen, might represent a **fettering of discretion** in terms of how a policy was applied in a particular case.

LIBRARY FACILITIES: DISABLED PEOPLE

If a person is **disabled** and **ordinarily resident** within the area of a local authority, then the authority has a **duty** to **make arrangements** for the provision of, or assistance to the person in obtaining, library facilities, if the authority is **satisfied** that it is **necessary** for it to make those arrangements in order to meet the person's **needs** (*CSDPA 1970*, s.2).

LIFTING AND HANDLING

Health and safety **legislation**, in the form of the Manual Handling Operations Regulations 1992 (SI 1992/2793), places a **duty** on employers to minimise the risk of **injury** to employees through lifting and handling at work. These **regulations** have had an impact not only in hospitals and other institutions, but also on the delivery of **personal care** services to people at home. Consequences within the NHS and local authorities generally have been (a) greater care taken in lifting and handling practices, (b) more awareness of the need to use hoists, and other lifting and turning equipment, and (c) increased levels of training for staff.

Concern about injury to staff arose in the *Goldsack* case when, at a local authority day centre, walking assistance was being given to a person under s.29 of the *National Assistance Act 1948*. The person's mother wanted the assistance to be given without the use of an extra support in the form of a wheeled walking frame, but the local authority refused because of fear of injury to staff. The judge ruled that such a health and safety issue was a **relevant** factor in determining what services should be provided.

LIGHT

Facilitating the use of a source of light by a **disabled occupant** is one of the statutory purposes for which a housing authority has a **duty** to approve an application for a **disabled facilities grant**, assuming various other conditions are also met (*Housing Grants, Construction and Regeneration Act 1996*, s.23).

LOCAL AUTHORITIES (GOODS AND SERVICES) ACT 1970

This Act gives local authorities certain powers to trade, either with other authorities or other specified bodies designated 'public'. It appears to give no power to trade with the public: for example, it is not possible to sell items of daily living equipment to members of the public who walk in off the street.

LOCAL AUTHORITY SOCIAL SERVICES ACT 1970

This Act governs various social services functions.

(1) **Complaints.** The Secretary of State has the **power** to order local authorities to establish **complaints** procedures. The procedure is open to all those people for whom the authority has a power or **duty** to provide services (s.7B). **Regulations** (SI 1990/2444), **Directions** (contained in DH 1990), and **guidance** (DH 1990 and SSI 1991) have been issued.

(2) **Adequate staff.** Local authorities are under a duty to appoint a **director of social services** and to secure the provision of **adequate staff** to assist him/her (s.6).

(3) **Guidance.** Local authorities have a duty, 'in the exercise of their **social services functions**, including the exercise of any **discretion** conferred by any relevant enactment, to act under the general **guidance** of the Secretary of State' (s.7(1)).

(4) **Directions.** Local authorities have a duty to exercise their social services functions 'in accordance' with Directions issued by the Secretary of State (s.7A).

(5) **Default powers.** The Secretary of State has the power to make an order declaring that a local authority is in **default** of its duty if he or she is satisfied that the authority has failed 'without **reasonable** excuse' to comply with any duties which are social services functions (s.7D).

(6) **Social services committees.** Local authorities have a duty to appoint a **social services committee** to deal with the discharge of social services functions (s.2).

LOCAL GOVERNMENT ACT 1972

This Act governs various functions of local authorities.

(1) **Delegation.** For instance, authorities have the **power** to delegate functions to its committees and officers (s.101) such as social workers or **occupational therapists**.

(2) **Extra powers?** Local authorities **may** also do anything which 'is calculated to facilitate, or is conducive or incidental to, the discharge of any of their functions' (s.111). Thus, Department of Health **guidance** suggests that s.111 is an appropriate legal basis for provision of **information** for **carers** and carer support groups, in connection with functions under schedule 8 of the *NHS Act 1977* (DH 1996).

However, recently the House of Lords ruled that **charges** for services cannot be made under this section (*Richmond* case). In the community care context, this ruling might affect a local authority which tried, for example, to use s.111 to charge interest when placing a charge on people's homes (see **Charges: residential accommodation**).

LOCAL GOVERNMENT AND HOUSING ACT 1989

This Act formerly underpinned, amongst other things, the provision of **disabled facilities grants**, **minor works assistance**, and **renovation grants**. The relevant parts of the Act have now been superseded by the *Housing Grants, Construction* *and Regeneration Act 1996*. The Act also contains the duty to appoint a **monitoring officer**.

LOCAL OMBUDSMAN

The local ombudsmen investigate alleged **maladministration** and resulting **injustice**. They are not permitted to question the **merits of decisions** (e.g. the professional judgement of a social worker) and are precluded from investigating situations where the complainant could have gone to a court of law or appealed to a government minister. However, they may waive this latter restriction, if they are **satisfied** that a complainant could not **reasonably** have been expected to use those avenues of redress (Local Government Act 1974).

There are several local government ombudsmen, each covering a different area of the country. Normally, the ombudsmen will only investigate if the complaint has first gone through the local authority's own, internal **complaints** procedure. Maladministration is not defined in **legislation**, a fact which allows the ombudsmen to operate with substantial flexibility. The decisions of the local ombudsmen are not enforceable in the law courts, and do not set legal **precedents**. At the conclusion of their investigations, the local ombudsmen might make various recommendations, relating to, for instance, financial compensation, provision of a service, or changes required to a local authority's procedures. Recommendations do not have to be accepted by local authorities, but in practice they are followed in about 95 per cent of cases.

The ombudsmen attempt to arrive at decisions which, overall, are fair to both parties. Much will depend on the individual circumstances of the case and although some local authorities attempt to develop 'ombudsman-proof' methods of working, this is not always easy. For instance, there is no absolute rule of thumb about an acceptable length of **waiting time**. Thus, the ombudsman might decide in one investigation that a four-month **delay** in **assessment** constitutes maladministration, but in another that eleven months does not.

LOGIC

Logical argument is deployed up to a point in **judicial review** cases, but is not necessarily decisive of the final outcome – notwithstanding that some court cases resemble logic-chopping medieval disputations.

For instance, at the House of Lords stage of the *Gloucestershire* case, the difference of opinion between two of the judges appeared to reduce to the contention about what **Parliament** must have intended in relation to the **needs** of **disabled people** and **resources**. Both claimed this in support of their opposing arguments, without obvious evidence either way. It was not clear that logic underlay either view: indeed, if it had, then the disagreement would presumably have been resolved, a unanimous judgment delivered, or perhaps the **right answer** obtained long before the case reached the House of Lords. Rather, what Parliament must have intended was called on almost as a self-evident truth of common sense.

This might suggest that law is an art rather than a science and hinges – for good reason, given the complexity and social significance of some of the issues considered – as much on considerations of public policy and judicial preference as mathematical or logical certainty.

■ **LYING-IN WOMEN:** see **Expectant mothers**

■ M CASE

This case illustrates the **buck-passing** which sometimes takes place between different statutory authorities when, short of **resources**, they attempt to exploit **grey areas** of responsibility.

Speech therapy: health or educational service? An education authority, having classed a child's **need** for **speech therapy** as an educational need, claimed that it had made a mistake – and that, as a matter of law, speech therapy could not be special educational provision (and so should be provided by the NHS). Thus, it was not empowered to provide the therapy even if it wanted to. The court ruled against the education authority, agreeing with a previous decision (*Oxfordshire* case) that speech therapy could be either educational or non-educational: i.e. it depended on the circumstances.

■ MACWAN CASE

This case illustrates how the courts might be reluctant to intervene in how, or how quickly, an authority carries out its **statutory duty**.

Delay not unreasonable. The case concerned a **delay** on the part of a housing authority in carrying out its acknowledged **duty** to find permanent **accommodation** for a person under **homelessness legislation**. The authority had decided to perform the duty in stages, the first of which was to provide **temporary accommodation** for three years. The relevant code of **guidance** for local authorities on homelessness stated that once the duty arose to provide permanent accommodation, the authority should set about providing it immediately. However, the court held that the code was not law, that the authority had to **have regard** to it but not necessarily follow it, and that its decision – in all the circumstances – was not **unreasonable**.

■ MAGNIFYING GLASSES AND MICROSCOPES

The last two or three years have seen judges, barristers, solicitors, local authorities and voluntary organisations all reaching for their magnifying glasses and microscopes in order to scrutinise words and phrases in community care **legislation** ever more closely, and conduct cases in the law courts which sometimes resemble **medieval disputations**.

This is a consequence of increasing pressure being placed on the community care system by the mismatch between **resources, needs** and **expectations**. For example, the *CSDPA 1970* had been in force for some 25 years before the *Gloucestershire* case was brought in 1995 about the meaning and implications of the word 'needs' in s.2 of the Act. Detailed analysis of particular words and phrases forms part of the **contortions** that local authorities execute in their search for **escape routes** from legal obligations.

■ MAKE ARRANGEMENTS

The term 'make arrangements' is widespread in community care **legislation**. For instance, under s.2 of the *CSDPA 1970*, the **duty** arising is 'to make arrangements' for the provision of various services. Similarly, many of the various **duties** and **powers** in relation to **residential accommodation** and **welfare** services under sections 21 and 29 of the *National Assistance Act 1948* are couched in terms of making arrangements. This term covers the situation in which, for example, a third party is paid by a local authority to make provision, rather than the local authority making direct provision itself. However, it does not cover the making of **cash payments** to service users; such payments are expressly forbidden for **welfare services** under s.29 of the 1948 Act, whilst the *Hammersmith and Fulham (no.2)* case confirmed that neither are they available in relation to residential accommodation under s.21 of the 1948 Act.

■ MALADMINISTRATION

Maladministration is the territory of the ombudsmen – local, health and Parliamentary – although the term is not defined in **legislation**. The Commission for Local Administration in England (i.e. the **local ombudsman**) has published a helpful booklet called *Good Administrative Practice* (CLAE 1993). The law courts have also stepped in to mark the boundary between their field of operations and that of the ombudsmen – pointing out in the *IRC* case that maladministration is not necessarily **unlawful**.

Maladministration might consist, for instance, of a breach of **statutory duty** (e.g. a failure to provide a community care **assessment** for a person appearing to be in need of services), of excessive delay in assessment or provision of services, of poor handling of **complaints**, of a breakdown of communication between two local authority departments (e.g. social services and housing), and so on. Of these examples, the first would also be an example of unlawfulness.

■ MANUAL HANDLING OPERATIONS REGULATIONS 1992: see Lifting and handling

■ MANCHESTER CASE

A case illustrating the confusion sometimes surrounding the status and legal effect of **guidance**.

(1) **Peremptory language in guidance.** It concerned a dispute between the Manchester Local Medical Committee and the Secretary of State about the reimbursement of funds to **general practitioners** in accordance with the relevant guidance. There was some uncertainty about the effect of the 'Red Book' and related guidance notes and whether in fact they contained a binding **Direction**, which the Secretary of State had the power to issue under s.97 of the *NHS Act 1977*. The judge stated that there was:

> 'no magic form of words that is required and I do not think that the use of the word 'direct' is necessary in order to constitute a 'Direction'. Nevertheless, it was obviously desirable that, if the Secretary of State was intending to direct, she should have made clear that she was indeed directing. Normally, the way to make that clear is to use the word 'direct' and it would have saved a lot of time and money in this case if only the Secretary of State had done just that... The language used in the guidance notes...is, in passages, peremptory.'

MANDAMUS

Mandamus is one of the remedies available in **judicial review** proceedings, ordering an authority to do something.

MANDATORY

This refers to something there is a **duty** to provide; for instance, mandatory as opposed to **discretionary, disabled facilities grants**.

MAY

The word 'may' in **legislation** usually signals the existence of a **power**, rather than a **duty**.

MCMILLAN CASE

This case illustrates a **balancing exercise** carried out by a local authority, when weighing up the **needs** of **disabled people** against available **resources**. It was heard in the High Court with the *Gloucestershire* case, and focused likewise on obligations arising under s.2 of the *CSDPA 1970.*

(1) **Notice of discontinuity in home care services.** Following meetings, conversations and visits from local authority staff, the applicant had been informed that his home care service might suffer from discontinuity in certain circumstances (e.g. when home carers were ill or on leave). The applicant complained about the discontinuity that duly followed.

(2) **Balancing exercise.** The judge found that the council had (a) performed a proper balancing exercise 'taking into account resources and the comparative needs of the disabled in their area'; (b) given clear notice about the possible interruptions to the service; (c) provided what they had undertaken to provide and what had been **assessed** as needed; (d) at no time **withdrawn** the service; and (e) not interrupted a service to a person for whom any interruption of the service would have been intolerable. For instance, missing a day's meal would not have been acceptable, but missing a day's cleaning would have been.

MEALS

Meals: disabled people. If a person is **disabled** and **ordinarily resident** within the area of a local authority, then the authority has a **duty** to **make arrangements** for the provision of meals either in the person's home or elsewhere, if the authority is **satisfied** that it is **necessary** for it to **make those arrangements** in order to meet the person's **needs** (*CSDPA 1970*, s.2).

Meals: elderly people. In order to meet the **needs** of **elderly people**, local authorities have the **power** to **make arrangements** to provide meals in people's own homes and elsewhere (Approval under *Health Services and Public Health Act 1968*, s.45). In addition, district councils have the power to make arrangements for providing meals for elderly people in their own homes or elsewhere (*HASSASSA 1983*, schedule 9).

Meals: illness. For the prevention of **illness**, the care of people who are ill, and the **after-care** of people who have been ill, local authorities have the **power** to **make arrangements** for the provision of meals at centres or at other facilities, and of meals-on-wheels for housebound people (Approval under *NHS Act 1977*, schedule 8).

MEDICAL ADVICE: SPECIALIST

Specialist medical advice is a an NHS **continuing care** service which, **guidance** explains, people – in **nursing** or **residential homes**, or in their own homes – might **require**, and for which **priorities** and **criteria of eligibility** should be set within available **resources** (HSG(95)8). Such advice is provided under the *NHS Act 1977*.

MEDICAL AND NURSING ASSESSMENT: SPECIALIST

Specialist medical and nursing **assessment** is listed in **guidance** as an **NHS continuing care** service for which **priorities** and **criteria of eligibility** should be set within available **resources** (HSG(95)8). Such assessment is provided under the *NHS Act 1977*.

MEDICAL AND NURSING EQUIPMENT: SPECIALIST

Specialist medical (eg. specialist feeding equipment) and nursing equipment are part of NHS **continuing care** provision which, guidance explains, people – in **nursing** or **residential homes**, or in their own homes – might **require**, and for which **criteria of eligibility** and **priorities** should be set within available **resources** (HSG(95)8. Such equipment is provided under the *NHS Act 1977*.

In practice, as more people use 'high-tech' equipment in their own homes, and some private **nursing homes** increasingly resemble 'mini-hospitals', there is considerable pressure on health authorities to implement adequate, responsible **policies** for providing a whole range of medical and nursing equipment (e.g. specialist pressure relief mattresses) and services.

MEDICAL AND NURSING TREATMENT: SPECIALIST

Specialist medical treatment is an NHS **continuing care** service which, **guidance** explains, people – in **nursing** or **residential homes**, or in their own homes – might **require**, and for which **criteria of eligibility** and **priorities** should be set within available **resources** (HSG(95)8). Such equipment is provided under the *NHS Act 1977*.

MEDICAL ATTENTION

Local authorities have a **duty** to **make arrangements** to enable people for whom **residential accommodation** has been provided to obtain medical attention during illnesses which are normally nursed at home (Direction under *National Assistance Act 1948*, s.21).

MEDICAL GROUNDS

Medical factors are sometimes relevant to decisions about community care and related services. For example, when drawing up public **housing allocation** schemes, housing authorities have a **duty** to give **priority** to households with a person who needs settled **accommodation** on medical grounds (*Housing Act 1996*, s.167). And, community care **guidance** points out that **general practitioners** have an important role to play in community care **assessment** (DH 1990). Nevertheless, medical grounds are only one of a number of relevant factors a local authority takes account of when assessing people's community care **needs**, and might or might not be decisive, depending on the circumstances.

- **MEDICAL OPINION:** see **Medical grounds**

MEDICAL SERVICES

The Secretary of State has a **duty**, exercised by health authorities, to provide medical services 'to such extent as he **considers necessary** to meet all **reasonable requirements**' (*NHS Act 1977*, s.3). This represents a vague duty, difficult to enforce in the law courts because of the wide **discretion** it confers on authorities, as illustrated by the *Hincks* case. Thus, denial of even lifesaving medical treatment to children does not in itself represent a **breach of statutory duty**.

MEDIEVAL DISPUTATION

For three days in the *Gloucestershire* case at the Court of Appeal stage, three judges and various barristers picked over, in painstaking detail, the purported **logic** and meaning of various words and phrases in community care **legislation**. The detailed and formal argument suggested a medieval disputation; ironically the straightforward judgments of the two majority judges belied the complexity which had gone before.

MENTAL DISORDER

A wide term used to cover a spectrum of conditions. It is defined in the *Mental Health Act 1983* as: 'mental illness, arrested or incomplete development of mind, psychopathic disorder and any other disorder or **disability** of mind'.

Mental disorder: after-care services. Under s.117 of the *Mental Health Act 1983*, local authorities and health authorities have a **duty** to provide **after-care** services for **any person** with a mental disorder to whom certain sections of the Act apply. These are sections 3 (people admitted for treatment), 37 (people for whom hospital or guardianship orders have been made), 47 or 48 (prisoners transferred by Direction to hospital).

(1) **Individual duty.** The duty is placed on both health and local authorities to continue to provide, in **co-operation** with voluntary agencies, after-care services for anybody to whom the section applies, until both authorities are '**satisfied** that the person concerned is no longer in need of such services'. This duty has been held, in the *Fox* case, to be a **specific duty** owed to each individual, and therefore to be stronger than the related **general duty** to provide after-care under s.3 of the *NHS Act 1977*.

(2) **Supervision orders.** In addition, under s.25A, supervision orders **may** be made when (a) people suffer from mental disorder – that is mental illness, severe mental impairment, psychopathic disorder or mental impairment; (b) 'there would be a substantial risk of serious harm to the health or safety of the patient or the safety of other persons, or of the patient being seriously exploited, if he were not to receive the after-care services to be provided' under s.117; and (c) the supervision order is 'likely to secure that he receives the after-care services'. The application for a supervision order must be made to the health authority, which must then consult the local authority (*Mental Health Act 1983*, s.25A).

(3) Good practice. Guidance issued in 1994 to both health authorities and local authorities suggested good practice in the discharge from hospital of mentally disordered people (LASSL(94)4), as did the statutory Code of Practice (DH 1993).

Mental disorder: prevention, care, after-care. In order to prevent mental disorder – or for people who are suffering, or have been suffering, from mental disorder – local authorities have a **duty** to **make arrangements** (a) for the provision of centres (including **day centres** or training centres) or facilities (including domiciliary facilities) for **training** or **occupation**; (b) for the appointment of sufficient approved **social workers**; (c) in relation to guardianship functions under the *Mental Health Act 1983*; and (d) for providing **social work** and related services to assist the **identification, diagnosis, assessment** and **social treatment** of mental disorder – and to provide **social work** support and other **domiciliary** and **care services** to people living in their homes and elsewhere (Direction under *NHS Act 1977*, schedule 8).

Mental disorder: residential accommodation (duty). A local authority has a **duty** to **make arrangements** to provide **residential accommodation** for people who are or have been suffering from mental disorder (or for the purpose of preventing mental disorder) and who are either **ordinarily resident** in the authority's area or have no **settled residence** (Direction under *National Assistance Act 1948*, s.21).

Mental disorder: residential accommodation (power). A local authority has the **power** to **make arrangements** for provision of **residential accommodation** for people who are or have been suffering from mental disorder (or in order to prevent mental disorder) and who are **ordinarily resident in another authority**, but have been **discharged from hospital** in the authority's area (Approval under *National Assistance Act 1948*, s.21).

Mental disorder: welfare services. The various **powers** and **duties** of local authorities to **make arrangements** to provide **welfare services** are expressed as being toward various groups of people, including those 'who suffer from mental disorder of any description' (*National Assistance Act 1948*, s.29, and therefore under the *CSDPA 1970*, s.2), or from 'mental disorder of any kind' (*Children Act 1989*, s.17).

This is taken to be mental disorder within the meaning of the *Mental Health Act 1983*. However, services for adults with a mental disorder are generally provided under schedule 8 of the *NHS Act 1977* (see immediately above) since anyway the *National Assistance Act 1948* contains a provision against **duplication** of services provided under the 1977 Act. Nevertheless, people with a mental disorder are eligible for services under s.2 of the *CSDPA 1970* (see: LAC(93)10); and see **Duplication**.

■ **MENTAL HEALTH:** see **Mental illness; Mental disorder;** and **Health: physical and mental**

■ MENTAL HEALTH ACT 1983, S.117

This section of the 1983 Act imposes a duty on both health authorities and local authorities to provide **after-care** services for people with a mental disorder: see **Mental disorder**. A code of practice on the Act has been issued (DH 1993) and an amendment added in relation to supervision orders (DH 1996).

■ MENTAL ILLNESS

Provision for the prevention of **illness**, the care of people who are ill and the **after-care** of people who have been ill is made (a) by local authorities under the *NHS Act 1977*, schedule 8, and the *National Assistance Act 1948*, s.21 (Approval); and (b) by the NHS under ss.1 and 3 of the *NHS Act 1977*. See also: **Mental disorder;** and **Care Programme Approach.**

The Secretary of State also has the **power** to give grants to local authorities, for services provided for people who are mentally ill (*Local Authority Social Services Act 1970*, s.7E). This power has been regularly exercised through the mental illness specific grant (MISG) system.

■ MERITS OF DECISIONS

In **judicial review** cases, the courts take pains to avoid ruling on the merits – as opposed to the lawfulness – of local authority decisions. For instance, in both the *Haringey* and *East Sussex* (Court of Appeal, the majority) cases, it was quite clear that the judges were disturbed about the merits of the decisions which had been made, but were not prepared to strike them down as **unlawful** on the basis of **irrationality** or **unreasonableness.**

■ MIGRATION OF SERVICES: see **Grey areas**

■ MINOR WORKS ASSISTANCE

Provided up to December 1996 under the *Local Government and Housing Act 1989*, minor works assistance has now been replaced by a more extensive scheme called **home repair assistance**. See: **Home adaptations**

■ MIXED ECONOMY OF CARE

Cited by **central government** as the optimum way of delivering community care, the mixed economy of care has developed rapidly.

For instance, policy **guidance** emphasises that local authorities should **consult** and contract with the independent sector, both voluntary and private sector bodies, for the delivery of services (DH 1990). **Directions** have stipulated that consultation must take place with the independent sector (LAC(93)4). The *National Assistance Act 1948* states that local authorities **may** contract for **residential accommodation** with private, as well as voluntary sector, bodies. And a condition of the community care 'special transitional grant' (STG) has been that 85 per cent of it should be spent on service provision by the independent sector. This reliance on local authorities for contracts has led to a number of court cases in which private sector care home owners have challenged the actions of local authorities, eg *Cleveland, Cumbria* and *Newcastle* cases.

MOBILE HOMES

Mobile homes are eligible for **home repair assistance** (*Housing Grants, Construction and Regeneration Act 1996*, s.78).

MOBILITY

Local authorities have a **duty** to **make arrangements** to provide – either at centres or elsewhere – facilities for **social rehabilitation** and **adjustment to disability**, including assistance in overcoming mobility limitations – for disabled people who are ordinarily resident in the area. In respect of those not ordinarily resident, the duty becomes a **power** only (Direction and Approval under *National Assistance Act 1948*, s.29).

For instance, the assistance with walking given to a person attending a local authority day centre in the *Goldsack* case was provided under s.29 of the 1948 Act. The occasional provision by local authorities of wheelchairs is presumably covered by s.29, if not more specifically by s.2 of the *CSDPA 1970* (**additional facilities** for **safety, comfort or convenience**).

MONITORING OFFICERS

Local authorities have a **duty** to appoint a monitoring officer who, in turn, has a duty to report on any proposal, decision or omission which has given rise, or is likely to give rise, to (a) a contravention of **legislation or code of practice**, or (b) **maladministration** or **injustice** which the **local ombudsman** might investigate (*Local Government and Housing Act 1989*, s.5).

MUSEUM ATTENDANTS

An example argued at the High Court stage of the *Gloucestershire* case was that of the chairless museum attendant who 'either needs a chair or he does not. The cost of the chair to the administrator of the museum does not come into it'. The parallel drawn was with disabled people, whose **needs** could surely not be assessed in terms of **resources**. The argument failed.

NATIONAL ASSISTANCE ACT 1948

This Act remains the bedrock of community care, covering care in **residential accommodation** (including **nursing homes**), as well as various **welfare services**. The *CSDPA 1970* is generally seen as an extension of the 1948 Act, since a pre-condition of provision of **welfare services** under the 1970 Act is that a person qualifies as disabled under s.29 of the 1948 Act.

In addition, although the Act abolished the Poor Law, it is at the same time seen by the courts as fulfilling a similar role in terms of a last resort or **safety net** in certain circumstances – i.e. when other channels of provision have failed. For instance, it was recently invoked by the Court of Appeal in the *Hammersmith and Fulham* case as an Act which, having replaced 350 years of the Poor Law, is 'always speaking' and should be interpreted in a way which allows for changes in society since the Act was first passed. Thus, destitute asylum-seekers – lacking food and accommodation, ignorant of the language, and under the stress of being refugees

– were held to be potentially eligible for assistance with residential accommodation.

National Assistance Act 1948: residential accommodation: see **Residential accommodation**

National Assistance Act 1948: welfare services. Local authorities have both **powers** and **duties** in respect of **welfare services** for people who are **ordinarily resident** in the local authority's area and who fall within the statutory definition of **disability**.

(1) Disability. Section 29 applies to people 'aged 18 or over who are **blind, deaf** or **dumb**, or who suffer from **mental disorder** of any description and other persons aged 18 or over who are **substantially and permanently handicapped** by **illness, injury,** or **congenital deformity** or such other disabilities as may be prescribed'.

(2) Directions and Approvals. The exercise of the powers and duties under s.29 is largely dependent on **Directions** and **Approvals** made by the Secretary of State. These are contained in Circular LAC(93)10.

(3) Duties. In respect of **disabled people** who are ordinarily resident in the area, local authorities have a duty (a) to maintain **registers of disabled people;** (b) to provide a **social work service** and such **advice** and **support** as needed for people at home or elsewhere; (c) to provide, whether at centres or elsewhere, facilities for the **social rehabilitation** and **adjustment to disability** including assistance in overcoming limitations of **mobility** or **communication;** (d) to provide, either at centres or elsewhere, facilities for **occupational, social, cultural** and **recreational activities** and, where appropriate, payments to persons for work they have done.

(4) Powers. The above duties are powers only in the case of disabled people who are not ordinarily resident within an authority's area.

There are also other powers which **may** be exercised in relation both to ordinary residents and to people who are not ordinary residents in the authority's area. These are to make arrangements: (a) to **inform** people about services available under s.29; (b) to give **instruction** to people at home elsewhere in methods of overcoming effects of their disabilities; (c) for providing **workshops** where such people may engage in suitable work and for providing associated **hostels**; (d) for providing suitable **work;** (e) for helping people dispose of their work; (f) to provide **holiday homes**; (g) to provide free or subsidised **travel** for people who do not otherwise qualify for other travel concessions; (h) to assist a person to find **accommodation** which will enable him or her to take advantage of arrangements made under section 29(1); (i) to contribute to the cost of employing a **warden** in warden-assisted housing; (j) to provide warden services in private housing.

NECESSARY

In principle suggestive of certainty (for example, that which is 'really needed') the implications of the term 'necessary' leave much to the **discretion** of the authority.

Necessary: NHS provision. To 'such extent as he **considers** necessary to meet all **reasonable requirements**', the Secretary of State has a **duty**, exercised by **health authorities, to provide various services** (*NHS Act 1977*, s.3). The term 'necessary' contributes to the overall vagueness of the duty, which is difficult to enforce because of the wide **discretion** it confers – as illustrated by cases such as *Hincks.*

Necessary: social services provision for disabled people. If a person is **disabled** and **ordinarily resident** within the area of the authority, then the local authority has a **duty** to **make arrangements** for the provision of various welfare services: if the authority is **satisfied** that it is necessary for it to **make those arrangements** in order to meet the person's **needs** (*CSDPA 1970*, s.2). Not only did the majority (House of Lords) in the *Gloucestershire* case rule that the local authority could take account of resources when deciding whether it was necessary for it to meet a person's needs, but even the minority view noted that there might be other factors affecting the decision. Thus, there:

> 'might be any number of reasons why, in the circumstances of a particular case, it might not be necessary for the local authority to make arrangements, for example, if the person's needs were being adequately met by a friend or relation. Or he might be wealthy enough to meet his needs out of his own pocket.'

Necessary and appropriate: disabled facilities grants. Housing authorities must be **satisfied**, before approving an application for **disabled facilities grants**, that the proposed works are 'necessary and appropriate'. See: **Home adaptations**

(1) Consultation with social services. Legally, the housing authority has a **duty** to **consult** the social services authority, where the two authorities are not one and the same (i.e. not a metropolitan or unitary authority). However, the final decision is that of the housing authority, since it is that authority which must be satisfied – not the social services authority (*Housing Grants, Construction and Regeneration Act 1996*, s.24). **Guidance** states that even where housing and social services departments are within the same authority, the latter should still be consulted (DoE 17/96).

(2) What is necessary and appropriate? Guidance states that the necessity and appropriateness of an adaptation concern: (a) whether it is needed to enable a **care plan** to be implemented and the person to remain in their own home and living as independently as possible; (b) whether it will meet the person's assessed **needs** (physical and medical); and (c) the distinction between the person's real needs, 'what is desirable' and 'possibly legitimate aspirations' (DoE 17/96).

(3) Continuing duty for the social services department. Local authority social services departments are often anxious about – and attempt to avoid – the following situation. They might recommend that an adaptation is necessary and appropriate, but the housing authority then fails, unexpectedly, to provide a grant, or leaves the applicant with a contribution he or she cannot afford. In this situation, they fear that a **continuing duty**, under s.2 of the *CSDPA 1970*, might compel the social services department to make provision – which they cannot afford (see e.g. DoE 17/96).

The anxiety would be well-founded, if a court were to question a local authority's decision that an adaptation is 'necessary' under one Act (the *Housing Grants, Construction and Regeneration Act 1996*) but not under another (the *CSDPA 1970*). On the other hand, a court might accept that a recommendation that adaptations are 'necessary and appropriate' under housing legislation is not the same as saying that they are 'necessary' under social services legislation. For instance, the converse situation arose in the *Tower Hamlets* case; simply because rehousing was not warranted under housing legislation did not mean that it might not be required under social services legislation (*Children Act 1989*, s.17).

Nevertheless, guidance explains that 'necessary and appropriate' refers in part to whether the adaptations will assist with the carrying out of a care plan (which is formulated by social services and might often involve s.2 of the *CSDPA*). Therefore, it is not clear how sustainable the distinction between the word 'necessary' in the two Acts really is.

NEEDS

The term 'need' or 'needs' recurs in **legislation**, is not defined but has played a central role in **judicial review** cases. Indeed, the *Gloucestershire* case, which revolved around the term, progressed through the High Court, the Court of Appeal and House of Lords. It took up a great deal of time, and elicited marked judicial disagreement along the way.

Various **guidance** contrasts need with **preference**, and practice guidance refers to need as a dynamic, relative concept which should be defined at local level and which will vary over time with changes in national legislation and local **policy**, availability of **resources** and patterns of local demand (SSI/SWSG 1991a). See also **Choice**.

Needs: clinical (NHS): see **Clinical need**

Needs: cultural and religious. Some local authority staff are aware that what is a mere **preference** for one person, might amount to a genuine **need** for somebody else because of the latter's **cultural** or religious background. For example, different cultures might have very different attitudes to **bathing** (and immersion in water), or even to the use of a stairlift in the house.

However, while taking account of cultural factors might seem daunting to local authority staff, who fear opening the floodgates of demand, it should not prove insuperable. Given that local authorities ought anyway not to have excessively **rigid policies** – since otherwise they risk a **fettering of discretion** – and that community care involves **assessment** of **individual needs**, there seems no reason why authorities should not be capable of considering cultural – amongst all the other relevant – factors when determining a person's needs (as guidance states they should: DH 1990 and SSI/SWSG 1991a).

Needs: individual: see **Individual needs**

Needs: medical. The recommendations of **general practitioners** or hospital consultants are sometimes an important factor to be taken account of by local authorities when assessing people's community care needs and deciding on service provision.

Community care policy **guidance** stresses the importance of the role of general practitioners in community care **assessment**, but also contains a warning. It notes that general practitioners have a personal duty to, and relationship with, their patients and that because of this they might not always be best placed to assess on behalf of the local authority. Instead, authorities might sometimes wish to obtain an **independent assessment** (DH 1990). This advice reflects the fact that, ultimately, it is local authorities which must make decisions about needs and provision of services – other agencies or practitioners cannot, ultimately, do this for them. Indeed this principle was illustrated, albeit in relation to different **legislation**, by a **homelessness** case;

where the housing authority had based its decision about a person's vulnerability on **medical opinion** alone and had not made wider enquiries in relation to social welfare and housing factors (*Carroll* case).

However, local authority policies sometimes appear **inconsistent** when they cite medical needs as a reason both for and against provision in different circumstances. For example, an authority might have a **policy** of not providing **bathing** equipment except in very limited circumstances – such as the existence of a medical need for daily immersion (e.g. because of a skin condition). Yet at the same time, some authorities might state that a person's need of a footstool for medical reasons (e.g. body fluid drainage) means that provision should be made by the NHS, and not by the local authority.

Needs: multi-faceted. Practice **guidance** refers to need as multi-faceted, including **personal care, social care, health care, accommodation,** finance, education, **employment, leisure, transport, access.**

Thus, arguably, a local authority which took an unduly narrow view of need might in some circumstances be acting **unlawfully**, as occurred in the Avon case when the authority refused to recognise the **psychological need** of a man with **learning disabilities** (see immediately below). The court agreed that **assessment** should be based on current need including psychological, educational, social and **medical factors**. It found that the entrenched **preference** of the man formed part of his psychological need. And, in the *Haringey* case, the local authority was ruled to have acted unlawfully by reassessing a disabled man's **personal care** needs – but not his social, **recreational** and **leisure** needs.

Needs: psychological: see **Psychological need**

Needs: resources. The crucial question in the *Gloucestershire* case was whether **resources** could sensibly – and legally – affect the **assessment** and meeting of the **needs** of **disabled people** under the *CSDPA 1970*, s.2. The final answer in the House of Lords was that resources could be taken into account in (a) assessing needs; (b) deciding whether it is **necessary** to meet those needs; and (c) deciding how to meet them. See **Resources**

Needs: urgent: see **Urgency**

NEEDS-LED ASSESSMENT

The community care **duty** of **assessment** is divided into two stages: the assessment of **needs** for **community care services**, followed by the decision as to what services the authority will provide.

(1) Twofold duty. Community care policy **guidance** and practice guidance explain that assessment of need should be separate from decisions about service provision. Indeed, the assessment is meant to be needs-led, so that services can be shaped to meet needs, rather than people's needs determined by whatever services happen to be available locally (DH 1990, SSI/SWSG 1991a).

(2) Assessing for absent services and unmet need. The courts have confirmed that even if an authority happens not to be providing a particular type of community care service at the time, a person's potential need for it must still be assessed (e.g. *Berkshire* case). Indeed, if this were not the case, then there could be no **unmet need** – a concept central to community care guidance.

(3) Unmet need under s.2 of the CSDPA. The conclusion reached by the House of Lords in the *Gloucestershire* case, was that under s.2 of the *CSDPA 1970*, assessment could also influenced by the local authority's **resources**.

Yet this judgment appears to make nonsense of the Department of Health's guidance, which stresses the importance of identifying unmet needs. In effect, if authorities take resources into account in the assessment of needs, there should never be any unmet needs; since needs would only ever be identified to the extent that resources were adequate to meet them. However, the House of Lords stated that resources can be taken into account in deciding about needs, and then about whether it is **necessary** to meet those needs. Therefore, identification of need, followed by a decision that it is not necessary to meet that need, could result in legally permissible unmet needs under s.2 of the *CSDPA 1970*.

(4) How to meet needs: cost considerations. A practical reason for separating needs from services under s.2 of the *CSDPA 1970*, is that once a local authority has accepted that it is necessary for it to meet a person's needs, it must do so (see: the *Gloucestershire* case). Therefore, how those needs are expressed has a considerable impact in terms of cost. For instance, in the *Lancashire* case, the court ruled that it was lawful for the authority to meet a person's needs by arranging **nursing home** care because the needs had been expressed as '24-hour care'. Had they been expressed as '24-hour care in the person's own home', then the authority would not have had the option of arranging nursing home care.

(5) Distinguishing needs from services in practice. In practice, the distinction between needs and service options is not always obvious from local authorities' **procedures** and **record-keeping**. Therefore, faced with a lack of (clarity in the) records, a court might itself have to distinguish between the two, finding – for example, in the *Goldsack* case – that 'walking assistance' was not itself the need, but one service option for meeting the mobility need generally. In the *Daykin* case, the judge found that a stairlift did not constitute the need, but was merely one way of meeting the need for access to and from a dwelling.

So, for instance, in assessing a person who is having difficulty washing, an authority might act defensively by assessing the need generally as 'personal care requirements including washing and toileting'. Various options to meet the need might then be identified, including a strip wash once a week, commode, stairlift or downstairs extension. The costs of these different options might vary enormously, but the authority could choose a cheaper option, so long as the assessed need were still met and the decision was not legally **unreasonable.**

Quite apart from the legal and financial advantages of setting out a range of options discrete from assessed need, such an approach accords also with professional good practice: i.e. considering how to meet a person's needs in a number of different ways, in order to identify the most appropriate solution (which is not always the most expensive).

NEGLIGENCE

Unlike **judicial review** which is a **public law** process, negligence actions are part of **private law** and involve people seeking **damages** in compensation for a personal wrong done to them. A finding of negligence involves identification of a *duty of care, breach* of that duty and *harm done in consequence* of the breach. Within the context of social services departments, the issue of negligence is somewhat confused; this contrasts with the health-care field, where negligence is well-established in relation to doctors, **nurses, therapists** and other staff.

(1) Duty of care independent of policy and statutory functions. Where the courts find that a common law duty of care exists independently of the statutory functions (i.e. the legislation) and **policies** under which local authorities and their staff are working, then they might in some circumstances consider that a duty of care exists (and that there might be liability in negligence). For instance, careless installation of a grab rail by a local authority's handyman, or the careless dropping of an elderly person by a personal care assistant, might amount to negligence (see e.g. *Vicar of Writtle, Enfield* and *Essex* cases, and comments in *Wyatt* case).

(2) Reluctance to impose a duty of care. On the other hand, if a court feels that to impose a duty of care would be to interfere with the local authority's statutory functions and policies, then it will not do so: for instance, if an allegation relates to whether an appropriate level of service was provided for a person's needs. And, for example, the courts have held that the failure to allocate a suitable social worker, to make proper investigations and to remove **children** at risk do not necessarily involve policy and statutory functions, but might do in some circumstances. However, the courts have gone further still in demonstrating their reluctance to impose liability on local authorities in respect of their social services functions. Even if the alleged negligence relates neither to statutory functions nor policy, nevertheless it might still be neither just nor **reasonable** to impose a duty of care on the local authority either directly or vicariously (i.e. in respect of its **social workers** (*Bedfordshire* case).

■ NEWCASTLE CASE

A case illustrating conflict between local authorities and the private sector over contracts for **residential** and **nursing home** care.

The case was brought by the Newcastle Association of Care Homes in protest at the local authority's standard form of agreement. The objection was that the contract terms went beyond the statutory requirements laid down in the *Registered Homes Act 1984*, with which home owners must comply. The court held that the authority had not behaved **unreasonably** by imposing a stricter contractual regime (when fulfilling its **duty** under the *National Assistance Act 1948*) than that provided by the 1984 Act.

■ NHS: SERVICES FOR RESIDENTS OF HOMES

Local authorities have a **duty** to **make arrangements** to enable people in **residential accommodation** to obtain the benefit of NHS services (Direction under *National Assistance Act 1948*, s.21).

■ NHS ACT 1977

The Act contains **duties** and **powers** not just in respect of the NHS but also local authorities **(social services functions)**.

NHS Act 1977 (Part 1, ss.1,3): health services etc. The provision of services by the NHS is governed by vague **duties** imposed on the Secretary of State (the s.3 duties are exercised by health authorities under SI 1996/708).

(1) Comprehensive health service. The Secretary of State has a duty 'to continue the promotion in England and Wales of a **comprehensive health service** designed to secure improvement (a) in the **physical** and **mental health** of the people of those countries, and (b) in the **prevention** of, **diagnosis** and **treatment** of **illness**, and for that purpose to provide or secure the effective provision of services in accordance with this Act' (s.1).

(2) **Reasonable requirements etc.** The Secretary of State has a duty to provide throughout England and Wales 'to such extent as he **considers necessary** to meet all **reasonable requirements**' various services including: (a) **medical, dental** and **nursing** and ambulance services; (b) **hospital** or other **accommodation**; (c) other facilities for **expectant** and nursing mothers and young **children**; and (d) 'such facilities for the prevention of **illness**, the care of persons suffering from illness and the **after-care** of persons who have suffered from illness as he considers are **appropriate** as part of the health service' (s.3). **Guidance** relating to **continuing care** provided by the NHS has been issued (HSG(95)8, and HSG(95)39).

NHS Act 1977 (Part 2): general medical services (general practitioners). Health authorities have a duty to ensure that general medical services are provided in their area through **general practitioners. Regulations** govern terms and conditions of service (SI 1992/635). See also: **General practitioners: fundholding**

NHS Act 1977: home help and laundry facilities (schedule 8). Local authorities have a **duty**:

> 'to provide on such a scale as is adequate for the needs of their area, or to **arrange** for the provision on such a scale as is so adequate, of **home help** for households where such help is **required** owing to the presence of...a person who is suffering from **illness**, lying-in, an **expectant mother**, **aged, handicapped** as a result of having suffered from illness or by **congenital deformity**...and every such authority has *power* to provide or arrange for the provision of **laundry facilities** for households for which home help is being, or can be, provided...'

NHS Act 1977: illness (schedule 8). Local authorities have a **duty** so far as directed – and the **power** so far as approved – by the Secretary of State, to **make arrangements** for the prevention of **illness**, the care of people who are ill, and the **after-care** of people who have been ill.

(1) **Directions and Approvals. Directions and Approvals** have been issued under Circular LAC(93)10 and are as follows:

(2) **Powers.** Local authorities have the power to make arrangements generally. In particular, they have the power to make arrangements for the provision of centres or other facilities for **training** or keeping people suitably **occupied**, for the equipage and maintenance of such centres, and for the provision for those people of ancillary or supplemental services.

Local authorities also have the power to make arrangements for the provision of **meals** at centres and at other facilities, and meals-on-wheels for housebound people not already provided for under other **legislation** (i.e. under s.45 of the *Health Services and Public Health Act 1968*, or schedule 9 of the *HASSASA* 1983); for the **remuneration** of people engaged in suitable work at centres or at other facilities; for the provision of social services (including **advice** and **support**) in order to prevent the **impairment** of **physical** or **mental health** of adults in **families** where such impairment is likely, or to prevent the break-up of such families, or for assisting in their **rehabilitation**. There is also a power to make arrangements for the provision of **night-sitter services; recuperative holidays;** facilities for **social** and **recreational activities;** services specifically for **alcoholic or drug-dependent people.**

(3) **Duties.** Local authorities have certain duties for the purpose of preventing **mental disorder**, or in relation to people who are, or have been, suffering from mental disorder. These duties are to make arrangements for the provision of centres (including **training** centres and **day centres**) for the training or occupation of such people; for the appointment of sufficient **approved social workers;** for the exercise of their functions towards people received into **guardianship** under Part 2 or 3 of the *Mental Health Act 1983*; for the provision of **social work and related services (a) to help in the identification, diagnosis, assessment** and **social treatment** of mental disorder, and (b) to provide **social work support** and other **domiciliary** and care services to people living in their homes or elsewhere.

NHS AND COMMUNITY CARE ACT 1990

This Act supplies the key to gaining **community care services** by erecting a gateway of **assessment** through which people have to pass. It also places various **duties** on authorities in relation to **community care plans**. Guidance relating to assessment includes *Community Care in the Next Decade and Beyond: Policy Guidance* (DH 1990); *Care Management and Assessment: Practitioners' Guide* (SSI/SWSG 1991a); *Getting the Message Across* (SSI 1991a); *Care Management and Assessment: Managers' Guide* (SSI/SWSG 1991b); *Implementing Caring for People: Assessment* (CI(92)34, now cancelled).

NIGHT-SITTER SERVICES

For the prevention of **illness**, the care of people who are ill, and the **after-care** of people who have been ill, local authorities have the **power** to **make arrangements** for the provision of night-sitter services (Approval under *NHS Act 1977*, schedule 8). In the *Farley* case, the court granted an interim **injunction** against the local authority which had **withdrawn** night-sitter services from a vulnerable, **elderly** woman.

NORTHAVON CASE

This case illustrates the reluctance of the law courts to intervene in matters of **co-operation** between authorities: in this case social services and housing.

Homelessness, Children Act 1989 and co-operation. A housing authority decided that it had no **duty** to secure permanent **accommodation** for a homeless family (because it judged that the **homelessness** was intentional). The social services authority then declined to exercise its **power** to give assistance in cash to the family, as part of its duty to safeguard and promote the welfare of the children under s.17(6) of the *Children Act 1989.* Instead it tried to rely on s.27 of the 1989 Act which stated that it had the power to request the assistance of other authorities, who 'shall comply with the request if it is compatible with their own statutory or other duties and obligations and does not unduly prejudice the discharge of any of their functions'. The housing authority, unsurprisingly, having already assessed the application in the negative, refused to offer long-term accommodation. On the issue of co-operation between authorities, the House of Lords stated that the:

> 'two authorities must co-operate. Judicial review is not the way to obtain co-operation. The court cannot decide what form co-operation should take. Both forms of authority have difficult tasks which are of great importance and for which they may feel their resources are not wholly adequate. The authorities must together do the best they can... In this case the housing authority were entitled to respond to the social services authority as they did.'

NURSING ATTENTION

Local authorities have a **duty** to **make arrangements** to enable people for whom **residential accommodation** has been provided to obtain nursing attention during illnesses which are normally nursed at home (Direction under *National Assistance Act 1948*, s.21).

NURSING CARE: SPECIALIST

Specialist nursing care is an NHS **continuing care** service which, **guidance** explains, people – in **nursing** or **residential homes**, or in their own homes – might **require**, and for which **criteria of eligibility** and **priorities** should be set within available **resources** (HSG(95)8. Such care is provided under the *NHS Act 1977*.

- NURSING EQUIPMENT: SPECIALIST: see **Medical equipment: specialist**

NURSING HOMES

Local authorities have a **duty** to **make arrangements** for the provision of **residential accommodation** (which might include nursing care) – for people in need of **care and attention** because of **age, illness, disability** or any **other circumstances** – which is not **otherwise available** to them. Before making arrangements for the provision of nursing home care, the local authority must obtain the consent of the health authority; except in case of **urgency**, when consent must be sought as soon as practicable after arrangements have been made (*National Assistance Act 1948*, ss.21 and 26). For details of the **powers** and duties to provide residential (including nursing home) accommodation generally, under the *National Assistance Act 1948*, see: **Residential accommodation**

The NHS, too, has the power to provide NHS inpatient care in **accommodation** other than its own hospitals – for example, by funding beds in independent nursing homes. The *NHS Act 1977*, s.3, refers to a **duty** to provide hospital and 'other accommodation' (see also Circular HC(81)1).

Nursing homes: independent sector. The provision of nursing home accommodation by the independent (voluntary or private) sector is governed by the *Registered Homes Act 1984* and by associated **regulations** (SI 1984/1578). This **legislation** covers a variety of matters, including registration and inspection, the fitness of people running the home, **record-keeping**, services and facilities to be provided, criminal offences etc.

Nursing homes: NHS services. Specialist **medical, nursing** or other **community health services** are NHS **continuing care** services which, **guidance** explains, people in nursing homes might **require**, and for which **criteria of eligibility** and **priorities** should be set within available **resources** (HSG(95)8). Such services are provided under the *NHS Act 1977*.

Nursing homes: services generally. There is a grey area between what services nursing homes will provide as part and parcel of the **accommodation**, what services will be provided by the NHS, and what residents or their relatives have to pay extra for themselves. For instance, whilst a nursing home might provide basic **incontinence** pads, it might attempt to **charge** extra, or simply not provide, for a person's special needs (e.g. in terms of type or quality of pad). Such uncertainty make it all the more important for local authorities to draw up carefully and monitor thoroughly their contracts for nursing home care. And, as some nursing homes increasingly come to resemble 'mini-hospitals', so the issue of what **continuing care** – such as specialised **equipment** (e.g. anti-pressure mattresses), **treatment** and **advice** – the NHS will provide also becomes crucial.

■ NURSING SERVICES

The Secretary of State has a **duty**, exercised by health authorities, to provide nursing services 'to such extent as he **considers necessary** to meet all **reasonable requirements**' (*NHS Act 1977*, s.3). The wide **discretion** conferred by this vague duty makes it difficult to enforce in the law courts, as illustrated by the *Hincks* case. Thus, even quite substantial **rationing** of nursing services or **equipment** or materials – such as **incontinence** pads – will not in itself contravene the **legislation**.

■ NURSING TREATMENT: see **Medical and nursing treatment**

■ O'ROURKE CASE

A **homelessness** case involving a claim for **damages** for **breach of statutory duty** in **private law** (rather than a **public law** action via **judicial review**). The case illustrates the extreme reluctance of the courts to consider awarding damages for breaches of health and **welfare** duties imposed by **legislation**. The similar reluctance expressed in the *Wyatt* case in relation to the *CSDPA 1970* was referred to.

(1) **Schemes of social welfare.** The court compellingly explained that the legislation was

> 'a scheme of social welfare, intended to confer benefits at the public expense on grounds of public policy. Public money is spent on housing the homeless not merely for the private benefit of people who find themselves homeless but on grounds of general public interest: because, for example, proper housing means that people will be less likely to suffer illness, turn to crime or require the attention of other social services. The expenditure interacts with expenditure on other public services such as education, the National Health Service and even the police. It is not simply a private matter between the claimant and the housing authority. Accordingly, the fact that Parliament has provided for the expenditure of public money on benefits in kind such as housing the homeless does not necessarily mean that it intended cash payments to be made by way of damages to persons who, in breach of the housing authority's statutory duty, have unfortunately not received the benefits which they should have done.'

(2) **Test for claims in damages for breach of statutory duty.** The court approved the test laid down in the *Bedfordshire* case. This was whether legislation shows an intention to afford a remedy in damages, and 'appears intended for the protection of a limited class of people but provides no other remedy for breach'. In the present case, judicial review was an obvious remedy; furthermore, there were other contra-indications to the existence of a private law remedy. First, the legislation involved social welfare (see immediately above). Second, the duty to provide the **accommodation** was dependent 'a good deal' on the **judgement** of the housing authority. For instance, it had to 'have reason to believe',

and it was 'necessary to **satisfy**' itself. Such **discretion** 'makes it unlikely that Parliament intended errors of judgement to give rise to an obligation to make financial reparation'.

In addition, the court attacked the reasoning in the *Cocks* case that if a housing authority is 'charged with executive functions' (i.e. involving the implementation or execution, rather than the taking, of a decision), then a private law duty automatically arises. Such executive functions are not enough to establish the duty: a 'careful examination of the statutory intent' is still required.

■ OCCUPATIONAL ACTIVITIES

See also **Training**

Occupational activities: adults. Local authorities have a **duty** to **make arrangements** to provide occupational activities for **disabled people** who are **ordinarily resident** within their area. In respect of people who are not ordinarily resident, there is a **power** only (Approval and Direction under *National Assistance Act 1948*, s.29).

Occupational activities: children. For **children in need** who are living with their **families**, local authorities have a **duty** to make what they **consider appropriate** provision for various services including occupational activities (*Children Act 1989*, schedule 2).

■ OCCUPATIONAL THERAPISTS

Occupational therapists (OTs) form a key professional group in community care, albeit one that has rarely received due recognition in the planning and delivery of **community care services**. Too often, OTs have been managerially sidelined in local authorities, despite the Social Services Inspectorate's national report on occupational therapy services which identified the large volume of community care referrals made to OTs. The skills of OTs lie in enabling people – through **advice, instruction, rehabilitation, disability equipment and home adaptations** – to remain in their own homes, the preferred aim of community care as stated by policy **guidance** (DH 1990).

■ **OLD PEOPLE:** see **Elderly people;** also **Age**

■ **OMBUDSMAN:** see **Local ombudsman;** also **Health service ombudsman**

■ ORDINARILY RESIDENT

Whether a person is deemed to be ordinarily resident within the geographical area of a local authority might affect; (a) the extent to which he or she is entitled to **community care services** from a particular local authority; and (b) which authority is liable to pay for any services provided. Unsurprisingly, therefore, the question of ordinary residence sometimes triggers disputes between local authorities.

(1) **Application to various legislation.** The ordinary residence condition converts powers into duties in respect of **residential accommodation** and **welfare services** arranged under the *National Assistance Act 1948*, and governs access to services under s.2 of the *CSDPA 1970*. However, it does not apply to services provided under schedule 8 of the *NHS Act 1977* (**home help, laundry facilities,** services in relation to **illness** etc.), or to services for **elderly people** under the *Health Services and Public Health Act 1968*.

(2) Meaning of term and disputes. Department of Health **guidance** states that the term 'ordinarily resident' 'should be given its ordinary and natural meaning' subject to the decisions of law courts. It explains the procedure for solving disputes via the Secretary of State under s.32(3) of the *National Assistance Act 1948*, and states unequivocally that a dispute about ordinary residence should be debated only after **assessment** and provision of services, not before (LAC(93)7). (This procedure does not apply to s.117 of the *Mental Health Act 1983*: after-care services.) In the *Shah* case, the House of Lords stated that unless **legislation** states otherwise, ordinary residence 'refers to a man's abode in a particular place or country which he has adopted voluntarily and for settled purposes as part of the regular order of his life for the time being, whether of short or of long duration'.

Guidance also states that if an authority places a person in a home within the area of another authority, then the first authority retains responsibility. But if a person has made his or her own arrangements to move to a residential home, or to live with relatives, within the area of another authority – then, when he or she comes to require assistance, the other, second, authority is responsible (LAC(93)10).

ORDINARY NEEDS

A feature of the **policies** of some local authorities is that assistance will not be provided, under s.2 of the *CSDPA 1970*, with items (e.g. **equipment** or other services) that non-disabled people would have to buy for themselves. The reason for such policies – which are often rigid – is obvious, since local authorities wish to avoid **relieving poverty** by, for example, furnishing people's homes from top to bottom.

(1) Example: holidays. The caution with which authorities should adopt such policies was illustrated by the *Hargreaves (no.2)* case, in which the judge ruled that the local authority had unlawfully **fettered its discretion** by refusing to assist a **disabled person** with her holiday under the *CSDPA 1970*. The authority had argued that everybody else has to have a holiday as well, that it was not in the business of generally **relieving poverty**, and that it was empowered only to pay the special (e.g. for special equipment or special accommodation) – but not the ordinary – costs of the holiday.

(2) Example: equipment. For the provision of ordinary, as opposed, to specialist **disability equipment**, under s.2 of the *CSDPA 1970*, see: **Additional facilities**

OTHER CIRCUMSTANCES

'Other circumstances' are one of the reasons – in addition to **age, illness** or **disability** – why, legally, a person might be in need of **care and attention** under s.21 of the *National Assistance Act 1948* and thus be eligible for **residential accommodation**.

Though a vague term, local authorities cannot simply ignore it, since it is of potentially wide application. For example, it was held by the Court of Appeal, in the *Hammersmith and Fulham* case, as being capable of applying to asylum-seekers on the streets and not necessarily limited in meaning by the words preceding it in the Act: age, illness or disability. The 'other circumstances' in this case were that the applicants were without food and accommodation, ignorant of the language, and under the stress of being refugees. The court pointed that even if the term were in fact limited in its meaning by the words preceding it, the circumstances facing the asylum-seekers could nevertheless bring about the illness or disability which would trigger eligibility for assistance: i.e. in relation to the provision of **temporary accommodation** or to the prevention of **illness**.

OTHERWISE AVAILABLE

The duty to **make arrangements** for the provision of **residential accommodation** is only triggered when the **care and attention**, because of **age, illness, disability** or **other circumstances**, is not 'otherwise available' to people. In the *Sefton* case (High Court stage), the judge held that in deciding whether care and attention is otherwise available, the authority should consider whether the physical, mental and financial **resources** of the person are such that he could make his own arrangements – even if the person's resources had dropped below the £16,000 threshold set by **regulations**. However, the Court of Appeal overturned this decision, stating that once the threshold was reached, care and attention could not, as a matter of law, be otherwise available.

OUTINGS: DISABLED PEOPLE

If a person is **disabled** and **ordinarily resident** within the area of a local authority, then the authority has a **duty** to **make arrangements** for the provision of outings if the authority is **satisfied** that it is **necessary** for it to make those arrangements in order to meet the person's **needs** (*CSDPA 1970*, s.2). See: **Holidays**

- **OWNER/TENANT CERTIFICATE:** see **Home adaptations: disabled facilities grants**

OXFORDSHIRE CASE

This case illustrates the **buck-passing** which sometimes takes place between different statutory authorities when, short of **resources**, they attempt to exploit **grey areas** of responsibility. The court held that an education authority was entitled to class **speech therapy** as a non-educational service which it did not have to provide (but which the NHS might), as opposed to a special educational service which it would itself have been obliged to provide. Speech therapy could be classed either way, depending on the circumstances, and therefore the authority's decision was certainly not **irrational**.

PALLIATIVE HEALTH CARE (NHS)

Specialist palliative care is an NHS **continuing care** service which, **guidance** explains, might be **required** by people in **nursing homes**, as well as in **residential homes** or in their own homes, and for which **criteria of eligibility** and **priorities** should be set within available **resources** (HSG(95)8). Such care is provided under the *NHS Act 1977*.

PARLIAMENT

When ruling on the meaning and implications of legislative words and phrases, judges sometimes refer to what '**Parliament** must have intended'.

In some, limited, circumstances where there is a lack of clarity in the **legislation**, the courts are now officially permitted to refer to Hansard (the reports of

Parliamentary proceedings) and to read what was said by government ministers when the relevant Bill was being debated. However, equally, the courts also refer to Parliament's intention without any such evidence, sometimes referring to it simply to reinforce a particular argument. For instance, the disagreement between the judges in the House of Lords in the *Gloucestershire* case appeared to reduce in part to conflicting views about what Parliament 'must' have intended the *CSDPA 1970* to mean – without any reference during the case to what was actually said in Parliament in 1969 and 1970.

■ **PARTICIPATION OF SERVICE USERS:** see **Choice**

■ PARTNERSHIP

A near-synonym, currently in vogue, for **co-operation.**

■ **PASSING THE BUCK:** see **Buck-passing and cost-shunting**

■ PATCHETT CASE

The case (referred to in Craig 1994) is of interest because it was about government Circulars, and some of the comments made are relevant to **guidance** generally, including that relating to community care. It concerned the **delegation**, through a Circular, by the Minister of Health of his **powers** to requisition buildings to town clerks. The judge stated, voicing obvious frustration, that whereas:

> 'ordinary legislation, by passing through both Houses of Parliament…is thus twice blessed, this type of so-called legislation is at least four-times cursed. First, it has seen neither House of Parliament; secondly, it is unpublished and is inaccessible even to those whose valuable rights of property may be affected; thirdly, it is a jumble of provisions, legislative, administrative or directive in character, and sometimes difficult to disentangle one from the other; and, fourthly, it is expressed not in the precise language of an Act of Parliament or an Order of Council but in the more colloquial language of correspondence, which is not always susceptible to the ordinary cannons of construction.'

■ PERSONAL CARE

The *Haringey* case indicates that local authorities should consider not just people's personal care **needs,** but also their social, **recreational** and **leisure** needs.

■ **PERSONAL INFORMATION:** see **Information: personal**

■ **PHYSICAL HEALTH:** see **Health: physical and mental**

■ PHYSIOTHERAPY

Physiotherapy is an NHS **continuing care** service which, **guidance** explains, people – in **nursing** or **residential homes**, or in their own homes – might **require**, and for which **criteria of eligibility** and **priorities** should be set within available **resources** (HSG(95)8). Physiotherapy is provided under the *NHS Act 1977*, and like **occupational therapy** plays a crucial role in **rehabilitation**.

POLICIES

Local authorities inevitably adopt policies, in accordance with which they set **priorities** and **criteria of eligibility**, and deal with the large demands made upon them. Both the law courts in judicial review and the **local ombudsmen** accept that local authorities have to make policies; but both will be vigilant to ensure that these are not excessively **rigid** or of a **blanket** nature. This is because authorities must be able to take account of exceptions and not make up their minds in advance – especially in community care, where so much depends on assessment of **individual needs**. Otherwise they are in danger of **fettering their discretion**.

In addition, of course (quite apart from avoiding fettering their discretion), authorities must ensure that their polices are not **illegal** in the first place. For example, a local authority which refused even to consider assisting **disabled people** with **home adaptations** under s.2 of the *CSDPA 1970* would have adopted a policy in blatant contravention of the wording of the **legislation** (e.g. *Leaman* case).

Formulation, application and representation of policies. An authority might find itself challenged in connection with a policy in at least three different ways, concerning *formulation, application* or *representation*. For instance, if a policy is flawed in its formulation. then it might be illegal. Or, the policy might be formulated legally, but misapplied by frontline staff – who have not had it properly explained, have misunderstood it, or simply been unable to adhere to it, given the pressure of work. Last, the policy might be both formulated and applied lawfully, but a letter – sent to a service user explaining the **reasons** for a particular decision – might be carelessly drafted and misrepresent the policy which has in fact been applied. In this case, although the letter might provoke a challenge, a court of law might look beyond the letter and not find fault with the authority, because the underlying policy and its application was lawful. Nevertheless, authorities will obviously wish to avoid sending misleading letters in the first place.

■ POLICY GUIDANCE: see **Guidance**

POLITICS

The scope of this book does not extend to politics: however, there is clearly a political dimension to community care. One has only to consider the remarks, critical of **central government**, made by Lord Lloyd at the House of Lords stage of the *Gloucestershire* case.

POWER (ENERGY)

Facilitating the use of a source of power by a **disabled occupant** is one of the statutory purposes for which a housing authority has a **duty** to approve an application for a **disabled facilities grant** – assuming various other conditions are also met (*Housing Grants, Construction and Regeneration Act 1996*, s.23).

POWER (LEGAL)

A power given to authorities in **legislation** should be distinguished from a **duty**. Powers – usually identified in legislation by the word **'may'** – *permit* but do not *oblige* authorities to act, whilst duties impose obligations. For example, local authorities have a power to – i.e. they may – provide **home adaptations** for **elderly people** (*Health Services and Public Health Act 1968*, s.45) or home repair assistance (*Housing Grants, Construction and Regeneration Act 1996*, s.76), but have a **duty** – i.e. they must – provide them for **disabled people** under certain circumstances (*CSDPA 1970*, s.2).

Clearly, it will be very much easier for local authorities to limit their spending in respect of powers than of duties. Nevertheless, even in the case of some powers, authorities should beware of **fettering their discretion** by the adoption of excessively **rigid policies**.

PRACTICAL ASSISTANCE IN THE HOME

In order to save money, local authorities have tended to reduce steadily practical assistance in the form of 'non-essential' housekeeping and cleaning services, and to concentrate more on **personal care** services (e.g. help with **bathing**, eating, physical transfers). For example, in the *Gloucestershire* case, one of the original applicants had been originally receiving **cleaning, laundry, shopping** and **meals** services: the authority then **withdrew** the cleaning service and reduced the laundry provision.

Although the House of Lords has ruled that **resources** can be a factor in determining, under the *CSDPA 1970*, both a person's **needs** and whether it is **necessary** to meet them, authorities should beware of imposing blanket policies about practical assistance in the home. This is because: (a) **assessment** is of the individual person and not a class of people; and (b) authorities must beware of **fettering their discretion**. For example, a **rigid policy** might result in cleaning services being withdrawn from, or denied to, a man with double **incontinence** and diabetes – conditions necessitating rigorous standards of hygiene. This could not only put him medically at risk but cause him acute psychological distress as well, and scarcely amounts to a genuine exercise of **discretion** directed towards **individual needs**. See also: **Home help**

Practical assistance in the home: disabled people. If a person is **disabled** and **ordinarily resident** within the area of a local authority, then the authority has a **duty** to **make arrangements** for the provision of practical assistance in the home if the authority is **satisfied** that it is **necessary** for it to make those arrangements in order to meet the person's **needs** (*CSDPA 1970*, s.2).

Practical assistance in the home: elderly people. In order to meet the **needs** of **elderly people**, local authorities have the **power** to **make arrangements** to provide practical assistance in the home, including assistance in the carrying out of works of **adaptation** or the provision of any **additional facilities** designed to secure greater **safety, comfort** or **convenience** (Approval under *Health Services and Public Health Act 1968*, s.45).

PRACTICE GUIDANCE: see **Guidance**

PRECEDENTS

Precedents: non-judicial. Local authorities are often anxious that setting local precedents will open the **floodgates**: for example, when provision of a particular service for one or two people will lead to many others **expecting**

or demanding the same thing. Anxiety gives rise to defensive practices, to vagueness in published **information** about **criteria of eligibility**, and even to potentially **unlawful** policies.

Precedents: the law courts. When the law courts make a ruling, they set a precedent – i.e. a rule which must subsequently be followed. This facilitates greater certainty and consistency in the law. However, precedent goes only so far toward such certainty and does not overcome the lack of **predictability** of the outcomes of cases. First, it is not always clear which particular words in a judgment form the precedent. Second, it can be difficult to work out which situations and disputes actually come within the precedent in practice. Third, judges sometimes find ways of not following a precedent – if they feel that it would be unjust to do so – by 'distinguishing' the case in front of them from the previous case which set the precedent in the first place.

For instance, two recent decisions in education law both went against local authorities which had been attempting to introduce **resources** as a factor in the assessment of **children's** educational **needs**. Both judges cited the *Gloucestershire* case. However, in the earlier case, the judge followed the still extant Court of Appeal decision, which had outlawed resources as a factor in assessing needs (*Hillingdon* case). But by the time of the later case (*East Sussex*: High Court stage), the House of Lords had overturned the Court of Appeal's decision in the *Gloucestershire* case, and so allowed resources into the picture. Yet the judge in this later case still managed to exclude resources, by stating that the House of Lords judgment did not apply because the education legislation was significantly different from the *CSDPA 1970* (in fact the High Court decision in the *East Sussex* case was subsequently overturned by the Court of Appeal).

■ PREDICTABILITY OF LAW

The outcome of **judicial review** court cases is unpredictable for a number of reasons, including the uncertain and confusing nature of some of the community care **legislation** and **guidance**, the unique circumstances of each case, and the ability of judges to depart from, as well as to follow, **precedent**. This unpredictability was illustrated by the marked judicial disagreement evident at the different stages of the *Gloucestershire* case, when, overall, six judges thought **resources** could be a factor in assessing **disabled people's** needs, and four thought not. See also: **Law: knowledge of**; and **Right answers**

■ PREFERENCES

The term 'preferences' is used by Department of Health **guidance** to contrast a person's **need**, which triggers a statutory obligation, with a **preference**, which does not. The distinction was particularly emphasised in a Circular – now cancelled – sent out to local authorities at the end of 1992 (CI(92)34). The issue can become a sensitive one when, for example, **disabled people** wishing to lead their lives independently, are told that their aspirations amount to preferences rather than needs.

At least two court cases demonstrate how authorities can go legally astray in relation to people's preferences. In the *Hargreaves* case, the court found that the authority was in breach of its **statutory duty** by failing to ascertain the preferences of a service user even though it had **consulted** her brother (who was also her carer). And in the *Avon* case, the court held that the preferences of a young man with learning disabilities amounted to a **psychological need**, which it was the **duty** of the authority to meet. See also: **Choice**

PREPARATION AND COOKING OF FOOD

Facilitating the preparation and cooking of food by a **disabled occupant** is one of the statutory purposes for which a housing authority has a **duty** to approve an application for a **disabled facilities grant**, assuming various other conditions are also met (*Housing Grants, Construction and Regeneration Act 1996*, s.23).

PREVENTION OF ILLNESS: see **Illness**

PRIMARY HEALTH CARE

Primary health care is a term used generally to refer to 'first line' community services provided by, for example, NHS professionals such as **general practitioners**, practice nurses, community/district nurses, health visitors, midwives, optometrists, community-based **therapists**, community dentists, and community pharmacists. Primary health care provided by the NHS is not legally part of the community care framework. Nevertheless, community care policy **guidance** makes it quite clear that effective primary care services are essential to the success of community care.

Primary health care is listed in **guidance** as an NHS **continuing care** service, for which **priorities** and **criteria of eligibility** should be set within available **resources** (HSG(95)8), and is provided under the *NHS Act 1977*.

PRINCIPAL FAMILY ROOM

Facilitating access by a **disabled occupant** to a room used or usable as the principal family room is one of the statutory purposes for which a housing authority has a **duty** to approve an application for a **disabled facilities grant**, assuming other conditions are also met (*Housing Grants, Construction and Regeneration Act 1996*, s.23).

PRIORITIES

Priorities in community care are closely related to **policies, criteria of eligibility** and **waiting times**. Priorities can sometimes be distinguished from eligibility criteria in that the former might determine how quickly people receive **assessments** or services, and the latter whether they receive them at all. However, priorities, like eligibility criteria, might also have the effect of total exclusion; for example, some local authority policies state that those people deemed to be a lower priority might never be assessed or provided with services.

As with policies and criteria of eligibility, local authorities should ensure that their priorities do not lead to **rigid policies** and a **fettering of discretion**, and do not lapse into **illegality**. In addition, as the **local ombudsman** has pointed out on a number of occasions, the allocation of priority to individual people should be based on adequate **referral** information (otherwise how can priority properly be allocated in the first place?).

■ **PRIVATE LAW:** see **Public law**

■ PROCEDURES

If local authorities wish to maximise the effectiveness of services to clients, and to minimise challenges through **complaints**, the **local ombudsman** or **judicial review**, then sound procedures are required. The absence of effective procedures can lead to, for example, poor **communication** with service users, a typical ground on which the local ombudsman might find **maladministration**. Furthermore, poor procedures might well be associated with a low standard of **record-keeping**. The situation will be made worse if, in addition to their poor implementation, the procedures do not even reflect underlying **legislation**; in which case it will be difficult for an authority to argue its case in **judicial review**.

■ **PROFESSIONAL JUDGEMENT:** see **Judgement**

■ PSYCHOLOGICAL NEED

In the *Avon* case, involving a young man with learning disabilities, the court held that his entrenched **preference** for particular **residential accommodation** amounted to a psychological **need**, which the local authority was obliged to meet. This case shows that, depending on individual circumstances, need can take various forms and is not simply physical. See **Needs: multi-faceted**

■ **PUBLIC HOUSING ALLOCATION:** see **Housing allocation**

■ PUBLIC LAW

Cases of **judicial review** are public law matters, and are primarily about the supervision of public bodies. In contrast, **private law** is used to enforce individual rights when, for example, **negligence** or **breach of statutory duty** are in issue.

■ PUBLICITY

In some instances, publicity rather than the **law**, might determine the outcome of disputes. Raising matters with local councillors, MPs or local newspapers puts pressure on local authorities to resolve matters. Nevertheless, local authorities should be wary of giving in to those who are **shouting loudest** or allowing **queue-jumping**; these could potentially land the authority in trouble with the **local ombudsman**.

Even so, adverse publicity only assists service users so far, if there really are no extra **resources**. For instance, the *Gloucestershire* case was fought right up to the House of Lords. And, although most local authorities comply with the recommendations of the local ombudsman, some do not – despite the sanction of having to publish a statement about the situation in the local newspaper. See: **Information**

■ **QUALIFIED DUTY:** see **Duty**

QUINN CASE

This was a case about **buck-passing and cost-shunting**. Essentially, it was a dispute between local and **central government** as to which would provide support out of public funds for people in **residential accommodation**. The particular residential home involved had originally been managed by the local authority under Part 3 of the *National Assistance Act 1948*, but had since been transferred by the authority to a voluntary organisation. The court held that since the transfer arrangements did not contain a provision satisfying s.26 of the 1948 Act – under which local authorities must pay the independent provider of residential accommodation at an agreed rate – the authority could not have been **making arrangements** under s.26. Therefore, higher rates of income support were payable to the relevant residents from central government (i.e. the Department of Social Security).

RADIO: see **Wireless**

RATE-CAPPING

Rate-capping is the system whereby **central government** imposes penalties, effectively to prevent local authorities raising money locally beyond a certain level. This system was identified by one of the dissenting judges at the House of Lords stage of the *Gloucestershire* case, as one of the reasons why the local authority was in a 'truly impossible' position and unable to carry out its **statutory duty** to meet the **needs** of **disabled people**.

RATIONING

Rationing is an emotive word, generally avoided by **central government**, local authorities and health authorities. It has always been present within the welfare state, but its scale and public profile seem to have grown in the last few years. Despite this, misconceptions and confusion remain. For instance, health authorities tend to announce that they are rationing services such as tattoo operations and fertility treatments, as though this were a new, ground-breaking phenomenon. Somehow forgotten or passed over is the silent rationing, in place for many years, of items such as **incontinence** pads, wheelchairs and **communication aids**. See also: **Criteria of eligibility; Policies; Priorities;** and **Resources**

RE J CASE

This case illustrates the reluctance of the law courts to overrule the **clinical judgement** of the medical profession. The High Court had ordered a health authority to administer various treatment including artificial ventilation to a severely handicapped baby. The Court of Appeal overturned the decision stating that it could 'envisage no circumstances in which it would be right directly or indirectly to require a doctor to treat a patient in a way that was contrary to the doctor's professional judgement and duty to the patient'.

REASONABLE

The word 'reasonable' is of fundamental importance in law, occurring regularly in **legislation**. It tends to give local authorities a certain amount of leeway within which to take decisions. In addition, **unreasonableness** is one of the key (common law) conceptual tools which the judges use in **judicial review**.

Reasonable: and practicable (disabled facilities grants). A housing authority must be **satisfied**, before approving an application for **disabled facilities grants**, that the proposed works are 'reasonable and practicable...**having regard to**' the age and condition of the dwelling, and must take into account whether the dwelling is fit for human habitation (*Housing Grants, Construction and Regeneration Act 1996*, s.24).

Reasonable: charges for non-residential services. Local authorities have the **power** to make reasonable **charges** for non-residential **community care services**, which are **reasonably practicable** for the person to pay (see *Hooper* case).

Reasonable: requirements (NHS). To 'such extent as he **considers necessary** to meet all reasonable **requirements**', the Secretary of State has a **duty**, **delegated** to health authorities – to provide various NHS services (*NHS Act 1977*, s.3). The overall duty is difficult to enforce in the law courts because of the wide **discretion** it confers: see, for example, the *Cambridge* and *Hincks* cases.

Reasonably practicable. Local authorities have the **power** to make reasonable charges for non-residential **community care services** under s.17 of the *HASSASSA 1983*, s.17, which it is 'reasonably practicable' for the person to pay. And, under the *Manual Handling Operations Regulations 1992*, employers have a duty, 'so far as is reasonably practicable' to avoid the need for employees to undertake **lifting and handling** which involve a risk of injury (SI 1992/2793).

So what does reasonably practicable mean? It is a term used frequently in **health and safety legislation**, and it imposes a less onerous duty than either 'practicable' alone, or 'physically possible' would. For instance, an employer might have to weigh up the degree of risk against the cost of implementing safety measures. At an extreme, if substantial cost were entailed in eliminating a remote risk, it might not be reasonably practicable to implement the measures.

REASONS

Sometimes a **duty** is imposed on local authorities to give reasons to service users for decisions by **legislation**. For example, under s.34 of the *Housing Grants, Construction and Regeneration Act 1996*, housing authorities have a duty to give reasons for refusal of applications for grants, including **disabled facilities grants**. Where legislation does not require reasons, the courts sometimes impose a common law duty to give them, and sometimes not: it depends on the context.

(1) **Community care.** In the community care context, legislation does not impose a duty on local authorities to give reasons for decisions. Indeed, s.3 of the *Disabled Persons (Services,*

Consultation and Representation) Act 1986, which would do so, has not been brought into force.

(2) NHS. In the NHS context, when a health authority denied lifesaving treatment to a child in the *Cambridge* case, the Court of Appeal ruled that the health authority could not be criticised for failing to explain the priorities underlying the decision, and that it would be 'totally unrealistic' to require the authority to provide details of its financial affairs in justification. The court was therefore saying that the authority did not have to furnish this type of reasoning, either to the court itself or to a service user.

(3) Recording reasons. Nevertheless, authorities generally should, as a matter of good practice, formulate and **record** their reasons for decisions, even if they do not necessarily give these to service users. This is so that if they are later challenged in **judicial review** on other grounds (e.g. **unreasonableness** or **illegality**), they are able to demonstrate to a law court that the decision-making process was lawful.

■ REASSESSMENT

The basis in community care **legislation** for reassessment is the same as for **assessment**: s.47 of the *NHS and Community Care Act 1990*. It is sometimes suggested that s.12 of the Interpretation Act 1978 should be cited in justification of reassessment, since it allows **powers** or **duties** to be exercised or performed from time to time.

The practical usefulness of reassessment is essentially twofold. First, it can take account of the changing **needs** of service users for different or more services, and is therefore professional **good practice**. Second, it has financial usefulness, in that a local authority can vary provision of services following reassessment – not only because of a change in the needs of service users, but also because of a change in the authority's own **policy** and **criteria of eligibility.**

In other words, even if a service user's circumstances are unchanged, his or her services might be **withdrawn** or reduced because the authority has judged that, in the light of a new policy, he or she is no longer eligible for the same level of services. This has excited some controversy, but was always envisaged in community care **guidance** (SSI/SWSG 1991a) and has been confirmed in the *Gloucestershire* case. Thus, a decrease in **resources** and a consequent raising of the threshold of need can affect adversely not only new applicants for services, but also – following reassessment – existing users. Thus it is that reassessments, made according to new policies and criteria of eligibility based on diminishing resources, lead to court cases such as *Gloucestershire, Haringey, Bucke, Farley* and *East Sussex.*

Another aspect of the *Gloucestershire* judgment (see especially the High Court stage) – that individual reassessment is necessary before services are reduced or withdrawn – was delivered in the context of s.2 of the *CSDPA 1970*. However, given that guidance envisages reassessment for all **community care services**, the courts might well apply the principle beyond the *CSDPA* to other community care legislation also. In any case, users of services could argue that reassessment is necessary to satisfy the principles of **legitimate expectation** and **consultation**.

RECORD-KEEPING

Good record-keeping is an essential consideration for local authorities, so that when they are challenged – as is increasingly likely – they are able to demonstrate that decisions were not taken **unlawfully** or with **maladministration**.

For example, poor record-keeping might make it difficult for the local authority to demonstrate that it has carried out a community care **assessment** either at all, or properly. In the *Goldsack* case, the judge pointed out that the 'assessment of...needs and the decisions taken about the need for arrangements to provide for them were not formally recorded. It cannot even be said with any certainty when the assessment was completed'.

Furthermore, defensive record-keeping can easily become poor record-keeping. For instance, legal advice to local authority staff not to record, or even not to tell **disabled people**, that assessment is being carried out under the *CSDPA 1970* – because challenges are easier when that **legislation** is involved – is surely dubious. First, it explicitly breaches s.47 of the *NHS and Community Care 1990* which states that if a person is disabled, he or she should be assessed for services under *CSDPA 1970*, and be *told what is happening and about his or her rights.* Second, it renders the authority's decision-making opaque and difficult to defend against any challenge.

- **RECOVERY:** see **Rehabilitation and recovery**

RECREATION

Recreational activities: children. For **children in need** who are living with their **families**, local authorities have a **duty** to make 'such provision as they **consider appropriate**' for various services including recreational activities (*Children Act 1989*, schedule 2).

Recreational activities: disabled people (adults). Local authorities have a **duty** to **make arrangements** for the provision of facilities for recreational activities for **disabled people** who are **ordinarily resident** in the area. In respect of people not ordinarily resident, the duty becomes only a **power** (Direction and Approval under *National Assistance Act 1948*, s.29).

In addition, if a disabled person is ordinarily resident in the area, then the authority has a **duty** to make arrangements for the provision of, or assistance to the person in obtaining, **wireless, television, library** or similar recreational facilities, or for the provision of **lectures, games, outings** or other recreational activities outside the person's home. However, before making the arrangements, the authority must be **satisfied** that it is **necessary** to make those arrangements in order to meet the person's **needs** (*CSDPA 1970*, s.2).

Recreation: elderly people. In order to meet the **needs** of **elderly people**, local authorities have the **power** to **make arrangements** to provide recreation in people's own homes and elsewhere (Approval under *Health Services and Public Health Act 1968*, s.45). In addition, district councils have the power to make arrangements for providing recreation for elderly people in their own homes or elsewhere (*HASSASSA 1983*, schedule 9).

Recreation: illness. For the prevention of **illness**, the care of people who are ill, and the **after-care** of people who have been ill, local authorities have the **power** to **make arrangements** for the provision of facilities for recreational activities (Approval under *NHS Act 1977*, schedule 8).

REDBRIDGE CASE

This was a dispute about **ordinary residence**. It concerned two autistic twins with **learning disabilities**, whose parental home had been in Redbridge, who attended a residential Rudolf Steiner school in East Sussex, and whose parents then sold their house in Redbridge and returned to Nigeria. The imminent closure of the school then sparked the dispute between the two councils about which would be responsible for **making arrangements** for the provision of **residential accommodation** under s.21 of the *National Assistance Act 1948*.

The judge, referring to the *Shah* case, found that the parents' departure and sale of the family home meant that the twins had ceased to be ordinarily resident in Redbridge, and that the **duty** to make provision fell to East Sussex.

REDEZEUS CASE

This case affords an example of what can happen if a local authority makes a decision on the basis of a policy falling 'outside the council's statutory powers': i.e. an instance of **illegality**.

It concerned the award of **renovation grants** under the *Local Government and Housing Act 1989*. The relevant parts (now superseded) of the Act clearly listed the specific and exclusive factors authorities should take into account when deciding how much grant to give. However, the authority had added its own rule that effectively limited the maximum grant payable to 20 per cent of the total cost of the works. The judge found nothing in the Act which gave the council a discretion 'to impose some arbitrary limit on the amount payable or to take account of financial resources or their absence'.

REFERRAL

The quality of referral information is crucial if local authorities are successfully to allocate **priorities** when deciding whom to assess, how quickly and at what level. The **local ombudsman** has sometimes criticised the quality of such information. See also: **Criteria of eligibility; Priorities; Screening**

REGISTERED HOMES ACT 1984

Governs a variety of matters, including registration and **inspection** of **residential accommodation**, in terms of both **residential** and **nursing home** care. Further detail is provided by associated regulations (SI 1984/1345 and SI 1984/1578).

- REGISTERED SOCIAL LANDLORDS: see **Housing associations**

REGISTERS OF DISABLED PEOPLE

Local authorities have a **duty** to keep registers of **disabled people**, although registration is not stated to be a pre-condition for the receipt of services (direction under *National Assistance 1948*, s.29). **Guidance** reinforces the point by explaining that registrability (rather than registration) is the condition that must be met (LAC(93)10). Local authorities also have a duty keep registers of **disabled children** (*Children Act 1989*, schedule 2).

REGULATIONS

Regulations, otherwise called statutory instruments, are secondary **legislation** and are made under Acts of Parliament (which are primary legislation). For instance, the details of the statutory **charging** scheme for **residential accommodation**, and of the rules governing community care **direct payments**, are contained in regulations.

REHABILITATION

Rehabilitation is, or at least should be, an important aspect of community care, since it assists people either to regain – or at least to develop compensatory – physical and mental functions. Timely rehabilitation can be crucial. For instance, following a cerebro-vascular accident (stroke), there is sometimes a window of opportunity when timely treatment provided by **therapists** determines whether people regain physical and functional abilities and return to their own homes, or whether they are consigned instead to **residential** or **nursing homes**.

Rehabilitation: disabled people. Local authorities have a **duty** to provide, for **disabled people** who are **ordinarily resident** in their area, facilities – at centres or elsewhere – for **social rehabilitation** and **adjustment to disability**, including assistance in overcoming **mobility** or **communication** limitations. For people who are not ordinarily resident, the duty becomes a **power** only (Direction and Approval under *National Assistance 1948*, s.29).

Rehabilitation: illness. For the prevention of **illness**, the care of people who are ill, and the **after-care** of people who have been ill, local authorities have the **power** to **make arrangements** to provide social services – including support and advice – to prevent the **impairment** of physical or mental **health** of adults in **families** where such impairment is likely, or to prevent the break-up of such families, or for assisting in their rehabilitation (Approval under *NHS Act 1977*, schedule 8).

Rehabilitation: and recovery (NHS). Rehabilitation and recovery are listed in **guidance** as NHS **continuing care** services, for which **criteria of eligibility** and **priorities** should be set within available **resources** (HSG(95)8). Such services are provided under the *NHS Act 1977*.

RELEVANT FACTORS

Just as authorities must exclude **irrelevant factors** from their decision-making, so they must include those which are relevant if they are to avoid **judicial review** by the law courts.

For instance, in the *Carroll* case, the housing authority's failure to consider social welfare and housing factors, in addition to the **medical opinion** obtained, meant that the final decision was flawed. The *Gloucestershire* case was about whether

resources were a relevant factor to take into account when local authorities **assessed** both people's **needs** and the **necessity** to meet them; and, in the *Bexley* case, the failure of the local authority to consider provision of assistance under the *CSDPA 1970*, s.2 – something it clearly had a duty to do – meant that it failed to take into account a 'material consideration' (i.e. a relevant one).

■ RELIEF OF POVERTY

Short of **resources**, and disturbed that social services **legislation** is sometimes viewed as a **safety net**, local authorities sometimes seek an **escape route** by arguing that their role is not the relief of poverty. Nevertheless, this argument failed in both (a) the *Hammersmith and Fulham* case concerning **residential accommodation** for asylum-seekers under s.21 of the *National Assistance Act 1948*; and (b) the *Hargreaves (no.2)* case about assisting a **disabled person** with **holiday** costs under s.2 of the *CSDPA 1970*. This was because in neither case was the assistance being requested simply a matter of relieving poverty.

■ REMOVING PEOPLE

In limited circumstances, local authorities have the power to remove people from their homes by obtaining a court order.

The circumstances are, basically; (a) if a person is suffering from a 'grave, chronic disease, or being **aged**, infirm or physically incapacitated' is living in insanitary conditions and cannot devote to himself or herself, and is not receiving from anybody else, proper **care and attention**; and (b) if the appropriate medical officer confirms that it is **necessary** that the person be removed (*National Assistance Act 1948*, s.47).

■ REMUNERATION: ILLNESS

For the prevention of **illness**, the care of people who are ill, and the **after-care** of people who have been ill, local authorities have the **power** to **make arrangements** for remuneration of people engaged in suitable work at centres or at other facilities (Approval under *NHS Act 1977*, schedule 8).

■ RENOVATION GRANTS

Housing authorities have a **power**, subject to various conditions being met, to award renovation grants for the improvement or repair of a dwelling, or for the provision of dwellings by conversion of a house or other building (*Housing Grants, Construction and Regeneration Act 1996*, s.12).

Prior to December 1996 (under the *Local Government and Housing Act 1989*), some renovation grants were **mandatory** (where fitness for habitation was in issue): this led to considerable problems in some areas where the demand for such grants far outstripped the **resources** available, because of limited **central government** funding and **rate-capping** rules. In some investigations, the **local ombudsman** has been reduced to criticising central government – in similar vein to one of the judges in the *Gloucestershire* case – for denying local authorities adequate resources with which to perform their **statutory duty**.

■ REPAIR (OF A DWELLING)

Repair is one of the purposes for which housing authorities have the **power** to provide **home repair assistance** (*Housing Grants, Construction and Regeneration Act 1996*, s.76).

■ REQUIREMENTS (NHS)

To 'such extent as he **considers necessary** to meet all **reasonable** requirements', the Secretary of State has a **duty**, exercised by **health authorities, to provide various NHS services** (*NHS Act 1977*, s.3). The overall duty is difficult to enforce in the law courts because of the wide **discretion** it confers, as illustrated by the *Hincks* case. See: **Clinical need**

■ REQUISITES: see **Residential accommodation: board etc.**

■ RESIDENTIAL ACCOMMODATION

Local authorities have both **powers** and **duties** to **make arrangements** for providing **residential accommodation** for 'persons aged 18 or over who by reason of **age, illness, disability** or any **other circumstances** are in need of **care and attention** which is not **otherwise available** to them' (Directions and Approvals under the *National Assistance Act 1948*, s.21).

(1) **Directions and Approvals.** The exercise of these powers and duties is dependent on **Directions** and **Approvals** made by the Secretary of State. These are contained in Circular LAC(93)10.

(2) **Duties.** Local authorities have a **duty** to make arrangements for residential accommodation for people in need (see immediately above) who are **ordinarily resident** within the area or who are in **urgent need**. In addition to this main duty, further duties are imposed to make arrangements for provision (a) for people who have an unforeseen, urgent need for **temporary accommodation**; or (b) for people who are, or have been, suffering from **mental disorder** (or in order to prevent mental disorder), and who are either ordinary residents in the authority's area or have no **settled residence**.

Authorities also have a duty to make arrangements in relation to the **welfare** of residents, supervision of **hygiene** of the accommodation, access to **medical attention, nursing attention,** access to **NHS services**, provision of **board** and other **necessary** services, **amenities** and **requisites** (except where the authority managing the premises believes their provision is not necessary), **review** of provision, and the making of improvements considered necessary. Authorities also remain under a duty to continue to make arrangements to provide accommodation for residents of what were local authority homes but which have been transferred to voluntary organisation management.

(3) **Powers.** Powers are conferred on local authorities to make arrangements for residential accommodation for people who have no settled residence, or who are ordinary residents of another authority (as far as the authority thinks desirable and with the other authority's consent). There is power to make arrangements for provision for people who are or have been suffering from mental disorder (or in order to prevent mental disorder), and who are ordinarily resident in another authority, but have been **discharged from hospital** in the authority's area.

Local authorities also have the power to make arrangements for the provision of accommodation to meet the needs of people for the prevention of **illness**, and the care or **after-care** of those who are **ill**. They have the power to make arrangements

– in such cases as the authority considers appropriate – for the **conveyance** of people to and from residential accommodation.

Authorities **may** make arrangements for the provision of residential accommodation – in particular mother and baby homes – for **expectant and nursing mothers** of any age who are in need of care and attention not otherwise available to them. Arrangements for residential accommodation may also be made specifically for people who are '**alcoholic** or **drug-dependent**'.

(4) Charges for residential accommodation. Local authorities have a **duty** to make **charges**, by operating a statutory charging regime (*National Assistance Act 1948*, s.22). **Regulations** (SI 1992/2977) and **guidance** (CRAG) have been issued. See: **Charges: residential accommodation**

(5) Independent sector. Local authorities have the **power** to **make arrangements** with both private and voluntary sector organisations for the provision of **residential accommodation**. If both **board** and **personal care** are involved, the provider must be registered under the *Registered Homes Act 1984*, as must providers of residential accommodation with nursing care. Arrangements for the provision of residential accommodation which includes nursing care cannot be made without the consent of the health authority, except in case of **urgency**, when consent must be sought as soon as practicable (*National Assistance Act 1948*, s.26). There are various rules concerning payment of charges for accommodation: see **Charges: residential accommodation**. In the *Beckwith* case, the House of Lords ruled that, contrary to Department of Health guidance (LAC(93)10), local authorities are not themselves obliged to provide accommodation (i.e. by running at least some homes directly), but can make arrangements for provision wholly with the independent sector.

(6) Different types of residential accommodation. When they **make arrangements** for residential accommodation, authorities have a **duty** to **have regard to** the **need** for providing accommodation of different types suited to the different types of people who might need residential care through **age, illness, disability** or **other circumstances** (*National Assistance Act 1948*, s.21). In this respect, it is envisaged that local authorities will sometimes provide accommodation for 'less-dependent' residents (SI 1992/2977) – i.e. those who do not require the normal level of **care and attention**.

Indeed, the *Hammersmith and Fulham* case confirms that the duty can, in some circumstances, entail provision of basic accommodation (i.e. food and shelter) and not just accommodation providing more intensive care. Nevertheless, the arrangements being made must involve residential accommodation of some type; in the *Gorenkin* case, the High Court ruled that food vouchers, without accommodation, could not be given to asylum-seekers under s.21.

(7) Community health services. Community health services are listed in **guidance** as NHS **continuing care** services for people in their own homes and in **residential homes**, for which **criteria of eligibility** and **priorities** should be set within available **resources** (HSG(95)8). Such services are provided under the *NHS Act 1977*.

(8) Health care support. Specialist heath care support for people in **residential accommodation** or in their own homes is listed in **guidance** as an NHS **continuing care** service, for which **criteria of eligibility** and **priorities** should be set within available **resources** (HSG(95)8). Such support is provided under the *NHS Act 1977*.

■ RESIDENTIAL HOMES

I.e. residential accommodation without nursing care: see generally under: **Residential accommodation**; also **Mixed economy of care**

Residential homes: independent sector. The operation of residential homes run by the independent (voluntary or private) sector is governed by the *Registered Homes Act 1984* and by associated **regulations** (SI 1984/1345). This **legislation** covers a variety of matters, including registration and inspection, the fitness of the people running the home, **record-keeping,** services and facilities to be provided, criminal offences for breach of the legislation etc.

Residential homes: provision of services generally. There is sometimes a **grey area** between what services residential homes (run either directly by a local authority or independently) will provide as part and parcel of their services, what services will be provided by the NHS, and what residents or their relatives have to pay extra for themselves. This uncertainty might apply, for instance, to **incontinence** pads or to other **disability equipment** which people require. For instance, **guidance** issued in 1986 (LAC (86)6 – no longer current) stated that under registered homes **legislation** (see immediately above), proprietors of homes should provide:

> 'adaptations and facilities necessary to make the home suitable for people with disabilities. However, this does not preclude local authorities from supplying individual aids such as walking-frames and dressing-aids to residents in private and voluntary homes provided such items are supplied individually for their personal use and on the same basis as for other people living in the community.'

RESOURCES

Resources are a fundamental issue in community care. Indeed it is shortage of resources, rather than confusing **legislation**, which underlies various problems within community care and most of the cases reaching the law courts. The *Gloucestershire* and *Sefton* cases are prime examples. Resources come in at four stages: (a) the local authority's **assessment** of **needs;** (b) its decision about whether the authority should provide services to meet those needs; (c) the decision about how to meet them; and (d) the actual making of arrangements to meet the needs.

Resources: assessment of need. Legislation does not state whether the **assessment** of people's community care **needs** can be influenced by the amount of money either the local authority or the service user (see below) has available.

In order to avoid incurring obligations in the first place, authorities might try to avoid inclusive or generous definitions of need, by introducing resources as a factor. The question in the *Gloucestershire* case was whether they could do this legally in respect of s.2 of the *CSDPA 1970*. After protracted litigation, the House of Lords finally ruled that resources could be taken into account when **disabled people's** needs are being assessed; although a **balancing exercise** will still be required, weighing people's needs against available resources: i.e. resources should not be the sole factor. The case would seem to confirm also that resources can be taken into account by local authorities when they assess, under s.47(1) of the *NHS and Community Care Act 1990*, people's needs for other **community care services**.

Community care is of course not alone in being afflicted by disputes about resources. In the field of education, the courts have grappled with the same problem (e.g. *East Sussex* and *Hillingdon* cases). On the same theme, but in the field of sewage treatment, they have ruled that resources cannot be relevant to establishing physical features of geography such as estuaries (*Kingston upon Hull* case).

Resources: are services necessary or called for? Having assessed **needs**, the next step for the local authority is to decide whether services are **necessary** or **called for**.

The House of Lords in the *Gloucestershire* case ruled that when deciding whether it is necessary for it to meet a person's assessed needs under s.2 of the *CSDPA 1970*, a local authority **may** take account of resources: 'It is not necessary to hold that cost and resources are always an element in determining the necessity. It is enough…to recognise that they may be'. As to the relevance of the service user's – as opposed to the authority's – resources, one of the judges remarked that if a person could afford to pay for services out of his own pocket, then it might not be **necessary** for the local authority to meet his needs under the *CSDPA*.

Under a community care **assessment** and decision about other (i.e. not under the *CSDPA*) **community care services** (s.47(1) of the *NHS and Community Care Act 1990*), cases such as *Gloucestershire, Rixon* and *Goldsack* would seem to indicate that, generally, the authority may take account of its own resources when deciding whether a person's needs call for provision by it: to the extent that, in individual cases, the authority may decide to make no provision at all (with the exception perhaps of s.117 of the *Mental Health Act 1983*). This is because of the presence of **general duties**, which are difficult to enforce.

The relevance also of the resources of the service user was considered in the *Sefton* case about provision of **residential accommodation** under s.21 of the *National Assistance Act 1948*. The judge accepted that while people had money remaining – and were able, physically and mentally, to make their own arrangements – residential care was 'otherwise available to them', and that the authority was under no duty to **make arrangements** under s.21 of the *National Assistance Act 1948*. He stated that the resources of service users were to be looked at in the broad sense of financial, physical and mental. (This judgment was overturned by the Court of Appeal – although the case might go on further appeal to the House of Lords.)

Resources: deciding how to meet the needs. Even though **needs** have been identified for which services are **necessary** or **called for** (see above), there might be different ways of meeting those needs. It is accepted that local authorities can take account of resources when deciding how to meet a need, as long as the option chosen does genuinely meet it (e.g. *Lancashire* and *Bucke* cases).

Resources: meeting the need. Once a local authority has agreed that it should meet a **need**, how enforceable is provision by the service user?

The House of Lords in the *Gloucestershire* case contrasted the **specific duty** under the *CSDPA 1970* (see immediately below), with the **duty** under other community care **legislation** such as s.29 of the *National Assistance Act 1948*. Thus, having come to a decision that it is **necessary** for it to meet a person's needs under the *CSDPA 1970*, the authority must do so irrespective of resources (subject only to a **reassessment**). This is because the Act gives **disabled people** 'a right to have their assessed needs met so far as it is necessary for the authority (as distinct from others) to do so'. (The specific duty under s.117 of the *Mental Health Act 1983* might have a similar effect, though it is not mentioned in the case).

As to other **community care services**, the court distinguished between s.2 of the *CSDPA 1970* and s.29 of the *National Assistance Act 1948* by stating that the former entailed 'not a general duty but a particular duty and it gave a correlative right to the individual which he could enforce in the event of a failure in its performance'. This might suggest that provision of what had been agreed in terms of other community care services (e.g. under s.29 of the 1948 Act) would be difficult to enforce – if, for example, the authority failed to provide them on grounds of lack of resources (see also the *Goldsack* case). Even so, this distinction between *CSDPA* services and other community care services is not totally clear; the Court of Appeal in the *Sefton* case stated that once a duty is triggered under s.21 of the 1948 Act (for **residential accommodation**), then resources cannot be cited as a reason for non-provision – just as they cannot under s.2 of the *CSDPA*.

There has been a supposition that particular, **specific duties** might be enforceable in **private law** claims for **damages** for **breach of statutory duty**; however, the *O'Rourke* case appears to restrict severely the circumstances in which such actions are likely to succeed.

Resources: providing NHS services. The courts have ruled that when deciding whether to provide services, health authorities can take account of resources. For instance, in the *Hincks* case, the Court of Appeal stated that the **general duty** to provide services under s.3 of the *NHS Act 1977* should be read on the following assumption: namely that services could only be provided 'within the resources available'. Thus, there was no question of a health authority being coerced by the law courts into providing **treatment** for which it lacked the money or facilities.

RESPITE CARE

Respite care consists of short-term breaks for the carer, when the person cared for goes elsewhere: for instance, into NHS care (*NHS Act 1977*), **residential accommodation** (*National Assistance Act 1948*, s.21), or on a **holiday** (*CSDPA 1970*, s.2; *NHS Act 1977*, schedule 8). Alternatively, somebody else might do the caring for a short period, and the carer goes away. This could even be, for instance, by way of **practical assistance in the home** (*CSDPA 1970*, s.2, *Health Services and Public Health Act 1968*, s.45), or **night-sitter services** (*NHS Act 1977*, schedule 8).

Respite care is listed in **guidance** as an NHS **continuing care** service, for which **criteria of eligibility** and **priorities** should be set within available **resources** (HSG(95)8), and is provided under the *NHS Act 1977*.

REVIEW OF NEEDS AND SERVICES

Review of people's community care **needs** and services is not a concept to be found in **legislation**, except for a fleeting and general reference in relation to **residential accommodation** (see immediately below). Arguably, 'review', as the term is commonly used, amounts to **reassessment**. Policy **guidance** states that the review process should look at whether services need to be increased, revised or **withdrawn**: taking account of changes not only in the person's **needs**, but also in **policies** (DH 1990). See: **Reassessment**

Review of needs and services: residential accommodation. A local authority has a **duty** to **make arrangements** regularly to review the provision made under arrangements for **residential accommodation** and to make improvements it **considers necessary** (Direction under *National Assistance Act 1948*, s.21).

RICHMOND CASE

This case established that **charges** cannot be made by local authorities under s.111 of the *Local Government Act 1972* (which otherwise enables authorities to do things to facilitate, or which are conducive or incidental to, the discharge of any of their functions).

It involved the giving of pre-application planning advice by the authority. This was in itself permissible since such advice facilitated, or was conducive or incidental to, the authority's statutory planning functions. What was not permissible was the making of charges for this advice, since such charges were at best 'incidental to the incidental and not incidental to the discharge of the [statutory] functions'.

RIGHT ANSWERS

It is easy to suppose that if only service users or local authorities knew the **law** in sufficient depth, they would regularly be able to alight on the right answer to a problem or dispute. However, this does not happen.

Although the outcome of some **judicial review** cases might be predicted with some confidence, one is not dealing in mathematical certainties. As one Law Lord (Lord Reid) put it, there used to be a belief that the right answer lay in some Aladdin's cave awaiting release by magic incantation of the correct judicial words; but, he noted, people do not believe in fairy tales any more (in: Lee 1989). The judicial disagreements in the *Gloucestershire* case, culminating in a three to two split decision in the House of Lords, support this view. Indeed, if judges in the higher courts spend several days discussing the implications of the term 'need' and still manage to disagree, how can anybody else be expected to know the right answer? This state of affairs reflects the complexity and difficulty of some of the issues facing the courts.

RIGID POLICIES

Rigid **policies** should be avoided by local authorities. First, if the policies do not in practice cater for **exceptions** – a particularly important consideration given that community care **assessment** is about people's **individual needs** – they expose authorities to the risk of **judicial review** on the grounds of **fettering of discretion** (e.g. *Hargreaves (no.2)* case). Second, some rigid policies, snatched at hastily by authorities, can all too easily bear the marks of **illegality** when they contravene the wording of **legislation** – as happened in the *Leaman* case, concerning the provision of holidays under the *CSDPA 1970*.

RIXON CASE

A community care case in which the court spelled out the extent of the obligations on local authorities to have regard to, and to follow, **guidance** issued by **central government;** and pointed to the authority's failure adequately to provide services to meet the applicant's social, **recreational** and educational needs. (Apart from community care obligations, the court also considered those owed by the local authority under education legislation and guidance.)

(1) **Background.** The case concerned a 25-year-old man who suffered from Seckels syndrome and who was **blind**, microcephalic, virtually immobile, doubly **incontinent** and mostly unable to communicate. He also suffered from severe deformities of the chest and spine, a hiatus hernia and a permanent digestive disorder. His weight and size were those of a small child, his dependency that of a baby. The dispute concerned the provision for his social, recreational and educational needs; having left a special needs school, the applicant had requirements which the local authority could not meet because, it pleaded, it was short of resources.

(2) **Provision of recreational facilities despite lack of resources.** The judge found that the local authority had failed to provide for the person's recreational needs under s.2 of the *CSDPA 1970*. The duty under the Act was 'owed to the applicant personally' to provide:

> 'recreational facilities outside the home to an extent which Islington accepts is greater than the care plan provides for. But the authority has, it appears, simply taken the existing unavailability of further facilities as an insuperable obstacle to any further attempt to make provision. The lack of a day centre has been treated, however reluctantly, as a complete answer to the question of provision'.

The judge accepted that although the exercise of assessment should be needs-led, resources could not be ignored. He also commented that 'even an unequivocal set of statutory duties cannot produce money where there is none or by itself repair gaps in the availability of finance'. But nevertheless, resources should be a 'balancing and not a blocking' factor, and there was no indication that the authority had in practice undertaken anything like the balancing exercise described in the *Gloucestershire* case (High Court) 'of adjusting provision to need'.

(3) **Care plans and guidance.** The judge stated that although legislation does not refer to care plans, nevertheless – given the status afforded them in community care guidance – 'a care plan is the means by which the local authority assembles the relevant information and applies it to the statutory ends, and hence affords good evidence to any inquirer of the due discharge of its statutory duties'.

He analysed the content of the care plan in question and found that it conformed neither to policy guidance nor practice guidance. The policy guidance refers to the recording of the objectives of social services intervention as well as of the services to be provided. The care plan failed to do this, and thus was in breach of the policy guidance. This, in turn, amounted to a breach of the law, in the absence of a considered decision for departing from the guidance: such departure would have to be with 'good reason, articulated in the course of some identifiable decision-making process even if not in the care plan itself'.

The care plan also breached practice guidance in respect of its contents, specification of objectives, agreement on implementation, leeway for contingencies and the identification and feedback of unmet needs. Practice guidance did not, the judge explained, carry the force of the policy guidance, but even so, the authority should have had regard to it: 'Whilst the occasional lacuna would not furnish evidence of such disregard, the series of lacunae...does, in my view, suggest that the statutory guidance has been overlooked'.

(4) **Individual and general duties**. The judge also dismissed the attempt to convert the general, target duties under s.29 of the *National Assistance Act 1948* into a more specific, stronger duty. This had been attempted by referring to the specificity of the **Directions** given under the 1948 Act, and to the gateway of individual assessment under s.47 of the *NHS and Community Care Act 1990*.

(5) **Limitations on the court.** The complexity of the case, as the judge pointed out, presented the court 'with problems some of which are beyond the competence of the law courts'. He was also tempted to exercise the **discretion** courts have in **judicial review** not to grant any relief (eg an **injunction** or **declaration**) because of 'the present fluid situation, and given the genuine endeavours being made on both sides to do the right thing'. However, two declarations were eventually granted.

■ **SAFE:** see **Safety**

■ SAFETY

Safety is a concept increasingly governing the provision of **community care services** by local authorities: as **resources** run dry, so authorities tend to award people **priority** according to the degree to which their physical safety is at risk.

Safety: disabled facilities grants. Making a dwelling or building safe for a **disabled occupant** – and for other people residing with him/her – is one of the statutory purposes for which a housing authority has a **duty** to approve a **disabled facilities grant**; assuming various other conditions are also met. However, it should be noted that safety is only one of a number of purposes listed; therefore, an authority which only considered providing grants where safety was in issue would be acting **unlawfully** (*Housing Grants, Construction and Regeneration Act 1996*, s.23).

Safety: unreasonableness. At the High Court stage of the *Gloucestershire* case, the court stated that if an authority were to deny assistance to a **disabled person** at severe physical risk on the ground of lack of **resources**, then it might be acting **unreasonably**. Safety and risk were among the grounds for the granting of an interim injunction in the *Farley* case, forcing the local authority to restore the **night-sitter services** it had **withdrawn**.

■ SAFETY, COMFORT OR CONVENIENCE

A legislative phrase which qualifies the provision of **home adaptations**, and of **disability** or **daily living equipment** for **disabled** or **elderly people**.

Safety, comfort or convenience: disabled people. If a person is **disabled** and **ordinarily resident** within the area of a local authority, then the authority has a **duty** to **make arrangements** for the provision of **home adaptations** or **additional facilities** for his or her 'greater safety, comfort or convenience', if the authority is **satisfied** that it is **necessary** for it to **make those arrangements** in order to meet the person's **needs** (*CSDPA 1970*, s.2).

Some local authorities appear to concentrate on the term 'safety' and to operate **policies** which explicitly exclude provision for people's comfort or convenience. The potential legal pitfall of such **blanket policies** was exposed in the *Leaman* case, concerning the provision of **holidays** under s.2 of the *CSDPA 1970*. The authority had adopted a policy which was inconsistent with the statutory wording by excluding consideration of assistance with certain types of holiday – much as some authorities might exclude consideration of comfort or convenience. The policy was held to be **unlawful**.

Nevertheless, having to consider comfort or convenience does not necessarily throw open the **floodgates**. First, as the House of Lords confirmed in the *Gloucestershire* case, authorities are permitted – up to a point – to take account of **resources** not only when determining people's **needs**, but also when determining whether it is **necessary** to meet them. Thus, if a person wants access to his garden, the authority might deem that this is simply not a need at all for that particular individual; and so no question of provision arises, whether for safety, comfort or convenience. Alternatively, the authority might decide that there is a need, but not one which it is necessary for it to meet; in the light of its high, though not **unreasonable**, threshold of intervention.

Safety, comfort or convenience: elderly people. In order to meet the **needs** of **elderly people**, local authorities have the **power** to **make arrangements** to provide **practical assistance in the home**, including the provision of any **additional facilities** designed to secure greater safety, comfort or convenience (Approval under *Health Services and Public Health Act 1968*, s.45).

SAFETY NET

Social services **legislation** is seen to some extent as a safety net, capable of being used for all manner of provision when other legislation fails to meet people's **needs**.

(1) **Example: asylum-seekers.** In the *Hammersmith and Fulham* case, when asylum-seekers were denied assistance under both social security and housing legislation, the Court of Appeal ruled that local authorities potentially had duties under the *National Assistance Act 1948* to assist. The High Court actually used the words safety net, although the Court of Appeal did qualify the scope of such a net.

(2) **Example: housing for children in need.** In the *Tower Hamlets* case, when the option of rehousing a family with a child in need had been rejected under housing legislation, the court ruled that the local authority should at least consider the option under the *Children Act 1989*, s.17.

(3) **Example: CSDPA 1970.** Under s.2 of the *CSDPA 1970*, a local authority has a **duty** – if it is **satisfied** that it is **necessary** for it to meet a **disabled person's** needs – to **make**

arrangements for the provision of various welfare services, including **additional facilities** for a person's greater **safety, comfort or convenience**. This last phrase is so vague that it could cover, for example, a huge range of **disability** and other **daily living equipment**. The problem for local authorities in limiting their obligations under the Act would appear to be as follows.

If for instance, the NHS, an education authority or a housing authority is prepared to provide certain types of equipment or **home adaptations**, then it will not be necessary for the local authority to provide them. But if these other agencies do not provide in a particular case, then the local authority might find itself with a **continuing duty** to do so – if it has accepted that the need is one which it is necessary for it to meet if nobody else does.

In order to preclude this continuing duty arising, local authorities might sometimes attempt to avoid assessing in the first place for particular services or equipment. However, to do this they would have to argue that they have no legal **power** to provide the equipment in issue, on the grounds that it could not, even in principle, be a facility for greater safety, comfort or convenience. Yet the wide import of the legislative wording, together with the existence of **grey areas** of responsibility, means that this argument will in some circumstances be difficult to sustain.

■ SATISFIED

Sometimes a **duty** is triggered by an authority being 'satisfied' that something is the case. For instance, the duty to provide services under s.2 of the *CSDPA 1970* arises only if the local authority is satisfied that it is **necessary** for it to **make arrangements** to meet a person's **needs**. Similarly, under the *Housing Grants, Construction and Regeneration Act 1996*, housing authorities have to be satisfied, before approving an application for a **disabled facilities grant**, that the proposed works are both **necessary and appropriate**, and **reasonable and practicable**.

Clearly, the term gives authorities considerable leeway, insofar as the satisfaction is **subjective** to the authority, rather than, for example, to the independent expert. However, the decision of an authority about its satisfaction can be challenged in some circumstances. For instance, in the *Gloucestershire* case at the High Court stage, the judge suggested that an authority which was not satisfied that it should intervene under s.2 of the *CSDPA 1970* – in the case of a person at severe physical risk – might be acting **unreasonably**. This safeguard for service users of arguing unreasonableness on the part of an authority was emphasised at the House of Lords stage of the same case, and illustrated in the *Farley* and *Haringey* cases.

The judicial undermining of a decision-maker's satisfaction was demonstrated in the *Tameside* case, when the House of Lords found that the Secretary of State for Education could not have been 'satisfied' as to certain matters because, the court ruled, the information and evidence before him could not possibly have warranted such satisfaction.

■ SCHOOL-LEAVERS: DISABLED

Local authority social services departments and local education authorities have a **duty** to carry out assessments, exchange information etc., in relation to each **disabled child** with a statement of special educational **needs** who is approaching school-leaving age (*Disabled Persons (Services, Consultation and Representation) Act*

1986, ss.5–6). The general aim is to ensure that disabled children receive the services they require on leaving school.

■ SCREENING

Policy **guidance** – although not **legislation** – states that local authorities should normally operate an initial screening process. This should be to determine either the appropriate form of **assessment** or, in some cases, to make a **referral** to another agency when the person's needs **appear** to be unconnected with the local authority's statutory responsibilities (DH 1990).

Local authorities might run foul of the **local ombudsman** or even the law courts if their screening procedures are inadequate. For example, the **duty** to carry out an assessment if a person appears to be in need of **community care services** does not amount to 'assessment on request' but does represent a potentially extensive duty. So, a screening procedure, which – on the basis of inadequate information – crudely removes the right to an assessment from individuals or whole groups of people, might be susceptible to challenge.

Similarly, screening procedures which do not deny an assessment to people, but which allocate **priorities** and **waiting times**, might be challenged if those priorities are awarded on the basis of clearly inadequate **referral** information. For instance, the local ombudsman has sometimes queried how authorities can possibly come to decisions about priority and **urgency**, without possessing good quality information in the first place.

■ SEFTON CASE

This case, about the provision of **residential accommodation**, illustrates how local authorities explore the **legislation** for **escape routes** when **resources** run short, and pose difficult questions for the law courts. The High Court delivered an apparently quite logical judgment in favour of the local authority, although it seemed to run contrary to Department of Health **policy.** The Court of Appeal overturned the decision in July 1997. The case might be appealed to the House of Lords; it is also possible that amending legislation will be passed to clarfiy the position.

(1) Background. The case was brought, with the assistance of the charity *Help the Aged* on behalf of two applicants in particular. Under challenge was a twofold policy adopted by the Council in relation to the provision of residential accommodation under ss.21 and 26 of the *National Assistance Act 1948*. The Council accepted that once it had arranged for accommodation under the 1948 Act then the **Regulations** governing the **assessment** of people's resources applied (see: **Charges: residential accommodation**). For example, capital of up to £10,000 is disregarded, capital of between £10,000 and £16,000 triggers a partial contribution by the resident, and capital over £16,000 means the resident has to pay the full cost of the accommodation until the capital reduces to the £16,000 figure.

The Department of Health had written a letter to the Council making clear that it had not intended that local authorities should take account of resources when deciding whether to make arrangements for residential care. However, Sefton found itself in a difficult situation, given that one area within its boundaries, Southport, attracts a large number of elderly, retired people – whilst another area is considerably disadvantaged.

(2) **The policy: first limb.** The Council maintained that if a person had already arranged for himself or herself, or needed to enter for the first time, residential accommodation – and thus in either case *the Council* had not so far made any arrangements – then it was under no obligation to **make those arrangements** simply because the person's capital had fallen below £16,000. Its policy of considering intervention only when the person's capital had fallen below £1500 was in fact based both on the lack of its own resources and those of the applicant. This was because, in the Council's opinion, a person with more than that minimum sum, had enough money to make their own arrangements. In turn this meant that accommodation was '**otherwise available**' to him or her – as envisaged, the Council claimed, by the legislation (s.21 of the *National Assistance Act 1948*).

(3) The policy: second limb. If the Council had originally made arrangements for accommodation for a resident, but the resident's capital subsequently rose above £16,000, then the Council would then regard itself as having ceased to make arrangements – even though the resident still remained in the same accommodation. This would mean that when the resident's capital sank below £16,000 again, the Regulations would not apply, and the Council could apply the first limb of its policy to the resident – as it could to a person for whom it had never made arrangements.

Sefton case: High Court. The judge decided that the first limb of the policy was lawful, though he added one or two qualifications. He decided – on the authority of the *Gloucestershire* (House of Lords) case – that the authority was permitted to take into account its own resources when deciding whether the **need** of an applicant should trigger the duty to provide residential accommodation.

He accepted also that, generally, people possessing **resources** of their own are able to make their own arrangements – and that therefore the duty of the local authority to make arrangements under s.21 of the *National Assistance Act 1948* will not necessarily arise. However, he did point out that there will be various circumstances in which, even if a person does have adequate resources, he might be unable to make his own arrangements – for example, because he is unable to obtain the advice and assistance required. Thus, the authority had to take account of the resources of the applicant in the widest sense: financial, physical and mental. In addition, the judge warned against the danger of pursuing an inflexible policy which could not take account of special circumstances. He also stated that, just like under s.2 of the *CSDPA 1970*, once the authority had identified a need which triggered a duty in a particular case under s.21 of the 1948 Act, it could not 'pray in aid' a lack of resources for failing to perform the duty.

The second limb of the policy – at least in respect of the particular applicant – was deemed **unlawful**, since nothing had been said or done to indicate that at any point the resident had ceased to be provided with accommodation arranged by the authority.

Sefton case: Court of Appeal. In overturning the High Court's decision, and stating that the authority's policy (i.e. the first limb) was unlawful, the Court of Appeal emphasised the following points.

(1) **Deferring payment for care: unlawful.** In distinguishing this case from the *Gloucestershire* case (in which the House of Lords stated that resources could influence the assessment of people's needs for services), the court stated that Sefton was not denying

that the applicant needed care and attention, but was simply deferring consideration and payment because of a shortage of resources. This was unlawful under s.21 of the *National Assistance Act 1948* – notwithstanding that the *Gloucestershire* judgment meant that in relation to welfare services under both the *CSDPA 1970* and s.29 of the 1948 Act, authorities were able to consider resources even after a person's needs had been established.

(2) Need for care and attention not otherwise available. The court came to this decision partly because s.2 of the *CSDPA 1970* requires that having established needs, an authority has to decide whether it is 'necessary' to meet them. Whereas the word 'necessary' did not appear in s.21 of the *National Assistance Act 1948*.

Nevertheless, s.21 of the 1948 Act contained the words 'not otherwise available', crucial to Sefton's position. Despite the apparent, if hard, logic of this position, the court simply dismissed it by equating these words with the statutory means-test: the 'statutory scheme rests upon the assumption that care and attention is not to be regarded as 'otherwise available' if the person concerned is unable to pay for it according to the means test regime provided for in section 22' (of the 1948 Act) – a statutory scheme which Sefton were totally defeating.

The court also had doubts about applying – to s.21 of the *National Assistance Act 1948* – the aspect of the *Gloucestershire* judgment which allowed authorities to take account of resources when assessing people's needs under s.2 of the *CSDPA 1970*. It found such an exercise 'very much more difficult to perform' in relation to residential care under s.21 of the 1948 Act; though the court was 'compelled to conclude that there is a limited subjective element in making the assessment of whether the ailments of the person concerned do or do not collectively establish a need for care and attention'.

■ SEMANTIC DISTINCTIONS

Significant legal implications flow from: (a) the logic-chopping of the law courts; (b) a fluid distinction between terms such as **'need'** and **'preference'**; (c) the fine line between **screening** and **assessment**; (d) confusion over the difference between assessment of **need** and the options for **service provision** to meet the need (see e.g. *Goldsack* case); and (e) **grey areas** of responsibility. This suggests that much hinges on the sometimes arbitrary semantic distinctions made by local authorities.

■ SENSORY IMPAIRMENT: see **Blind; Deaf;** and **Disability**

■ SERVICE PROVISION

Decisions about whether **community care services** are **called for** or are **necessary** are distinguished from **assessment** of need, might depend on **resources** and be subject to **delay**.

■ SETTLED RESIDENCE

Local authorities have the **power** to **make arrangements** to provide **residential accommodation** for people who have no settled residence – i.e. who are not **ordinarily resident** in the area of any local authority. However, authorities have a **duty** to make arrangements to provide accommodation for people who have no settled residence and who are, or have been, suffering from **mental disorder**, or for the prevention of mental disorder (Direction and Approval under *National Assistance Act 1948*, s.21).

SHAH CASE

This was an education case about **ordinary residence**, an issue which regularly triggers disputes in the community care context. It concerned the application for educational awards of several students who had entered the United Kingdom at least three years previously. The education authorities involved claimed that the students had failed to establish that they were ordinarily resident within the areas of the authorities under s.1 of the Education Act 1962. The House of Lords ruled in favour of the students. One of the judges stated that unless:

> 'therefore, it can be shown that the statutory framework or the legal context in which the words are used requires a different meaning, I unhesitatingly subscribe to the view that 'ordinarily resident' refers to a main's abode in a particular place or country which he has adopted voluntarily and for settled purposes as part of the regular order of his life for the time being, whether of short or of long duration.'

SHALL

A word in **legislation** which normally signifies the existence of a **duty**.

SHAMS

The courts might try to see through and expose **policies** which are 'shams'. So, for example, an authority might claim that its policy is not excessively **rigid**, because though strict, it allows for appeals against decisions. However, when 300 appeals – i.e. potential exceptions – were brought over three years and all failed, the court held that the policy of considering **exceptions** was simply not genuinely applied, even if there was no bad faith involved (*Collymore* case).

Conversely, the courts might not fault an authority whose decisions deviate sufficiently from a policy which *in principle* is **unlawful**, so as to amount to lawful *practice* (e.g. *Bristol* case).

SHOPPING

Shopping might be part of **home help** or **practical assistance in the home**.

SHOUTING LOUDEST

Local authority staff sometimes lament the fact that people who shout the loudest and the most frequently obtain services more quickly than other people who are in greater **need**. It appears that on occasion they might be provided with services for which they would not normally be assessed to be in need at all. This might be to avoid both excessive consumption of staff time in dealing with a vexatious complainant, and adverse publicity.

However, local authorities should be aware that the **local ombudsman** is likely to regard **queue-jumping** as **maladministration**. And, if, for example following an assessment under the *CSDPA 1970*, an authority were to provide services which were not really needed in order to 'get rid' of a persistent complainant, it might – *in principle* at least – be acting outside the **legislation** and **illegally**, since **arrangements** under s.2 are to meet people's assessed need, not their wishes alone.

SHOWER

Facilitating access to this by, provision of it for, or facilitating its use by, a **disabled occupant** is one of the statutory purposes for which a housing authority has a **duty** to approve an application for a **disabled facilities grant** – assuming various other conditions are also met (*Housing Grants, Construction and Regeneration Act 1996*, s.23). See also: **Bathing services and equipment**

SIGHT IMPAIRMENT

People with a sight impairment are eligible for **welfare services** under s.29 of the *National Assistance Act 1948*, s.2 of the *CSDPA 1970*, and Part 3 of the *Children Act 1989*; and also for **disabled facilities grants** under the *Housing Grants, Construction and Regeneration Act 1996*, s.100. See: **Disability**

SOCIAL ACTIVITIES

Social activities: children. For **children in need** who are living with their **families**, local authorities have a **duty** to make 'such provision as they consider **appropriate**' for various services including social activities (*Children Act 1989*, schedule 2).

Social activities: disabled people (adults). Local authorities have a **duty** to **make arrangements** for the provision of facilities for social activities for **disabled people** who are **ordinarily resident** in the area. In respect of people not ordinarily resident, the duty reduces to a **power** only (Direction and Approval under *National Assistance Act 1948*, s.29).

Social activities: illness (adults). For the prevention of **illness**, the care of people who are ill, and the **after-care** of people who have been ill, local authorities have the **power** to **make arrangements** for the provision of facilities for social activities (Approval under *NHS Act 1977*, schedule 8).

SOCIAL CARE

This term is often used (a) to refer to the services which fall to local authority social services departments to provide, and (b) in contrast to **health care**. However, the vagueness of **legislation** and resulting **grey areas** sometimes blur the distinction.

SOCIAL FUND

Under the Social Fund (run by the Department of Social Security and Benefits Agency), people can receive assistance in certain circumstances in the form of, for instance, budgeting loans and community care grants. Neither of these can be given for medical items, whilst community care grants cannot be given towards expenses which a local authority has a **duty** to meet. These seemingly straightforward rules do not preclude uncertainties arising.

(1) **Grey areas of responsibility.** The existence of vague **legislation, grey areas** of responsibility between statutory services, and variable local practices, mean that responsibilities are not always clear. Thus, in the *Connick* case, the judge ruled that in the particular circumstances the Social Fund Officer could not exclude provision of **incontinence** pads. This was because they were not necessarily medical items: they could be

items in 'ordinary everyday use' as well. The Fund has sometimes been used in relation to outdoor electric wheelchairs and non-allergenic bedding. Indeed, advice notes issued to Social Fund Officers suggest that items such as built-up shoes, adapted beds and wheelchairs are not necessarily excluded – since they, too, are all capable of being ordinary, everyday items.

(2) **Safety net beneath even the Social Fund?** However, local Social Fund budgets are cash-limited and local authorities could find themselves under pressure to provide a **safety net** beneath even the Social Fund. For instance, the **policy** of a local authority might state that if a **disabled person needs** a high-seat chair in the living room, it will not provide it unless he or she already has a chair. The rationale for such an odd-looking policy appears to be that if there is no chair at all, and the person cannot afford to buy one, then it is the Social Fund's responsibility. Indeed, if the Fund does provide a grant or loan, then it is clearly not **necessary** for the local authority to meet the needs. But if assistance is not forthcoming from the Fund, then the local authority would appear to remain under a **statutory duty** at least to consider whether it might assist in the particular circumstances (under the *CSDPA 1970*, s.2).

SOCIAL REHABILITATION AND ADJUSTMENT TO DISABILITY

Local authorities have a **duty** to **make arrangements** to provide – whether at centres or elsewhere – facilities for social **rehabilitation** and adjustment to **disability** for disabled people who are **ordinarily resident** in the area. In respect of disabled people not ordinarily resident, there is a **power** only (Direction and Approval under *National Assistance Act 1948*, s.29).

SOCIAL SERVICES COMMITTEES

Local authorities have a **duty** to appoint a **social services committee** (*Local Authority Social Services Act 1970*, s.2). In the *Gloucestershire* case, at the House of Lords stage, both majority and minority views agreed that it is social services committees which should set the **standards** against which the **needs** of **disabled people**, and the **necessity** to meet them, are to be **assessed**.

SOCIAL SERVICES DIRECTORS

Local authorities have a **duty** to appoint a director of social services and to ensure that **adequate staff** are provided to assist with the performance of his or her functions (*Local Authority Social Services Act 1970*, s.6).

SOCIAL SERVICES FUNCTIONS

Social services functions are listed in **legislation** (*Local Authority Social Services Act 1970*, schedule 1). All matters relating to the discharge of these functions must be referred by a local authority to its **social services committee**. The list embraces functions under, for example, part of the *NHS and Community Care Act 1990*, the *CSDPA 1970*, the *National Assistance Act 1948*, part of the *NHS Act 1977*, the *Children Act 1989*, the *Carers (Recognition and Services) Act 1996*, and the *Community Care (Direct Payments) Act 1996*.

SOCIAL TREATMENT OF MENTAL DISORDER

Local authorities have a **duty** to **make arrangements** for the provision of **social work** and related services to help in the social treatment of **mental disorder** (Direction under *NHS Act 1977*, schedule 8).

SOCIAL WORK SERVICES

Local authorities have a **duty** to **make arrangements** to provide a social work service for **disabled people** who are **ordinarily resident** in the area. For people not ordinarily resident, there is a **power** only (Direction and Approval under *National Assistance Act 1948*, s.29).

For preventing **mental disorder**, or for people who are – or have been – suffering from mental disorder, local authorities also have a duty to **make arrangements** for the provision of social work and related services for the **identification, diagnosis, assessment** and **social treatment** of mental disorder, and for providing support and other **domiciliary** and care services to people living in their own homes or elsewhere (Direction under *NHS Act 1977*, schedule 8).

SOCIAL WORKERS

For preventing **mental disorder** or for people who are – or have been suffering from – mental disorder, local authorities have a **duty** to **make arrangements** for the appointment of sufficient approved social workers in relation to the *Mental Health Act 1983* (Direction under *NHS Act 1977*, schedule 8).

SOUTHWARK CASE

This case suggested that the Secretary of State's **default powers** – rather than the law courts – should be used for enforcement of a **duty** under the *National Assistance Act 1948*.

(1) **Background.** The case concerned two families, who – at a time of extreme housing shortage in London – sought assistance from a squatters' association and made an orderly entry into empty council property. When the local authority applied to the court for an order of immediate possession, the families relied on two defences: that the authority was under a duty to provide temporary accommodation under the *National Assistance Act 1948*, and that there was also a defence of necessity.

(2) **Breach of duty, defaults powers, and necessity.** The court doubted whether s.21(1)(b) applied, since it was relevant only when the circumstances could not reasonably have been unforeseen: this was not so in this particular case. Furthermore, even if the council had been in breach of its duty, enforcement of that duty could only be achieved through exercise of the Secretary of State's default powers. The defence of necessity was also rejected on the grounds that only extreme need could justify it. An example, from an old case, was of shipwrecked sailors who, in order to save their own lives, killed the cabin boy and ate him: even these circumstances did not constitute necessity. Liberal use of the defence 'would open a way through which all kinds of disorder and lawlessness would pass', and 'open a door which no man could shut'. Thus, the courts had to deny 'the plea of necessity to the hungry and the homeless: and trust that their distress will be relieved by the charitable and the good'.

SLEEPING ROOM

Facilitating access to this room by, or provision of it for, a **disabled occupant** is one of the statutory purposes for which a housing authority has a **duty** to approve an application for a **disabled facilities grant** – assuming other conditions are also met (*Housing Grants, Construction and Regeneration Act 1996*, s.23).

SPECIFIC DUTY: see **Duty**

SPEECH AND LANGUAGE THERAPY

Speech and language therapy is listed by **guidance** as an NHS **continuing care** service which people – in **nursing** or **residential homes**, or in their own homes – might **require** and for which **criteria of eligibility** and **priorities** should be set within available **resources** (HSG(95)8). Such therapy is provided under the *NHS Act 1977*.

Speech and language therapy is also provided under the Education Act 1996, and could arguably be provided as a **community care service** under s.29 of the *National Assistance Act 1948* (assistance with **communication**). Nevertheless, occupying the **grey area** between statutory services (particularly in relation to children), speech and language therapy has triggered a number of disputes involving both the **local ombudsman** and the law courts, concerning which authority – education or health – is going to provide (e.g. *Harrow, M* and *Oxfordshire* cases).

SPEECH IMPAIRMENT

People with a speech impairment are eligible for **welfare services** under s.29 of the *National Assistance Act 1948*, s.2 of the *CSDPA 1970*, and Part 3 of the *Children Act 1989*. See: **Disability**

STAFFORDSHIRE CASE

An education case about looking to the future, not just the present, when performing a **balancing exercise** in weighing up efficient use of **resources** against **needs**.

(1) Background. The case concerned a four-year-old child with quadriplegia, cerebral palsy and consequent **mobility** problems, and whether she could continue to attend the Birmingham Institute for Conductive Education. Although the authority claimed that an alternative, a nursery, would be cheaper and still meet the child's needs, the parents argued that continued attendance at the Institute would accelerate her entry into mainstream education and therefore save the authority resources in the longer term.

(2) Resources and longer term considerations. The Special Educational Needs Tribunal stated that she should remain at the Institute because this might expedite mainstream education for her (though it did not mention resources). The education authority challenged the Tribunal's decision. The court found that the Tribunal had been entitled to come to this decision by:

> 'not accepting that the authority was necessarily right to say that simply because [the nursery] costs less now, therefore it is an efficient use of resources to send [the child] there, because one would clearly have to do a balancing exercise to decide whether the more expensive education now, which would be likely to lead to mainstream education earlier, would overall create a greater efficiency in the use of resources.'

■ STANDARDS

Various **guidance** suggests that local authorities should be publishing performance standards such as response times for **referral, assessment,** service provision etc. (e.g. SSI/SWSG 1991b, LAC(94)24). Although the rigour of such standards can be softened by including phrases such as 'in 90 per cent of cases', nevertheless defensive legal advisers will suggest that authorities do not publish detailed standards. This is because the fact that an authority has not adhered (or come anywhere near) to its own response times becomes one more piece of unfavourable evidence – for instance, when the **local ombudsman** is investigating **maladministration**.

Local authorities develop their own sets of standards and also utilise those set nationally by the Social Services Inspectorate at the Department of Health. One of the difficulties is to distinguish clearly between, on the one hand, standards which represent professional good practice going beyond **legislation** and the principles of administrative law (i.e. concepts applied in **judicial review**); and, on the other, standards relating to basic legal compliance.

■ STANDING

In order to bring a **judicial review** case, the applicant has to have the standing – i.e. 'sufficient interest' in the matter – to do so. Sometimes it is accepted that representative voluntary organisations have sufficient interest even if they are not directly involved in the dispute – for instance, the *Royal Association for Disability and Rehabilitation* in the *Lancashire* case, and *Help the Aged* in the *Sefton* case.

■ STATUTORY DUTY: BREACH OF

A breach of statutory **duty** is one of the grounds (i.e. **illegality**) on which the law courts rule against authorities in **judicial review** proceedings, and on which the **local ombudsmen** might find **maladministration**.

However, judicial review is a **public law** remedy, and compensatory **damages** are not usually available. Therefore, people sometimes try to bring a **private law** action for breach of statutory duty. In the field of community care and other welfare law – as opposed, for example, to **health and safety** at work law – the courts are reluctant to allow cases for breach of statutory duty to succeed, and impose a strict test about whether **Parliament** could have intended such a remedy (e.g. *Bedfordshire* case). Nevertheless, in some **homelessness** cases (e.g. *Cocks*), the courts have in the past accepted that if the breach of duty does not concern the exercise of public law **discretion**, then claims for damages might be possible. This would be where an *executive* function (i.e. implementing a decision) is in issue, rather than actual *decision-making*. Nevertheless, the *O'Rourke* judgment in June 1997 still further restricted the circumstances in which a court is likely to entertain a claim for damages for breach of welfare duties.

■ **STATUTORY GUIDANCE:** see **Guidance**

■ **STATUTORY INSTRUMENTS:** see **Regulations**

STEANE CASE

Similar to the *Quinn* case, this case also exposed the **buck-passing and cost-shunting** to which public bodies – in this instance, a local authority and **central government** – resort when **resources** are scarce.

It concerned a 79-year-old woman with diabetes and problems of mobility who went to live in a **residential home** run by the Isle of Wight County Council. A limited company, Islecare, was then set up to manage the home formerly run by the council. The woman claimed attendance allowance, on the basis that she was no longer in **residential accommodation** arranged by the council under s.26 of the *National Assistance 1948*, and thus could claim the allowance (she could not have claimed it if arrangements were still being made under the 1948 Act). The House of Lords ruled that, because the local authority was not making payments to Islecare in conformity with s.26 of the 1948 Act, no accommodation was being provided under that Act and thus the attendance allowance could be claimed.

STOMA CARE

Stoma care (for people with a colostomy or ileostomy, for instance) is an example of an NHS **continuing care** service which, **guidance** explains, people – in **nursing** or **residential homes**, or in their own homes – might **require** and for which **criteria of eligibility** and **priorities** should be set within available **resources** (HSG(95)8). Such care is provided under the *NHS Act 1977*.

STRIP-WASH

Strip-washing is sometimes recommended as one way of meeting people's **needs** to keep clean. If a local authority is deciding how to meet a **disabled person's** needs following **assessment** under s.2 of the *CSDPA 1970*, a regular strip-wash might be one of the possible options. Others might include, for instance, a downstairs bathroom extension, or a stairlift (for access to an existing bathroom). Depending on available **resources**, the authority can choose a cheaper or even the cheapest option, even if this does not accord with a person's **choice**, so long the need is still met (e.g. *Lancashire* case). See: **Bathing services and equipment**

SUBJECTIVE

When an authority comes to a decision under **legislation** by being **satisfied** about, having an opinion on, or **considering**, something – or if something **appears** to an authority to be the case – much is left to the subjective view of the authority. However, the courts might intervene, for example, if an authority has come to an **unreasonable** decision by refusing to assist a **disabled person** at severe physical risk (*Gloucestershire* case, High Court), or if there was simply no evidence on which the authority could have come to the particular decision it did (*e.g. Tameside* and *Farley* cases).

Even if language tends to the less subjective – for instance, if the authority must 'have reason to believe', rather than be 'satisfied' about something – even so, the 'subject-matter might incline a court to allow a housing authority some latitude in decising whether it has 'reason to believe' the facts giving rise to the duty' (*O'Rourke* case).

■ **SUBSTANTIALLY AND PERMANENTLY HANDICAPPED:** see **Disability**

SUPERVISION ORDERS

Supervision orders **may** be made to ensure that certain **mentally disordered** people receive **after-care** services under s.117 of the *Mental Health Act 1983* (*Mental Health Act 1983*, s.25 as amended).

SUPPORT

Support: illness. For the prevention of **illness**, the care of people who are ill, and the **after-care** of people who have been ill, local authorities have the **power** to provide support to prevent the **impairment** of physical or mental **health** of adults in **families** where such impairment is likely, or to prevent the break-up of such families, or for assisting in those families' **rehabilitation** (Approval under *NHS Act 1977*, schedule 8).

Support: social work (disabled people). Local authorities have a **duty** to **make arrangements** to provide support for **disabled people** who are **ordinarily resident** in their area. For people who are not ordinarily resident, there is a **power** only (Direction and Approval under *National Assistance Act 1948*, s.29).

Support: social work (elderly people). In order to meet the needs of **elderly people**, local authorities have the **power** to **make arrangements** to provide social work support (Approval under *Health Services and Public Health Act 1968*, s.45).

Support: specialist health care. Specialist health care support is an NHS **continuing care** service which, **guidance** explains, people – in **nursing** or **residential homes**, or in their own homes – might **require**, and for which **criteria of eligibility** and **priorities** should be set within available **resources** (HSG(95)8). Such care is provided under the *NHS Act 1977*.

TAMESIDE CASE

A case illustrating how the courts – if they are minded to – interfere with the decisions of public bodies, even if the **legislation** apparently allows the decision-maker to come to a **subjective** view.

A local council, which had recently changed political hands, decided to modify the previous local policy on comprehensive education. However, under s.68 of the Education Act 1944, the Secretary of State decided that he was **satisfied** that this was unreasonable and issued a **Direction** to the authority, which he subsequently tried to enforce through a court order. The House of Lords ruled against the Secretary of State, finding that there were no grounds on which he could have been satisfied that the local authority had behaved unreasonably.

■ **TARGET DUTY:** see **Duty**

TELEPHONE: DISABLED PEOPLE

If a person is **disabled** and **ordinarily resident** within the area of a local authority, then the authority has a **duty** to **make arrangements** for the provision of, or assistance to the person in obtaining, a telephone and any special **equipment necessary** to enable him or her to use the telephone, if the authority is **satisfied** that it is **necessary** for it to make those arrangements in order to meet the person's **needs** (*CSDPA 1970*, s.2).

TELEVISION

If a person is **disabled** and **ordinarily resident** within the area of a local authority, then the authority has a **duty** to **make arrangements** for the provision of, or assistance to the person in obtaining, television if the authority is **satisfied** that it is **necessary** for it to make those arrangements in order to meet the person's **needs** (*CSDPA 1970*, s.2).

TEMPORARY ACCOMMODATION

Local authorities have a **duty** to **make arrangements** for the provision of temporary accommodation for people who have an unforeseen, **urgent** need of it (Direction under *National Assistance Act 1948*, s.21).

- THEORY AND PRACTICE: see **Law: practice**

THERAPISTS

Long overshadowed by social workers in local authorities, and by doctors and nurses in the NHS, **occupational therapists** (in social services and the NHS) and physiotherapists and **speech and language therapists** (in the NHS) play a fundamental, although sometimes ill-understood and under-valued, role in community care. In particular, these therapists enable people to regain or develop a wide range of daily living functions (physical, sensory, cognitive etc.) and make the key contribution to **rehabilitation**.

THRESHOLD OF NEED

Following the *Gloucestershire* case, it seems clear that as a local authority's **resources** diminish, so it can correspondingly raise the threshold of what it means both by **'need'** and by **'necessity'** to meet need, so that it avoids the trap of incurring obligations which it cannot afford to meet under s.2 of the *CSDPA 1970.*

TILLEY CASE

A case pre-dating the *Children Act 1989*, but indicating nonetheless (a) that local authorities should beware of **fettering their discretion** by failing to consider provision of **accommodation** for **children in need** (see also *Tower Hamlets* case); and (b) that even in the case of a generally-expressed **duty**, authorities might need to consider the **individual needs** of children.

Policies, fettering discretion and individual needs. The case concerned the generally expressed duty under s.1 of the Children and Young Persons Act 1963 to make available **advice, guidance** and **assistance** etc. to promote the welfare of children by diminishing their need for care. The Court of Appeal held that a resolution (**mandatory** in appearance) of the authority not to provide accommodation under this section of the Act was **unlawful**, since such provision could be covered by the word 'assistance'. The court also stated that even if the resolution had allowed of **exceptions** and had been a general policy and not a mandatory order, nevertheless this:

> 'would not get rid of the vice that a local authority, dealing with individual children, should not make a policy or an order that points towards fettering its discretion in such a way that the facilities offered to the child do not depend on the particular circumstances of that child or of its family, but follow some policy which is expressed to apply in general...Dealing with children, the discretion and powers of any authority must depend entirely on the different circumstances of each child before them for consideration.'

Arguably, such a ruling about the **general duty** contained in s.1 of the 1963 Act remains to some extent relevant to its successor, s.17 of the *Children Act 1989*, despite the explicit incorporation of the term 'general duty' in the latter.

TOLLING THE BELL OF TIGHT RESOURCES

This phrase was used by the High Court (before its judgment was overturned by the Court of Appeal) in the *Cambridge* case, when the judge stated that the health authority had to do more than toll the bell of tight **resources** in order to justify its decision to deny a child potentially lifesaving treatment.

TOWER HAMLETS CASE

This case illustrates that even where there is only a somewhat vague and **general duty** to provide for people's **needs**, local authorities should beware of limiting the scope of **assessment**.

(1) **Background.** The case concerned a **family** with various problems. The mother was severely **disabled**, suffering from epilepsy (leading to double **incontinence**) and arthritis. The family was subject to very considerable harassment in the area. This included bullying of the 11-year-old son, abusive telephone calls, attempted arson and the daubing of phlegm and faeces over the front door and car. The family applied for rehousing and also requested comprehensive **assessment** under the *NHS and Community Care Act 1990*, the *CSDPA 1970*, and the *Children Act 1989*. The request for rehousing was turned down on the grounds that the family had been assessed as having no points for medical priority. However, it was clear that the child was a **child in need** under the *Children Act 1989*, since he was experiencing a number of problems including the bullying, and was failing to attend school.

(2) **Unlawful limitation of scope of assessment under the Children Act 1989.** The essential point before the court was whether, in addition to considering rehousing under housing **legislation**, the local authority should have assessed also the possibility of rehousing the family under s.17 of the *Children Act 1989* – which places a general duty on the authority to safeguard and promote the welfare of children in need. The local authority believed that it could not, in principle, provide **accommodation** under s.17 – since s.20 of the Act (which did not apply in this situation) explicitly referred to the provision of accommodation, whilst s.17 did not. The judge found that:

> 'those responsible for the assessment approached it with a fundamental misunderstanding of their powers in relation to rehousing under the Children Act 1989...the assessment that was made was fundamentally flawed and that whilst...it was done without any deliberate or improper intent, the undertaking given [previously] to the Court to assess [the child's] needs under section 17 has not been fully and properly complied with.'

TRAINING OR OCCUPATION: CENTRES AND OTHER FACILITIES

For preventing **illness**, and caring for people who are, or have been ill, local authorities have the **power** to **make arrangements** for the provision of centres or other facilities for training or for keeping people suitably occupied, and to equip and maintain such centres (Approval under *NHS Act 1977*, schedule 8).

For preventing **mental disorder**, or for people who have been suffering from mental disorder, local authorities have a **duty** to make arrangements for the provision of centres – including training centres and **day centres** – for training or occupational purposes (Direction under *NHS Act 1977*, schedule 8).

TRANSPORT: SPECIALIST

Special transport is an NHS **continuing care** service which, **guidance** explains, should be included in local **policies**, and for which **criteria of eligibility** and **priorities** should be set within available **resources**. On the basis of patients' **needs**, it might include transport to and from hospitals or hospices, emergency admissions to **residential** or **nursing homes**, and non-emergency transport to and from health care facilities for people in residential or nursing homes or in their own homes (HSG(95)8. Such transport is provided under the *NHS Act 1977*. See: **Travel**

TRAVEL

Travel: children. For **children in need** who are living with their **families**, local authorities have a **duty** to make 'such provision as they **consider appropriate**' for various services including **home help**; which may include facilities for, or assistance with, travel to and from the home, in order to take advantage of services provided under the *Children Act 1989* or similar services (*Children Act 1989*, schedule 2).

Travel: disabled people (adults). Authorities have a **power** to **make arrangements** to provide free or subsidised travel for **disabled people** who do not otherwise qualify for travel concessions – but only in respect of travel arrangements for which concessions are available (Approval under *National Assistance Act 1948*, s.29).

In addition, if a person is disabled and **ordinarily resident** within the area of an authority, then the authority has a **duty** to make arrangements for the provision of facilities for, or assistance, with travel, in order for the person to participate in services arranged by the authority or similar services. However, the authority must first be **satisfied** that it is **necessary** for it to meet the person's **needs** by making those arrangements (*CSDPA 1970*, s.2).

Travel: elderly people. In order to meet the **needs** of elderly people, local authorities have the **power** to **make arrangements** to provide assistance or facilities for people in travelling to and from the home, so that they can participate in services provided by the authority or similar services (Approval under *Health Services and Public Health Act 1968*, s.45).

Travel: residential accommodation. Local authorities have the **power** to **make arrangements** to provide – in such cases as the authority **considers appropriate** – for the **conveyance** of people to and from **residential accommodation** (Approval under *National Assistance Act 1948*, s.21).

■ TREATMENT OF ILLNESS: COMPREHENSIVE HEALTH SERVICE

The treatment of **illness** is one of the purposes for which the Secretary of State has a **duty** to provide a **comprehensive health service** (*NHS Act 1977*, s.1). The overall duty is difficult to enforce in the law courts because of the wide **discretion** it confers: see for instance the *Hincks* case.

■ TUCKER CASE

A case illustrating the failure of an authority (a) to perform the duty of deciding what services were **called for** under s.47 of the *NHS and Community Care Act 1990*; and (b) to formulate a lawful **care plan**. It is also an example of a dispute, held by the court, to be suitable for resolution via **judicial review**, rather than by means of **alternative remedies** such as local authority **complaints** procedures or the Secretary of State's **default powers**.

(1) **Background.** The case concerned a 32-year-old woman with **learning disabilities, sensory impairments,** consequent social and **communication** difficulties and various **physical** and **mental health** needs. She had profound bilateral deafness, congenital nystagmus and myopia. Essentially the dispute centred around the fact that the local authority had made an **assessment** under s.47 of the *NHS and Community Care Act 1990*, but subsequently failed either to make a decision about the services she needed or to provide them.

In November 1993 she was placed in NHS premises for assessment; by 13 April 1994 she had received the assessment and was ready for discharge by July 1994. At the time of the hearing in 1996 she was still resident at the NHS premises, even though they had only ever been intended as an interim measure and had since become an emergency respite centre, making them even more unsuitable. Some disagreement had arisen between the woman's mother and the local authority: the mother favoured the recommendation of a consultant from SENSE (National Deaf, Blind and Rubella Association), which suggested a specialist, local placement. The authority had decided that this placement, which would mean setting up a two-person residential unit, would not be viable.

(2) **Alleged lack of a care plan.** It was argued not only that the authority had failed to come to a decision about service provision, but it had also not produced an adequate care plan as envisaged by community care **guidance**. For example, there was no stated overall objective in terms of long-term obligations, no criteria for measurement of any objectives, no costings, no considerations of long-term options for residential care, no recorded points of difference between the parties, no reference to a date for **review**.

(3) **Breach of guidance and statutory duty.** The judge accepted the argument that the authority had no lawful care plan and that the situation was similar to that which occurred in the *Rixon* case. He found a clear breach of, in particular, two paragraphs of the policy guidance: 3.24 (care plans and their objectives) and 3.41 (**hospital discharge**, and the undesirability of a person remaining in hospital when care could be provided more appropriately elsewhere). He also found the authority to be in breach of its **statutory duty** under s.47(1)(b) of the 1990 act, since it had 'still not made the decision which is

called for by that section'. The authority had 'used its undoubted discretion to make short term and interim decisions in relation to the care of the applicant', but such **discretion** could not 'replace the duty to make a service provision decision as to the long term future of the applicant'.

(4) **Alternative remedies?** Rejecting the authority's argument that even if it had breached its duty, **judicial review** was not the appropriate remedy, the judge explained that the case involved consideration of a 'discrete point of law', for which neither the Secretary of State's **default powers** nor the local authority **complaints** procedure were adequate remedies. For example, the latter would have involved the woman's mother arguing points of law before a non-qualified body: that would not have been 'convenient, expeditious or effective'. Judicial review was therefore appropriate.

■ UNFAIRNESS

Unfairness – sometimes referred to as procedural impropriety – is one of the grounds on which the law courts rule against public authorities in **judicial review** proceedings. There are various aspects to the concept: the following are examples.

(1) **Bias.** Either an appearance, or a very real danger, of bias might constitute unfairness: for instance, the **assessment** of a close relative by a social worker, even if the social worker has, actually, been scrupulously fair.

(2) **Fair hearing.** Having a fair hearing (i.e. making oral or written representations) is also a crucial element of fairness, although its application will differ with context. In community care, this common law principle of a fair hearing might be less relevant in some circumstances, since community care **guidance** itself is full of statements to the effect that service users should be allowed to participate fully in assessments and that their **preferences** should be taken account of. For instance, in the *Hargreaves* case, a failure to **consult** the service user was held to be a breach of policy **guidance**, which in turn amounted to a **breach of statutory duty**, rather than a lack of fairness.

(3) **Legitimate expectation, and giving of reasons.** Other aspects of fairness might, depending on the context, include the giving of **reasons** and **legitimate expectation**.

■ UNLAWFULNESS

A general term used by the law courts in **judicial review** to indicate, for example, **illegality, unfairness** or **unreasonableness**.

■ **UNMET NEED:** see **Needs-led assessment**

■ UNREASONABLENESS

Unreasonableness is one of the grounds on which the law courts sometimes rule against public authorities in judicial review proceedings. The classic definition of unreasonableness is a tautology: an unreasonable decision is one that is 'so unreasonable that no reasonable authority could ever have come to it'. A later reworking of this definition was made under the heading of **irrationality**.

The courts are apt to apply the term with varying degrees of strictness, depending on whether they wish to intervene in the case before them. When applying the term restrictively, they will say that the authority would have to have 'taken leave of its senses' – a rare occurrence. However, if a court wishes to intervene, then the term will be applied more loosely. For instance, at the High Court stage of the *Gloucestershire* case, the judge stated that it would be unreasonable to deny assistance to a **disabled person** at severe physical risk. Similarly, in the *Cleveland* case, the court ruled that in drawing up its contract terms with local providers of **residential accommodation**, the local authority had behaved unreasonably because the homes might have had to close as a result of the stringency of the terms. This would in turn have meant that the purpose of the *NHS and Community Care Act 1990* – to provide a choice of accommodation for people – would have been **frustrated**. Yet neither situation is suggestive of authorities taking leave of their senses.

The House of Lords in the *Gloucestershire* case regarded the test of unreasonableness as the safeguard against abuse by local authorities of their **discretion** to assess people's **needs** under the *CSDPA 1970*, s.2. However, whether this is an adequate safeguard in practice – i.e. from the point of view of **disabled people** – is doubtful. First, as **resources** diminish, so the 'reasonable' practice of the average local authority is likely to become more restrictive. Second, the judge in the *Bruce* case formulated just how difficult it might be for an applicant to demonstrate unreasonableness on the part of a local authority. Nevertheless, the *Farley* and *Haringey* cases indicate circumstances in which courts might intervene, overcoming their reluctance to become involved in the **merits of decision**.

■ URGENCY

Community care **legislation** takes account of people who are in urgent **need**.

Urgency: assessment. Before providing any **community care services** (whether residential or non-residential), authorities must first carry out a community care **assessment** – unless the person is in urgent need, in which case the services **may** precede the assessment. The assessment must follow as soon as practicable (*NHS and Community Care Act 1990*, s.47).

Urgency: health authority's consent. Local authorities **may** not **make arrangements** for the provision of **residential accommodation** with nursing care without the health authority's consent except in case of urgency. Consent must then be sought as soon as practicable after arrangements have been made (*National Assistance Act 1948*, s.21).

Urgency: ordinary residence. Local authorities do not have a **duty** to **make arrangements** for providing **residential accommodation** for people who are not **ordinarily resident** in the area, but only a **power**. However, if people are in urgent need, then even if they are not ordinarily resident, a duty arises (Direction and Approval under *National Assistance Act 1948*, s.21).

■ VISITING SERVICES: ELDERLY PEOPLE

In order to meet the needs of **elderly people**, local authorities have the **power** to **make arrangements** to provide visiting services (Approval under *Health Services and Public Health Act 1968*, s.45).

■ VICAR OF WRITTLE CASE

A case illustrating the circumstances in which a court might impose a **duty of care** in **negligence** on a local authority in respect of social services. It concerned a child, with a record of fire-raising and in the care of the local authority, who set fire to a local church. The vicar, churchwardens and other people interested in the church brought an action alleging negligence. The court found that in failing to warn his head office, a social worker was not exercising a statutory **discretion**, and that therefore (a) a common law duty of care arose; (b) it had been breached; and (c) damages would be awarded against the authority.

■ **WAITING TIMES:** see **Delay**

■ WANTS

People's wants are in practice (and legally) distinguished from their **needs** for the purpose of **assessment** and provision of various **community care services**. See: **Choice; Needs; Preferences**

■ WARDENS: OLD PEOPLE

In order to meet the **needs** of **elderly people**, local authorities have the **power** to **make arrangements** to contribute to the cost of employing wardens for welfare functions in warden-assisted housing schemes and to provide warden services for private housing (Approval under *Health Services and Public Health Act 1968*, s.45).

■ WASHHAND BASIN

Facilitating of access to this by, provision of it for, or facilitating its use by, a **disabled occupant** is one of the statutory purposes for which a housing authority has a **duty** to approve an application for a **disabled facilities grant**, assuming various other conditions are also met (*Housing Grants, Construction and Regeneration Act 1996*, s.23).

■ WELFARE

Welfare: children. Local authorities have a **general duty** 'to safeguard and promote' the welfare of **children in need** within their area by providing a range of **appropriate** services.

Welfare: disabled facilities grants. Making a dwelling or building suitable for the welfare of the **disabled occupant** is one of the statutory purposes for which a housing authority has the **power** to approve an application for a **disabled facilities grant**, assuming various other conditions are also met (*Housing Grants, Construction and Regeneration Act 1996*, s.23).

Welfare: grounds for housing allocation. When drawing up public **housing allocation** schemes, housing authorities have a **duty** to give preference to households with a person who needs settled **accommodation** on various grounds including welfare (*Housing Act 1996*, s.167).

Welfare: residents. Local authorities have a **duty** to **make arrangements** for the welfare of all residents for whom **residential accommodation** is provided (Direction under *National Assistance Act 1948*, s.21).

Welfare services. This term is sometimes used generically to refer to non-residential **community care services**, such as **home help, day centres, equipment** and **home adaptations, occupational activities, social-work support, advice.**

WHIM

This term was reportedly used by the local authority during the *Avon* dispute, which hinged on whether the entrenched **preference** of a man with **learning disabilities** for particular **residential accommodation** amounted to a **need**. The court decided that the preference, in the particular circumstances, did amount to a **psychological need** and was far from just a whim.

- **WILL OF PARLIAMENT:** see **Parliament**

WIRELESS

If a person is **disabled** and **ordinarily resident** within the area of a local authority, then the authority has a **duty** to **make arrangements** for the provision of, or assistance to the person in obtaining, wireless (i.e. radio) facilities – if the authority is **satisfied** that it is **necessary** for it to make those arrangements in order to meet the person's **needs** (*CSDPA 1970*, s.2).

WISHES

People's wishes are distinguished in practice (and legally) from their **needs** for the purpose of **assessment** and provision of various **community care services**. See: **Choice; Needs; Preferences**

WITHDRAWING SERVICES

Following an individual **reassessment**, entailing a **balancing exercise** involving **resources** and people's **needs**, a local authority can withdraw **community care services** from people either because of a change in their own **needs**, or because of a change in the authority's **policies** and **criteria of eligibility** (e.g. *Gloucestershire* case).

WOOLGAR CASE

A case concerning the **delegation** of a housing authority's **duty**, under the Housing Act 1985, to investigate (i.e. make an **assessment** of) a person's **homelessness** status and **eligibility** for **accommodation**. The court ruled that it was lawful for the authority to transfer the 'active and dominant' part of the investigations to a housing association, so long as 'all decision-making…is kept exclusively within the local authority'. (The legislation has since been altered to allow transfer of such decision-making: see SI 1996/3205).

WORK

Authorities have a **power** to **make arrangements** for providing suitable work for **disabled people**, either in their own homes or elsewhere. They also have a power to make arrangements for helping those people dispose of their work (*National Assistance Act 1948*, s.29). In addition, for the **prevention of illness**, the

care of people who are ill, and the **after-care** of people who have been ill, local authorities have the **power** to pay people engaged in suitable work at centres providing **training** or **occupational** activities (Approval under *NHS Act 1977*, schedule 8). See: **Employment**

WORKSHOPS AND HOSTELS

Authorities have the **power** to **make arrangements** for providing **workshops** where **disabled people** can engage in suitable work, and also for providing associated **hostels**. Where they make arrangements for the provision of such hostels, **charges** are made in the same way as for **residential accommodation** (*National Assistance Act 1948*, s.29).

WYATT CASE

This case, concerning the *CSDPA 1970*, illustrates the reluctance of the law courts to entertain claims for **damages** for **breach of statutory duty** or in **negligence**, for failure to provide **welfare services**.

(1) **Background.** The case concerned a woman who suffered from disseminated sclerosis and who, with her husband, claimed damages against the authority – in negligence and/or breach of statutory duty – in relation to provision of **home help, practical assistance in the home**, and an 'invalid bed' under s.2 of the *CSDPA 1970.*

(2) **Default powers more appropriate for dispute about 'comforts to the sick and disabled'.** The judge found that any remedy for breach of statutory duty lay through the Secretary of States's **power** to declare an authority in **default** of its functions under s.36 (now obsolete) of the *National Assistance Act 1948*, which was relevant because of the interaction between the 1948 and the 1970 Acts. He went further and stated (the following passage has recently been cited with approval by the House of Lords in the *O'Rourke case*):

> 'a statute such as this which is dealing with the distribution of benefits – or, to put it perhaps more accurately, comforts to the sick and disabled – does not in its very nature give rise to an action by the disappointed sick person. It seems to me quite extraordinary that if the local authority...provided, for example, two hours less home help than the sick person considered herself entitled to that that can amount to a breach of statutory duty which will permit the sick person to claim a sum of monetary damages by way of breach of statutory duty.'

The claim in **negligence** was also rejected, since the duty in issue arose from the Act of Parliament only (i.e. it did not constitute a free-standing common law duty of care). However, the court noted that a claim in negligence might have been possible if, for example, a home help had dropped the woman, or the bed provided by the local authority had been defective, collapsed and caused injury.

YARDSTICK OF NEED

The House of Lords in the *Gloucestershire* case was concerned to identify a suitable yardstick against which local authorities could measure people's needs. The minority opinion alighted on the standards of a **civilised society**, the majority on **resources**.

ZAKROCKI CASE

A community care case illustrating how the law courts can undermine the **satisfaction** of decision-makers and conclude that decisions have been made **unreasonably**.

(1) **Background.** The case concerned a Polish couple in their sixties who came to the United Kingdom to care for their ageing mother. Their leave to remain was extended so that they could care for the wife's brother, a British Citizen who suffered from epilepsy, had learning difficulties and spoke no English. They again applied for leave, with support of Hackney Council who pointed out that the high cost of alternative residential care was not acceptable to the brother. The Secretary of State refused the couple leave to remain any longer.

(2) **Balancing exercise, satisfaction and unreasonableness.** The judge stated that the critical point was that the brother was a British citizen who was entitled to remain in the United Kingdom and be cared for in accordance with the **policies** and **duties** (i.e. in relation to community care) applying to citizens in general. He (a) drew a parallel with another immigration case in which the Secretary of State had not performed the appropriate **balancing exercise** in comparing immigration issues with the rights of British citizens; (b) found that there was no evidence supporting the Secretary of State's assertion that he was satisfied that alternative arrangements could be made for the brother; and (c) ruled that the Secretary of State's decision was **unreasonable** and should be overturned.

APPENDIX I

REGULATIONS

The following are referred to in the A–Z list, but do not have their own entry.

SI 1984/1345. *Residential Care Homes Regulations 1984.*

SI 1984/1578. *Nursing Homes and Mental Nursing Homes Regulations 1984.*

SI 1987/1904. *Data Protection Subject Access Modification) (Social Work) Order 1987.*

SI 1989/206. *Access to Personal Files (Social Services) Regulations 1989.*

SI 1990/2444. *Local Authority Social Services (Complaints) Procedure Order 1990.*

SI 1992/635. *National Health Service (General Medical Services) Regulations 1992.*

SI 1992/2793. *Manual Handling Operations Regulations 1992.*

SI 1992/2977. *National Assistance (Assessment of Resources) Regulations 1992*

SI 1996/706. *National Health Service (Fund-holding Practices) Regulations 1996.*

SI 1996/708. *National Health Service (Functions of Health Authorities and Administration Arrangements) Regulations 1996.*

SI 1996/2887. *Home Repair Assistance Regulations 1996*

SI 1996/2888. *Disabled Facilities Grants and Home Repair Assistance (Maximum Amounts) Order 1996.*

SI 1996/2889. *Housing Renewal Grants (Services and Charges) Order 1996.*

SI 1996/2890. *Housing Renewal Grants Regulations 1996.*

SI 1996/2891. *Housing Renewal Grants (Prescribed Form and Particulars) Regulations 1996*

SI 1996/3119. *Housing Renewal Grants and Home Repair Assistance (Amendment) Regulations 1996.*

SI 1996/3205. *Local Authorities (Contracting Out of Allocation of Housing and Homelessness Functions) Order 1996.*

SI 1997/486. *National Assistance (Sums for Personal Requirements) Regulations 1997.*

SI 1997/734. *Community Care (Direct Payments) Regulations 1997.*

APPENDIX 2

DIRECTIONS

Those not contained in circulars: otherwise see below. The following is referred to in the text, but does not have its own entry.

Complaints Procedure Directions 1990. Contained in an appendix of policy guidance (DH 1990).

APPENDIX 3

GUIDANCE AND OTHER MATERIAL

The following are referred to within the text of the A–Z list, but do not have their own entry. Unless otherwise stated, titles are published by the Department of Health (DH). Some items are available from the Stationery Office (SO), formerly Her Majesty's Stationery Office (HMSO) at a price, rather than through the Department of Health's distribution centre at Wetherby.

CI(92)34. *Implementing caring for people: assessment.*

CLAE (1993). Commission for Local Administration in England. *Good administrative practice.* London: CLAE.

CRAG. *Charging for Residential Accommodation Guide* (CRAG) (looseleaf).

DH (1989). *Caring for people: community care in the next decade and beyond.* HMSO.

DH (1990). *Community care in the next decade and beyond.* HMSO.

DH (1991). *Children Act 1989 guidance and regulations, volume 6: children with disabilities.* HMSO.

DH (1991a). *Children Act 1989 guidance and regulations, volume 3: family placements.* HMSO.

DH (1993). *Code of Practice: Mental Health Act 1983.* HMSO.

DH (1996). *Carers (Recognition and Services) Act 1995: policy guidance.*

DH (1996a). *Mental Health (Patients in the Community) Act 1995: guidance on supervised discharge (after-care under supervision) and related provisions. Supplement to the Code of Practice published August 1993.*

DH (1996b). *Complaints: guidance on implementation of the NHS complaints procedure.*

DH (1997). *Community Care (Direct Payments) Act 1996: policy and practice guidance.*

DH (1997a). Department of Health; Department of Environment. *Housing and community care: establishing a strategic framework.*

DH (1997b). *Purchasing effective treatment and care for drug misusers: guidance for health authorities and social services departments.*

DH (1997c). Department of Health. *The Patient's Charter and you.*

DHSS 12/70. *Chronically Sick and Disabled Persons Act 1970.*

DHSS 19/71. *Welfare of the elderly: implementation of section 45 of the Health Services and Public Health Act 1968.*

DoE 10/92. Department of Environment, Department of Health. *Housing and community care.* HMSO.

DoE 17/96. Department of Environment. *Private sector renewal: a strategic approach.* Stationery Office.

EL (95) 97. *New drugs for multiple sclerosis.*

HC(81)1. *Contractual arrangements with independent hospitals and nursing homes.*

HC(90)23,LASSL(90)11. *Care Programme Approach for people with a mental illness referred to the specialist psychiatric services.* (The circular was due for cancellation in September 1995).

HSC (1994). Health Service Commissioner. *Report of the Health Service Commissioner: failure to provide long term NHS care for a brain-damaged patient.* HMSO.

HSG(94)5. *Introduction of supervision registers for mentally ill people from 1 April 1994.*

HSG(94)27. *Guidance on the discharge of mentally disordered people and their continuing care in the community.*

HSG(95)8, LAC(95)5. *NHS responsibilities for meeting continuing health care needs.*

HSG(95)39, LAC(95)17. *Discharge from NHS inpatient care of people with continuing health or social care needs: arrangements for reviewing decisions on eligibility for NHS continuing inpatient care.*

HSG(96)46. *GP fundholding: revised list of goods and services.*

LAC(86)6. *Registration of residential homes.*

LAC(87)6. *Disabled Persons (Services, Consultation and Representation) Act 1986: implementation of sections 4,8(1),9 and 10.*

LAC(88)2. *Disabled Persons (Services, Consultation and Representation) Act 1986.*

LAC(91)6. *Secretary of State's Direction, s.46 of the NHS and Community Care Act 1990: community care plans.*

LAC(92)17. *Health authority payments in respect of social services functions.*

LAC(92)15. *Social care for adults with learning disabilities (mental handicap).*

LAC(92)27. *National Assistance Act 1948 (Choice of Accommodation) Directions 1992.*

LAC(93)2. *Alcohol and drug services within community care.*

LAC(93)4. *Community Care Plans (Consultation) Directions 1993.*

LAC(93)7. *Ordinary residence.*

LAC(93)10. *Approvals and Directions for Arrangements from 1 April 1993 Made Under schedule 8 to the National Health Service Act 1977 and sections 21 and 29 of the National Assistance Act 1948.*

LAC(93)12. *Further and Higher Education Act 1992: Implications for sections 5 and 6 of the Disabled Persons (Services, Consultation and Representation) Act 1986.*

LAC(94)1. *Charges for residential accommodation: CRAG amendment no.2. Charges for non-residential adults services under section 17 of the Health and Social Services and Social Security Adjudication Act 1983.*

LAC(94)12. *Community Care Plans (Independent Sector Non-Residential Care) Direction 1994.*

LAC(94)24. *Framework for local community care charters in England.*

LAC(97)9. (Issued with equivalent circular: HSG(97)14). *Purchasing effective treatment and care for drug misusers.* Encloses: DH (1997b).

LAC(97)11. *Community Care (Direct Payments) Act 1996.* Encloses DH (1997).

LASSL(94)4. *Guidance on the discharge of mentally disordered people and their continuing care in the community.*

LASSL(96)10. *List of current circulars.*

LASSL(97)9. *Community Care (Direct Payments) Act 1996.* Enclosed training materials on the new Act.

Prime Minister (1991). *The Citizen's Charter: raising the standard.* HMSO.

SSI (1991). Social Services Inspectorate (Department of Health). *Right to complain: practice guidance on complaints procedures in social services departments.* HMSO.

SSI (1991a). Social Services Inspectorate (Department of Health). *Getting the message across: a guide to developing policies, principles and procedures on assessment.* HMSO.

SSI (1994). Social Services Inspectorate (Department of Health). *Advice note for use by Social Services Inspectorate: discretionary charges for adult social services.*

SSI (1996). Social Services Inspectorate (Department of Health). *Carers (Recognition and Services) Act 1995: practice guide.*

SSI/SWSG (1991a) Social Services Inspectorate (Department of Health), Social Work Service Group (Scottish Office). *Care management and assessment: practitioners' guide.* HMSO.

SSI/SWSG (1991b). Social Services Inspectorate (Department of Health), Social Work Service Group (Scottish Office). *Care management and assessment: managers' guide.* HMSO.

APPENDIX 4

FURTHER READING

Listed below are a number of books relevant to community care and judicial review, and which have been useful reference and check points – in addition to primary materials in the form of legislation, guidance and cases.

Bailey, S.H. (1997) *Cross on Principles of Local Government Law.* 2nd edition. London: Sweet & Maxwell.

Clements, L. (1996) *Community Care and the Law.* London: Legal Action Group.

Craig, P. (1994) *Administrative Law.* London: Sweet & Maxwell.

Fordham, M. (1997) *Judicial Review Handbook.* 2nd edition. Chichester: John Wiley.

Gordon, R. and Mackintosh, S. (1996) *Community Care Assessments: A Practical Legal Framework.* 2nd edition. London: FT Law & Tax.

Jones, R. (ed) *Encyclopaedia of Social Services and Child Care Law.* London: Sweet & Maxwell (continually updated looseleaf work).

Lee, S. (1989) *Judging Judges.* London: Faber & Faber.

Mandelstam, M. (1995) *Community Care Practice and the Law.* London: Jessica Kingsley Publishers.

Richards, M. (1996) *Community Care for Older People: Rights, Remedies and Rationing.* Bristol: Jordans.